GOD NEVER MAKES MISTAKES – EVER

~

An autobiography which contains BJ's spiritual journey of life-long miraculous circumstances with growing faith. You will learn that nothing is impossible with God. But you will also learn this requires surrender of one's fears and relinquishing one's constant pursuit of perfectionism. This can only be accomplished by trusting God completely. With everything. Lasting peace and fulfillment can be yours. It's a choice!

~

BJ Jacobson

REVIEWS

"What an amazing journey you have had in your life. Many will benefit from your experiences, bravery and the goodness of God so evident in your writing. I hope all who read this book will recognize the value of medical and financial records being shared by both spouses. Your writing touched my heart. Thank you."

Shirley Jenkins

~

"BJ has given us a powerful testimony of a Miracle Working God. She honestly shares her joyful loving relationships as well as the physical failures and emotional uncertainties she has faced. She teaches us how we can trust God even through pain, doubt and fear. BJ shares the necessity of *repeatedly* making *conscious* choices to focus on Trusting HIM, our living God. She inspires us to do the same. This book is a keeper giving us examples of how Biblical scripture can minister to us through our earthly dilemmas."

Dr. Sonja Kvale: Pastoral Counselor, AG licensed minister, Author and Director of International Mirror Images Retreats, Retired LPC, Author and Artist.

~

"What do you do when the doctors say, 'We found cancer in three places. We recommend a double mastectomy?' What do you do when the doctors tell you, 'Your child is dying of complications of Juvenile Rheumatoid Arthritis. There is nothing more we can do?' What do you do when doctors give your husband an incurable diagnosis and you begin the longest and most painful goodbye of your life?

In *God Never Makes Mistakes – Ever*, BJ Jacobson shares her intimate and transparent story of how she and her husband,

Arne, faced **all** of these crises and more. You will laugh and you will cry, but most of all

You will find encouragement and hope for your own journey. BJ will tell you she is no one special, just an ordinary person who has learned to place her trust in an extraordinary God. She learned that all things are possible through the power of God's Word and the Holy Spirit. BJ experienced a constant presence of God in her life and believes that God can and will be there for your life as well. By the time you finish reading *God Never Makes Mistakes – Ever,* I hope you will come to the same conclusion."

Pastor Jeffrey D. Rasanen: Master of Divinity Assemblies of God Theological Seminary

~

"Having been a long-time friend and confidant of the author, I know these writings to be factual. I have been a witness to the workings of the Lord in her life and family. I know that her desire is that God will be glorified by putting to print much of her life's story. She wants others to know the saving power of the Lord and Savior that she serves."

Mary Henry

~

"Jacobson's autobiography traces the faithfulness of Christ in her and others' lives. She and her family struggle with glaucoma, juvenile rheumatoid arthritis, meniers disease, breast cancer, thyroid cancer and heart conditions to name a few. From the childhood journals she kept for each of her sons, she gives us snapshots that highlight their poignant and humorous journeys toward trusting Jesus. We see her compassion as she walks beside strangers with love and patience pointing them to Jesus. But her poignant, stark and novel details of her husband, Arne's declining health become firsthand for us. While we're there she recognizes our struggles and encourages us. She shows us that in the thick of it – there is God.

Jane Spunaugle , Master of Science in Education

Contents

~ INTRODUCTION FROM THE AUTHOR ~

I am not afraid of tomorrow for I have seen yesterday and I love today.

There is nothing outstanding about me. I'm just an ordinary gal with an Extraordinary God. This is my story of the many ways God has shaped my life through what may seem like difficult circumstances. I feel very fortunate and blessed. I have made mistakes but God has been faithful to me always! He has ordered my steps and kept me close to Him. May you be inspired through my experiences of God's amazing grace within the pages of this book.

My desire in writing this memoir is that you will be drawn to the Jesus I love and serve. Because of His forgiveness, love and tenderness I am His today. I pray that you will find strength and hope for your situation, realizing that God has no favorites. I'm just one of His kids and feel so privileged to have Him as my heavenly Father. He will do for you what He has done for me. His Word is full of promises that are for us today if we have Jesus as our Lord and Savior. I have found Him to be very Faithful and Trustable. Please sit back and enjoy the ride of my life!

"Do not worry about your life, what you will eat or drink; or about your body, what you will wear. Is not life more important than food, and the body more important than clothes?" Matthew 6:25

This means every aspect of your life, taken together in totality: mentally, physically, emotionally, and spiritually. It means your yesterdays, todays, and all your tomorrows!

Jesus is simply saying not to worry about anything! We are to trust our Heavenly Father about everything!

Overheard in an Orchard
By Elizabeth Cheney

Said the Robin to the Sparrow,
"I should really like to know
Why these anxious human beings
rush about and worry so?"

Said the Sparrow to the Robin,
"Friend, I think that it must be,
That they have no Heavenly Father
Such as cares for you and me."

~ ONE ~

2011   My Cancer Journey

April 2011: It was just my annual, routine mammogram. Then I received **the letter from my doctor stating the mammogram was suspicious and they wanted me to** have a magnified mammogram. No big deal! In the past, I had already had a lumpectomy in each of my breasts and both were benign.

May 9th, 2011: Another mammogram. The radiologist took me into his darkened office and we sat down together as he pulled up my films. I saw one tiny spot that looked like a fine line pen dot on the screen. He then pointed out three almost indiscernible dots and told me they were micro calcifications and I needed to have a biopsy performed. I asked him the percentages of benign vs. cancer in these cases and he replied that 75% are benign and 25% are cancerous but only a biopsy would tell definitively. Quite honestly, although I have a deep faith in God and His healing ability, I knew in my heart at that moment that I was embarking on a journey that I really did not care to take.

In January of 2011, I had told the Lord that I wanted ALL He had to give. I wanted to KNOW Him in the deepest possible way. I wanted a walk of deep friendship that surpassed the wonderful relationship I already had with Him. I wanted to be constantly tuned into the Holy Spirit ~ not just during devotions or special times, but a walk that made me hear that still small voice every minute of my day, in everything I did and would make me more useful in listening and ministering to others. I was hungry for more! The Lord simply answered,

"You will shine for me." That was it! It was almost disappointing, but I thought, *"Well, that's nice. I want to shine for Him."*

I was given an appointment with a surgeon and as Arne and I sat in his waiting room, I noted the walls needed fresh paint, the shelves needed dusting in the over-all dingy atmosphere. When we were ushered into the exam room, the first thing I noticed was there was no washbasin in the room. Oh well ~ I'm sure he washes his hands before coming in and it's not like he's putting his fingers into my mouth!!

He was very compassionate, almost fatherly, as he proceeded to examine the wrong breast. I told him it was the 'other' breast. He said he just wanted to check them both. OK. Then he palpitated the wrong places in the correct breast – and these were microscopic and could not be felt. I finally told him it was the upper, outer quadrant and he was examining the inner part. I asked him if he had looked at the x-ray I had brought that clearly showed and told exactly where these "suspicious" areas were.

He said he had, but "...*perhaps I had the X-ray backwards.*"

That did it for me.

I thought, *"If you think I'm going to let you operate on my breast and you don't even know how to properly read an x-ray, you have another think coming!"*

He made an appointment for me to have a biopsy done at the Women's Clinic in our area, which was the only good that came from this visit!! Arne and I agreed to pray for wisdom and discernment regarding our doctors and that is exactly what we did. At this point we had not shared any of this with anyone. After all, ~ it may turn out to be nothing. Right?

Biopsy

I had a biopsy performed on the day after a devastating tornado leveled Joplin, MO just 50 miles from us in 2011. Dr. P, a lovely, young physician and a woman's health specialist who performs many breast biopsies, tried multiple times to get a needle biopsy of the suspicious areas. After 6 mammograms and several hours, she asked if we could try another procedure. Her technician, Lisa, was nervous and her hands were shaking as she performed the final mammogram.

I asked her if she was okay. No, she wasn't. The tornado had come very close to their home, they had no basement, her hubby was out of town and another tornado was already predicted as possible for tonight. I asked if I could pray with her. I touched her arm and asked Jesus to comfort her, protect her and give her wisdom for tonight. I felt a peace just descend on us as I said amen. Then I told her to prepare their bathtub with pillows and some kind of hard surface over their heads and go there if there was any chance of another tornado. She was weeping, thanked and hugged me. It took the entire afternoon until 5:15 to finally get the biopsy.

Dr. P said, *"Your tissue looks so healthy, I can almost assure you it will be benign."*

She said to call the next afternoon after 2:30 PM for the early results.

On the morning of the biopsy, during my regular devotions, I had glanced across the page of my Bible and the following literally jumped out at me:

"He is my strength and song in the heat of battle, and now he has given me the victory. Songs of joy at the news of our rescue are sung in the homes of the godly. The strong arm of the Lord has done glorious things! I shall not die, but live to tell of all his deeds." Psalms 118:14-17 Living Bible

I knew whatever was ahead I would give God the glory for the victory that would come.

Arne had some work to do for someone and said he would be back so we could call the doctor for the results together. However, at 1:45 pm Dr. P called me.

She said, *"Mrs. Jacobson, I am so sorry I gave you false hope yesterday. I am so sorry to tell you your biopsy came back positive. You have cancer in three places."*

It was moderately aggressive, non-invasive ductal carcinoma insitu. I thanked her for taking the extra time in getting the biopsy and said because of her efforts, she probably saved my life.

She was quiet a moment, and then asked, *"Are you going to be alright? Are you OK?"*

I replied, *"Dr. P, fussing is not going to add one moment to my life. My times are in my Heavenly Father's hands and He has all my days planned. Furthermore, He is awake all night, so I might as well sleep and let Him take care of me."*

She said, "OK" and we ended our conversation.

I stood in my kitchen, alone with the Lord. I was overwhelmed with a sense of His awesome presence and lifted my arms and praised Him and thanked Him for trusting me with this diagnosis. I didn't know what was ahead, but I knew I would not be alone! Arne came home just moments later and I told him the results. He got tears in his eyes, took me in his arms and just held me tightly as he wept.

He held me away from him, looked deep into my eyes and said, *"Honey, we are in this together and God will walk with us through whatever is ahead."*

It hurt my heart to see his concern and tears in his eyes. But I had that assurance that no one could ever take away. I knew that I knew that I knew, MY GOD. I trusted Him. And He never makes mistakes -Ever!

Gifted Breast Surgeon

We prayed for wisdom because we knew we needed a surgeon ~ where to start? We were from Rochester, Minnesota, home of the famous Mayo Clinic. All our surgeries and babies born etc. had been there. We KNEW who to ask for there. But here ~ in Bella Vista, Arkansas? We only had a family doctor and the VA. We had lived here 16 years but I had only needed minimal care in the past. We both prayed for wisdom and discernment and good doctors throughout the next couple of days.

Dr. P called me two more days in a row, wanting to be sure I was all right. She said she just could not get me out of her thoughts. I think she, perhaps, thought I was in denial, or in la-la land or something. She couldn't quite believe I was not all bent out of shape. Each day I assured her I was fine, believing and trusting my Heavenly Father with the future.

The third day she asked who my doctor was and I told her I didn't have one. She suggested Dr. C., a breast specialist in Fayetteville. She said he was the very best. Then I asked one of the nurses in our church if she knew a good breast surgeon and she said, Dr. C., and that he was fantastic! The next day a close friend asked me who I was seeing ~ you guessed it, she recommended Dr. C. My former personal physician had moved to Oklahoma and I had emailed and asked her recommendation: Yep ~ Dr. C., a brilliant breast doctor.

I said to Arne, *"Do you think God is trying to tell us Dr. C. is to be my doctor?"* Thank you, Lord.

Dr. C. was everything and more than everyone had said. Furthermore, he loved Jesus and was actively involved with the Jews in Jerusalem and believed the Lord's coming again was getting very close. He epitomized everything we had known at Mayo Clinic as a competent and to-the-point physician. He was state of the art and he was thorough! Very thorough! For the next two months, I jumped through every hoop, had every test, saw every specialist and began to think I may not be finished with all of this before our National RV Maps Convention in September/October.

RV MAPS

RV Maps stands for Recreational Vehicle Missions America Placement Service and is a mission arm of the Assembly of God church. It involves retired (or not) persons who want to donate their skills to help build buildings and change lives for eternity. We mostly build new churches, repair broken down or disaster destroyed churches, parsonages, Teen Challenge facilities and campgrounds. Arne and I were also first responders for disasters where Convoy of Hope is on the job. It is an entirely volunteer organization.

RVers provide our own RV rigs, fuel, food etc. and the only requirement for the facility's help is to provide a full hook up for our rigs. This is all coordinated through our National RV Maps office in Springfield, Missouri, headquarters of the Assemblies of God. In the Fall we have a week's convention where we are encouraged and uplifted. We hear of needed projects for the coming year. I was the choir director and Arne the sound technician at these conventions and it was the highlight of our year. This ministry is the most gratifying thing we have ever done and much has been done for the Lord that only eternity will tell. The RV Maps theme is, "Building churches, Changing lives". That is our goal always.

I was having trouble sleeping at night, a common occurrence with cancer patients I've been told. One night in June, I began to be filled with fears and panic attacks. Up to this point I had only told a few close friends what was going on in my body. I somehow felt embarrassed and shy about such a personal thing, yet I knew I needed prayer support. Our Discipleship Pastor, Mark, preached one Sunday night and shared his story of God's bringing him through leukemia and near death several times. He shared how when he was in isolation for 5 months, Satan harassed his mind and told him he'd never come out alive.

Mark got angry with Satan and finally told him, *"You may be right. I may die here, but YOU don't make that decision. God does!"*

I said in my heart, *"Yes – that's it!"*

The battle ended. It had been a war in my mind, knowing God was in charge, but constantly hearing the negatives of Satan. I turned off his voice and simply talked of Jesus, His power and His might. I played worship music LOUD all day long. I praised every time I turned a corner. Whatever happened was in His plan and that is where I would rest. I then decided to share my situation with my Sunday School class who became my under girding of encouragement and prayer for the remainder of the journey.

On June 29th I, once again, had to have more blood work. My CA 27-29 was high and worrisome. God spoke into my heart that day:

"I will go before you, BJ, and level the mountains and smash down city gates of brass and iron. I will give you treasure hidden in darkness and you will know that I am doing this. I have created you and cared for you since you were born. I will be your God through all your lifetime, yes, even when your hair is white with age. I will carry you along and be your Savior." **Isaiah 45 and 46** *Living Bible*

At my next appointment, Dr. C. recommended a double mastectomy. It was a shock! I wasn't prepared for that.

After he left the room and I was about to get dressed, I turned to Arne trying to lighten the moment said,

"I guess you better take a good long look at these girls because it doesn't look like they're going to be with us much longer."

Tears pooled in his eyes and he said, *"Sweetheart, I never married you for your body. You are precious to me and I married you because I fell in love with you. Didn't you hear what the doctor said? He said you would live if you have this done. I'll have you by my side and we'll grow old together. And that's all that matters."*

I broke down and cried for the first time. I didn't know that over the next few months those words would sustain me in times of doubt.

Next came a breast MRI. Dr. H, the scientist/inventor of the MRI Rodeo Breast Machine (and a team from Duke University) was my radiology doctor.

He looked at the images and said, *"It is amazing that the technician who did your original mammogram could even find this cancer. He must be one sharp cookie. This is microscopic and even the MRI machine doesn't always show everything."*

He also said that if there were three places of cancer, there were probably more that had not shown up yet and my other breast had an abnormal shape. He confirmed what all the specialists had said. He recommended a double mastectomy. He, too, was a born again Christian and we shared a special time of conversation together about the Lord. However, this wasn't going to be an easy ride.

Lymph Node Surgery

On July 7th I underwent surgery to remove two lymph nodes under the right arm and three from under the left arm. Dr. C. called me late Friday to tell me the good news: there was no cancer in the lymph nodes. This was a huge blessing because it meant no chemotherapy, no radiation and no toxic drugs after the mastectomy. I had a choice. I could start reconstruction at the same time as the mastectomy or wait until I was completely healed. I wanted this all over and done with as quickly as possible so I chose the reconstruction to begin at the same time as the double mastectomy.

We met with Dr. S. a young plastic surgeon. He explained what would happen and asked if I had any questions.

I said, *"Yes, a personal one."*

He swung around toward us and said, *"OK."*

I asked, *"Are you a born-again Christian? Do you personally believe in Jesus Christ as your savior?"*

He stuck out his hand and said, *"I sure am!"*

And his little RN assistant, Amy, squealed, *"Yeah!!"*

He asked if I would like Dr. C. and him to pray with me before surgery. Yes, yes, thank you, Jesus, for going ahead and making the crooked places straight once again.

I averaged about 3-5 hours of sleep per night and I was physically and mentally exhausted. I mentioned this to Pastor Mark, our Sunday school teacher when he asked how I was doing. He then asked the class of about 50 if they would be willing to fast and pray one meal for the coming week for me to be able to sleep. Almost everyone in the class raised hands. I was overcome with emotion! And I slept 8 hours every single night that following week. Oh, the power of prayer! God hears and answers. He is alive and loves us so very much and is concerned about our rest.

One last round of tests, chest x-ray and pre-op appointments at the Women's Hospital in Johnson, Arkansas and I would be ready. We were so impressed with all the efficiency, cleanliness, friendliness and thoroughness of everyone we were seeing. God gave us wisdom and directed us to exactly the right doctors and facilities. Our insurance company gave us waivers twice for out of network doctors. God gave us loving favor all along the way and I became closely acquainted with our insurance company as I navigated its procedures and policies.

One of the things I had been very concerned about was the financing. We had an Arkansas insurance that required our co-pay to be 20% on everything. I had talked to the Lord about this and He had said in my heart that we would have the money for every bill that came in. Now we don't usually have an excess of hundreds of dollars each month, so this was something of a stretch for me to see HOW God would accomplish this.

"I know in whom I have believed and am persuaded that He is able to keep that which I have committed unto to Him...." 2Timothy 1:12b

Every single bill that came in for the entire time was just after I received my Social Security check and we were able pay each bill immediately. God stretched our finances to meet each obligation. Only once did we put a payment on our credit card, which we would quickly pay. God also provided extra handyman work for Arne.

"My God shall supply all your need according to His riches in glory by Christ Jesus." Philippians 4:19 And He did!

It had been one week since the lymph nodes were removed and I was in excruciating pain. Back to the doctor we went. The lymphatic fluid was trying to go back into the non-existent lymph nodes under my left arm. A golf ball size bulge in the incision was the culprit. With nothing to deaden the pain, Dr. C. guided his needle via an ultrasound machine into the incision and withdrew 8 oz of lymphatic fluid. It hurt like the dickens and I was perspiring from the pain. The relief was instantaneous.

Two days later, on our 48th wedding anniversary, it happened again. This time Dr. C. extracted 12 oz of lymphatic fluid and said,

"My experience is that if it happens twice it will happen a third time. "

In my heart, I said, *"Not on my watch!"*

When I got home, I put my fingers into my left armpit and commanded, *"In Jesus name, body of Betty Jacobson, you must obey the spirit of God and I command you, lymphatic fluid, to return to where you are supposed to go and don't you try to come back into this incision again. I take authority over you and speak healing into this area of my body in the powerful name of Jesus Christ, whose healing is mine."*

The fluid never formed again! Once again, another victory was mine. I was weak and in pain just from the surgery, but I wouldn't have to deal with the complications of that painful lymphatic fluid anymore.

You may think that weird, and me strange, but I know the Bible clearly states we can take authority over many things in the powerful name of Jesus. Why isn't everyone healed? Why doesn't it always 'work'? I don't have the answers. I just know that it is mine to take at face value and ask. I was beyond angry at this terrible pain. I meant business. All I know is, God took over and I never had to endure any more painful lymphatic fluid extractions again.   This was the beginning of many new experiences of belief and trusting in God's word and in whom

Jesus said He was, and testing all the religious teachings I had been given over my lifetime.

On July 12th, I wrote: *"Arne has been so tender, so special, so awesome with his faith and hope so strong. Thank you, Jesus, for my wonderful husband. Arne, I love you, in my mind where my thoughts reside, in my heart where my emotions live, and in my soul, where my dreams are born. I love you. You make me complete and so happy. I am so full and blessed."*

We often do not appreciate what we have until we no longer have it. I am sorry to confess that I did not treasure my husband, nor appreciate him as much as I do now. I knew I had an exceptional husband, but I realized, through this cancer trauma, just how priceless and precious was this hubby I had. I knew he loved me, but his love just exploded and enveloped me during this time. I am so thankful today for all God gave us during this *'SPECIAL'* experience of cancer as we navigated this journey together.

~ TWO ~

Robert the angry Vietnam Vet

Someone drove into our driveway and I heard voices. This is how it went: Arne was working in the garage when a man pulled into our driveway, asking directions to a local nursing home. Arne started to give him directions when smoke began billowing out of the front of the stranger's car. Arne had him quickly back away from our house and our truck and lift the hood of his car. The man swore and Arne told him God had nothing to do with the failure of his car, but He probably did have something to do with his turning into our driveway.

The man replied, *"Don't talk to me about God."*

Arne proceeded to take this man to get some parts for his car – taking the remainder of the afternoon and into the evening. Calling me about 8 pm, Arne asked if I minded if this man spent the night with us. He was a Vietnam veteran and Arne had watched him carefully and felt in his spirit that this man came into our lives for a reason. I was hesitant, but trusted my husband. My only concern was I couldn't wear a bra and I was weak and in pain. They brought home supper and I met Robert.

Robert had long stringy gray-streaked hair in need of a good washing. He was unkempt, smelled of smoke and talked a lot. Arne asked a blessing on our meal and asked God to help them get his car fixed and to bless Robert's time with us. I noticed Robert had a tear in his eye.

During our visit Robert revealed he didn't want to go to bed too early because he sometimes walked in his sleep! He also told us that he always carried a loaded pistol on his person wherever he went, including in our home.

I thought to myself, *"Oh great ~ just what I need."*

Then he revealed he had post-traumatic stress syndrome and really didn't have any relationships with other people, except vets.

I went to bed, shaking and thinking, *"This is how people get murdered in their own homes."*

Satan had a hay-day with my thoughts. I called my older sister in Oregon. After all, if something happened to us, someone ought to know who it was that did the dastardly deed!! And yet I did trust my husband. Still, I was upset with him at the same time for placing me in this situation. I was upset with God for letting this situation happen in the first place. My sister heard my story, then prayed.

After praying, she said, *"Betty, God is in this. You have to trust Him and Arne. You are going to sleep better tonight than you have slept in months."* And I did.

Robert stayed with us 3 nights while his car was repaired. Arne took him to our mechanic and transported him all around, taking time to help him with whatever he needed.

The morning he left, he stood in the garage and broke down and wept and told Arne,
"I had given up on human beings. I had given up on God. But you and your wife have restored my faith in both. My life has been changed."

Arne prayed with him as he renewed his faith in Jesus. We exchanged email addresses so we could keep in touch. We sent him on his way with a copy of the book, "<u>Heaven is for Real</u>", by Todd Burpo and Lynn Vincent.

Robert helped other Vietnam Vets get on their feet and we will only know in heaven how many lives he touched in the future. God was, indeed, in this visit. God knew he could trust Arne, despite <u>my</u> physical and mental weakness. I look back with thanksgiving for this opportunity. Another soul was touched by God's love and we were privileged to be a part of it. God is so faithful – even in our weakness. We kept in touch with Robert for the next 3 years as he grew in the Lord and pointed others to Christ. He died unexpectedly of a heart attack just about 3 ½ years from when he entered our lives. God was faithful to redeem Robert's life and make it count for eternity. This wasn't the first time we had been privileged to be a part of restoration for a Vietnam Veteran.

Kevin the Vietnam Vet

His name was Kevin. Kevin had long thin gray-streaked hair and was extremely thin and weak looking. He appeared to be the shell of the man he once was. Arne met Kevin, a Vietnam Vet, when Arne was having a kidney stone blast, called Lithotripsy, at the VA hospital Oct 2010. Arne had always been an outpatient when having this procedure in the past. Although everything looked good, the doctor insisted he remain in the hospital overnight. This annoyed Arne, but God had a plan. And He never makes mistakes – Ever!

In late afternoon, Kevin's doctor came to speak with him. He pulled the drape closed around him and proceeded to tell Kevin that he had cancer all over his body and he had only a limited time to live.

After the doctor left and some time passed, Arne got out of bed and went to Kevin's bedside and began to talk with him about his condition, and Jesus, and where Kevin was going to spend eternity. Kevin wept as he admitted that he had gotten away from his youthful faith and Arne prayed with him as Kevin made things right with the Lord.

The next morning as I arrived to take Arne home from the hospital, I stopped first at Kevin's bedside and told him that Arne had shared with me the diagnosis he had received the day before. I asked if I could pray with him. I held his hand and felt the presence of the Holy Spirit as I prayed over Kevin that God would enfold him in His mighty arms and give him everything he needed in the coming months. It was a precious time as tears streamed down Kevin's gaunt face. He assured me he had, indeed, made things right with his Heavenly Father and had put his trust in Jesus.

Kevin, a single father, had been unable to work for some time due to his progressing illness so his 19-year-old son, Harley, had become his full-time caregiver. They had a very limited income. Two years earlier, Kevin's younger son, Kaos, had not liked Dad's rules and told authorities that his father had abused him. The authorities believed Kaos and placed Kaos into his uncle's home. The Father/Son relationship had come to an end in these previous two years, and Kevin was grieving over the situation. We began praying for this family's restoration and healing, calling Kevin periodically to check on him and just show him love.

In July Kaos was invited to a Youth Camp where he gave his life to Christ. The entire family began attending church together as the love of Jesus healed a broken family and mended wounded hearts.

Arne and I delivered a Thanksgiving food box to them the Monday before Thanksgiving. I noticed that the cupboard was virtually bare.

Son, Harley, kept saying, *"Wow – so much food,"* and *"I'll be able to fix Dad a good meal tonight."*

He was impressed with the Christmas music CD enclosed and the New Testament, which he said he would really like to have himself. They just could not get over all the food our church was giving them, especially because they lived about 50 miles from us. Harley was so excited as he saw the cupboard completely filling up.

Kevin was in constant pain and didn't have much time left on this earth. As Arne prayed for him, there was a peace even as tears fell down on to Kevin's bearded face. Kevin knew where he would spend eternity and our church's love gift touched their hearts in their meager surroundings. Harley's eyes filled with tears as he thanked us for everything and for providing his father a memorable last Christmas.

Kevin went to be with Jesus in January of the next year, just 13 months after we met him. What a privilege to be a part of this family's restoration and healing. There is no problem that God cannot solve.

"Eternity" by BJ Jacobson

When this time on earth is ended,
I'll not be one bit sad.

What joy to see my Savior's face
And join Him in His land.
No sickness, No sadness,
No pain, just gladness.
Soul's saved, lives changed,
And Treasures stacked up for Eternity.

We will praise and love our Lord together,
Loved ones will be re-united.
What a Gift we have been given
When our sins are all forgiven.
For all that really matters
Is that we are on our way to heaven.
When we face the last day of our life, now passed,
Only what's done for Christ will last.

We can enjoy this life and all God has given us, but in the end, we take nothing with us except those we have pointed to the love of God. This is my ardent desire.

~ THREE ~

Surgery Day 2011

August 16th: Surgery day. I didn't want any visitors or even pastors in the waiting room. I knew I would be in pain, look terrible (you can't wear make-up going into surgery – I know, I know: pride, pride) and coming from Mayo Clinic we were unaccustomed to the "crowd" of well-meaning friends and relatives that flooded the waiting room during a loved one's surgery. I didn't even want my children there. Their love and support via telephone was all I needed. I knew they loved me and were praying. Arne brought his laptop to keep himself occupied. We really didn't want or need anyone with us, but how do you tell those who love you to please stay away?

The dilemma was solved for us: no one was allowed in the area of any breast surgeries due to the personal nature of the surgery, except the spouse or person of choice. Thank you, Lord, for that one. We told everyone what Arne's mother always said, _"There is no distance in prayer."_ And we accepted all the prayers we could get.

Dr. C. prayed with us before surgery and I then prayed for his "surgery hands" and for everything to go smoothly. We had been told to expect anywhere from 3 ½ - 5 hours for the surgery. At just under 2 hours the doctors came out and told Arne everything went like clockwork, smooth as silk and that my recovery should go more quickly due to less time under anesthesia. It was just another gift from our Heavenly Father.

Ohhhh, I hurt so badly! It felt like my chest was on fire.

I kept saying, *"Jesus, oh Jesus, help me, please help me. It hurts so bad."*

Moving me from the gurney to the bed was excruciating. There was nowhere anyone could touch me to lift me. They couldn't pull on my arms, lift my arms or touch me near my surgical sight at all. I had to scoot my hips over using my elbows and the pressure on my elbows sent debilitating, horrendous, agonizing pain into my chest that took my breath away and eventually I must have blacked out from the pain because I awoke in the bed with tubes attached to the normal poles beside the bed and my loving hubby at my side.

Arne asked me how I was doing and I said, *"I feel like an elephant is sitting on my chest."*

Dr. S. came in and said all went well, but they were unable to save my nipples and areola,

but said, *"Don't worry, Mrs. Jacobson, I'll make you a cute little pair."*

What a strange thing to remember. But that was all I remembered until later in the afternoon when the nurse came to take me for my first walk.

I was so thankful for walking on my treadmill and having strong leg muscles prior to this surgery. I had to wiggle my fanny to the edge of the bed where the nurse swung my legs on to the floor and I used my leg muscles to stand up. Okay, so far so good! Once to the door and back. Enough for now. An hour later we repeated the exercise, this time making it to the nurse's station and back. I stayed close to the handrail on the wall as it became my new best friend. Then Arne took over and he walked up and down the halls with me all hunched over – it hurt so much to try to stand up straight. I simply could not do it. It felt like suspenders were pulling my front downward.

I encouraged my loving hubby to go home because he would be bringing me home the next morning and he needed some rest too. Yes ~ one night in the hospital after such major surgery. It was amazing to me too.

I received a picture message on my cell phone shortly thereafter. It was of the small leather elephant in our family room.

The caption read, *"I captured the elephant."*

My thoughtful, loving hubby was trying to get me to smile. Oh, how I loved him! God has blessed me so much with this beautiful man!

My nighttime nurse never blinded me with lights to check my vitals. She told me to *"not wake up"* because I needed my rest and she could check on me without needing me to be awake. Bless that thoughtful nurse, dear Lord. I slept peacefully all night!

I was up and walking by myself at 6 AM and had the path well worn by the time Arne came to retrieve me at 11:00 AM that morning. We stopped for a vanilla milk shake, which tasted divine! I was actually feeling pretty good, as long as I didn't move even a smidgen.

At home, Arne helped me into bed. For a long while I couldn't sit up nor lie down by myself, nor could I swing my legs up into the bed or down on to the floor by myself. The pain was beyond belief. Sharp, searing pain that made me want to scream out loud and a couple of times, the pain elicited outbursts of *"Ohhhhhh"* that was an understatement to the pain I was enduring.

Arne would first lift my legs to the bed, then place a hand behind my back and another hand behind my neck, tell me to *"relax,"* then lower me to the pillow. Once down, I really couldn't change my position except for lifting my hips very carefully and scooting over inch by inch. At this point, I was happy to just let the sleeping and pain pills take me into blissful sleep. I could feel God's arms around me. I knew many were praying and I depended on those prayers. I rested in those prayers. I was so thankful for those prayers! And Arne's tender ministrations of whispered love and encouragement made me feel so comforted and secure. I often felt so undeserving of his devoted love. He seemed to do and say what I needed just when I needed it. How grateful I was for my husband of 48 years. God forgive me for not valuing him more in years past.

I continued to have excruciating pain on my left side from time to time and found out it was a traumatized nerve that would have to heal on its own, which happens occasionally. Of course, they don't tell you this ahead of time because you might 'imagine' that horrific pain. They said it would go away gradually within 60 days.

The surgical nurse said, *"Hold it gently and massage it until the pain goes away."*

Yep ~ I've been holding it alright – quickly grabbing my side, praying, crying, squinching my face and gritting my teeth ~ then letting out a loud ~

"Oh Babes, it hurts SO much." So, I think I've been giving it dutiful therapy.

This too shall pass...I can FEEL pain, so I am ALIVE. OK ~ I am very, very thankful for this! That pain still exists, on occasion, to this day but it is a subtle reminder of all God has done in my body. I am filled with His goodness.

I had a choice to begin reconstruction at the time of the double mastectomy or have it later after my wounds had healed. I wanted to get it 'over with' as soon as possible so chose the reconstruction to begin simultaneously with the double mastectomy.

Dr. C. removed the tissue from both breasts, then Dr. S., the plastic surgeon, placed 'expanders' underneath the pectoral muscles and filled the expanders with the first 200cc of saline solution. I was put back together with drain tubes sutured into each breast. At the end of the tubes were little plastic bulbs that resembled plastic hand grenades. Blood and fluids were draining from my breast cavities. They placed a wide elastic band wrapped several times very tightly around my entire chest area. It hurt to breathe. Those little plastic hand grenades were pinned to my elastic band. Arne had to measure, document, empty and sanitize these 3 times daily. This was time consuming, but I was still shaky and weak and unable to do this myself. Bless my hubby. I couldn't even pull my own panties down to visit the restroom. He never complained and usually had some dry humorous remark to make me smile. Yes, I was blessed.

I had been home 4 days and each day was better than the day before. However, the large ace chest bandage was getting bunched up and digging into my flesh in places, causing me great discomfort. It was a Sunday afternoon. Arne had been told exactly what to do and how to change, dress and medicate my wounds so we decided to remove the bandages and put on new ones. I had not seen what had been done to me.

As Arne unwrapped my chest and I saw what was left, I was filled with horror and shock! It looked so mangled, ugly, distorted, bruised and discolored plus I had unspeakable scars that were jagged and gross to me.

All I could think of was, *"If this is so repulsive to me, what must Arne be thinking now?"*

I almost couldn't bear to look at his face, but I quickly looked up to see what his reaction would be. He never blinked an eyelash. He continued to gently swab my wounds, tenderly put the ointment over the huge scars and replace new gauze over my chest. He then took my face into his hands and gently kissed my nose, then kissed me ever so tenderly on the lips and reminded me of his love, to be patient and that it did not matter to him. He assured me that this was Our Journey together. No matter what!

Arne was in-charge of sound at church that evening, and when he left for church, I had a giant meltdown. I cried and ached from the depths of my insides. The sorrow was raw, like when I had lost my mother and father in death. I realized I WAS grieving the loss of my body parts, the loss of my femininity, the loss of my life as I knew it. I couldn't imagine how I would ever be desirable to my husband again when I couldn't even look at my own body. I could visualize myself looking awful in a bathing suit. Arne almost always purchases a lovely, slinky nightgown for me every Christmas; just how would I look now? I sobbed until I was exhausted and spent. I tried to believe all Arne had said to me, but I just couldn't believe it in my heart. Doubts circled my head like swarming flies on a hot summer night.

I desperately needed to talk to someone, right now! But all my close friends were in church, and I really didn't know if I truly wanted to talk to them anyway. I wanted someone who would not just give me platitudes. Someone I could trust that would not judge me for my weakness. There was no one available right then.

So, I decided to send an email to my pastor's wife, a very attractive, young lady in her twenties, but someone I did trust. I knew she would pray when she received the email. I poured out my pain to her, my doubts about my self-worth now and my horror of a body I deemed deformed and ugly. She responded that very night.

Jennifer wrote, *"My beautiful BJ, God has you in the very palm of His hand and He is going to bring you through this more valued and useful than ever before. Your lovely smile will radiate His glory and He is going to surround you with peace and be your comfort in all the days ahead."*

She went on to encourage me and remind me that an entire congregation of wonderful, loving people were praying continually for me and I was, indeed, going to make it through all my tomorrows.

As I sat in my recliner, feeling very sorry for myself, the Lord gently spoke to my heart.

It felt like He was saying, *"Are you about done now? When will you turn to me for your comfort? I know the plans I have for you; plans for good and not evil. When are you going to completely trust me?"*

I then thought of all the men and women who have given their lives for our freedom; those who have lost arms, legs, and eyes and some completely paralyzed. My body part could be replaced and I would be cancer free with a full life ahead of me. I felt ashamed and yet I hurt inside. One cannot change what is, but one can change his perception of what is. I chose to, once again, place my trust and hope in my heavenly Father. It was the beginning of still another journey.

"It's OK to feel shock. We need to give ourselves the opportunity to wait before God with our disappointments and allow Him to touch our pain. We need to be in touch with what is genuinely happening to us and deal with it — to let the Lord help us to understand. Healing is a process. Sometimes it takes longer for one person than another, but time is a great healer."

"Let us always reach out and touch those who are hurting inside, when all we see is hurt in their eyes. Touch that one who is visibly in physical pain. Pain is pain. Different maladies cause pain, but pain can be just as debilitating to one person as it is to another, regardless of the cause. We live in a broken, hurting world and our job is to bring The Healer of all pain to each individual we meet, so he or she can enter into a relationship of love and completeness through Jesus Christ."

The Plastic Surgeon

The next day was my first visit with my plastic surgeon since the mastectomy.

Dr. S. unwrapped my bandages and asked how I was doing. I replied that I was doing remarkably well, pain wise, but how could he do ANYTHING with how ugly and awful my defaced body looked? I had wondered what kind of a plastic surgeon he was that he couldn't even cut a straight line. Mine was all jagged and looked like a drunk had cut the incision.

He just smiled and said, *"Mrs. Jacobson, those are not Sutures. You had plenty of breast skin, so I just rolled them up and glued you together and when this is over you will have a nice fine line that will fade in time."*

Arne came flying out of his chair and said, *"You GLUED her together?"*

We had gotten a good laugh out of that many times. God taught me a valuable lesson that day.

The Lord quietly spoke to my heart, *"You see, you are looking at this through your human eyes, but Dr. S. is looking at you through his master plastic surgeon's eyes, knowing what the end-result will be. And that is how I look at you."*

Our all-seeing God knows all that we are and more. He sees what we shall be when He has completed His work and we stand before Him, holy and without blemish: the exact likeness and image of Jesus.

"Being confident of this very thing, that He which hath begun a good work in you will perform it until the day of Jesus Christ." Philippians 1:6

I have never forgotten that lesson! That was the last melt down I ever had with this issue. I knew my Heavenly Father had it all under control!

As Arne said to me one day shortly after this: *"Hon, when your life seems like an impossible jigsaw puzzle, remember, God has the puzzle cover!"*

It was a beautiful Fall day in September and I decided to enhance my body with some vitamin D by lounging in my outdoor swing as I read a book. After about 3 hours I thought I had absorbed enough sunshine and went inside to prepare supper. My legs and arms started burning like wildfire. I wasn't sunburned and not even pink yet the burning sensation was intense but deep inside. I was SO HOT the next 5 days that I thought I surely must be running a temperature, but I was not running any temperature at all.

It finally dawned on me: anyone taking certain antibiotics is NOT supposed to be exposed to direct sunlight. Great! I had probably sun burned the tissues deep within my skin*!*

"Oh Lord, protect me from myself!"

When facing a crisis, trust God and move forward. Eventually the burning stopped and I prayed I would have no lasting-affect. I would probably develop a few more wrinkles than desired, but that was really the least of my concerns at this point!

My breast surgeon dismissed me into the complete care of my plastic surgeon for the remainder of my reconstruction. Everything was going according to plan and every 4 weeks we had a 'fill'. This became a very intriguing part to both Arne and me. The expander that was placed under the pectoral chest muscle had a tiny magnet in it where a needle syringe could be placed to add the saline solution which would then expand the muscle and fill the breast cavity, creating a pocket that would eventually hold the breast implant. The pectoral muscle is flat and needs to be expanded to accommodate this procedure gradually. The doctor would use another magnet to find the proper place and simply administer 100cc – 200cc at a time of saline, according to the comfort level of the patient. Over a period of months, the desired breast size could be achieved.

The feeling this procedure provoked was tightness in my chest, but there wasn't any real pain until near the end of the fills. It literally hurt to take a deep breath then. It became impossible to find any comfortable position in which to sleep. Sides were out of the question and eventually it was best to just sleep sitting up. My boobs felt like hard footballs and I wondered if this was all really a good idea.

2011 Ear Infection

One week after the double mastectomy in August 1, had developed a severe ear infection and was treated w/3 rounds of Augmenten, Steroid shots and Mucinex D. The infection 'appeared' to disappear, but my left ear had a 'full' feeling in it, that made it feel like it was going to burst. My ENT doctor suggested we put in ear tubes/buttons, like they do with children, so the ears could drain and then the punctured hole in the eardrum would heal and close on its own. Unfortunately, that did not happen. This was Sept 16, 2011.

I had an audiometric exam (hearing test) at that time and my hearing was normal in both ears. Because of the antibiotics I was on from my double mastectomy and reconstruction throughout the remainder of 2011, the infection was incubating and growing in my body. I was unaware of this. I just knew the hearing in the left ear sounded like I was under water and I heard little clinking sounds in my left ear also.

The doctor said I *"should be able to hear."* I kept insisting I couldn't and something was very wrong. Over about four months my ENT doctor put on four "acid patches" in an attempt to close the now Very Large hole in my left eardrum. She said she could see all three tiny bones of the inner ear. This was still in Nov of 2011. None of the patches would stay on my ear. They simply "blew off" within a couple of days. This acid patch thing was an excruciating process! I might add, that at least the pain only lasted about 10 minutes each time. I lost all hearing in that ear and was feeling more tired with each passing week.

We carried on our normal life, participating in RV Maps projects and attending our RV Maps Convention. RV Maps is an organization of our denomination that uses volunteers to build churches, campgrounds, Teen Challenge centers, disaster assistance and other worthy projects, as I previously mentioned. It consists of traveling in our RVs to a designated area and remaining there as long as needed to finish a project, donating our labor completely. It is a phenomenal organization that has become our second family after over 25 years of being members.

Just before Thanksgiving (2011) I was scheduled for the breast 'exchange' to occur. Back into the hospital I went. The plastic surgeon opened me back up, took out the expanders and replaced them with soft, silicone gel. I went home the same day, in pain once again, but looking and feeling feminine once again. We were both amazed at how natural and good the final-result was. Yes, my master plastic surgeon knew what he expected to be the end result. Just like my Heavenly Father,

"who knows the plans He has for me, for good and not for evil – for a hope and a future." Jeremiah 29:11

My children took care of Thanksgiving and Christmas and I just continued to function from doctor appointment to doctor appointment. We flew to Florida for 10 days with our Son and family in January and the sunshine was marvelous, yet my ear was not improving at all.

In Feb 2012, I finally requested a swab culture be taken so we would know what we were dealing with. The culture came back indicating that I had a bacterial/fungal/candida yeast infection in my body, coming from that left ear. The ENT doctor decided to place me on a very strong antibiotic that was supposed to eventually get rid of this infection but had risks of permanently damaging my liver.

I also began taking additional remedies: thieves oil, oregano oil, lauricidin (anti- bacterial/fungal/candida yeast herbal meds), peroxide combo by mouth, various other "healing" herbal remedies, and probiotics. I was desperate. I tried EVERYTHING I had ever read on the internet or heard about from friends. Still the infection raged in my body, causing me to be very weary, having daily headaches and my body was stressed to the breaking point. Had it not been for the Lord and my faith during this time, I would have given up. There were times I told the Lord to just take me home – I had had enough and my bands were stretched to the breaking point. Most of the time His Grace helped me be cheerful and upbeat, but there were days I became a complainer to God. This was getting old!

An MRI of my brain was done in April, which showed the infection had progressed to the mastoid also. It appeared the auditory nerve was not damaged at this point. It was a "keep on doing what we are doing, wait and see" scenario.

Surgery was suggested but I was told I would have to sign a document absolving the doctor from any lawsuits if my auditory nerve was damaged, causing permanent hearing loss, or if the facial nerve was damaged, causing paralysis on the left side of my face. These were possible side-affects of this type of surgery. I asked my ENT how many of these surgeries she had done in her career and she said, *"Four."* Not a warm, fuzzy feeling. I might add, that without the antibiotic I was on, the infection would eventually travel to my brain and could do untold damage and eventually kill me. I wasn't excited about the options, obviously! It seemed like this nightmare was never going to end. More discouragement set in as my body became weaker from the infection raging inside me.

~FOUR ~

A Ray of Hope

In August 2012, on the way home from my nephew's wedding in Minnesota, my hubby said,

"That's it, sweetheart, you are going to Mayo."

We had been told Mayo Clinic was no longer taking Medicare patients and we had found out from a Physician friend at the wedding that, that information was incorrect. And we were former patients already in the system.

We had lived in Rochester, MN for over 35 years and I had worked at Mayo for over 5 years so we were familiar with their system and knew many of the physicians there. I called my Insurance company and was assured I could go anyplace and had the best coverage available on the market. Our 2011 co-pays for my Breast Cancer had taken a very large chunk out of our budget/savings and we could not have afforded another high dollar year medically. Once again, God had provided for us by our changing insurances.

I called and made my own appointment and because we had done all our doctoring at Mayo for over 30 years and had a clinic number, I got in immediately, but scheduled my appointment for after our RV Maps Convention in Carlinville, Illinois – a highlight of our year of volunteer missions work.

I must insert something here that is of significance. I had been struggling to hear correctly for over a year. The infection in my body was zapping my strength and I barely had enough energy to make it from week to week. I felt like I was being sucked down into a deep hole and although I trusted the Lord and I cried out to Him daily, I felt like He was just not hearing nor answering my pleas for help. I was going under physically, emotionally and becoming discouraged spiritually.

I told Jesus one morning that If He was not going to answer my cries for help; if He was not going to give me the grace to get through this; if He was not going to restore my joy, which is my strength, then He could just take me home. I told Him that His Word promised all of the above, but He was not giving me what I needed. So, either deliver me and give me grace and joy, or take me home. I was tired. I just didn't want to live this way any longer ~ and I meant it. Jesus had done so much for me during my mastectomy and strengthened me and was my Rock, yet here I was – alone, tired, discouraged, fighting depression and I just wanted out. This was the week of Sept 21, 2013.

I put on a happy face, tried to be pleasant but I just wanted to stay home and not be around people. It was an effort to smile when folks asked how I was doing.

I always said, "Still trusting God to heal me."

And I did. Yet I could also tell my personality was becoming reclusive and very subdued. I've always been out-going, and I knew I wasn't "me" anymore, but I felt helpless and at the mercy of this insidious ear malady. I felt I was shriveling up inside. My eldest son noticed this at our grandson's high school graduation in May 2012 and remarked later,

"My Mom is starting to get old."

I just did not have any more reserve to draw from. I functioned on "tired" and missed most of what was said as it was distorted and sounded like I was underwater or had clogged ears most of the time. I had constant headaches every day and could only sleep about 5-6 hours a night. I tried not complaining and after almost 2 years, I felt people were getting tired of me always asking for prayer – so I quit asking. I felt God knew exactly what I needed, and I talked to Him all the time anyway. I was just waiting for Him to do something! Anything! I knew I couldn't keep going on like this much longer.

Pastor's Prayer for Me

My nerves were at their breaking point; I was exhausted when I awoke in the morning and I could scarcely wait to take an afternoon nap. I went to bed very early every night yet never seemed to feel rested and was constantly depleted, no matter what I did. The very thought of doing anything beyond what was absolutely necessary put panic into me because I just didn't think I could do anything more. I struggled to be pleasant and became very quiet and withdrawn. I didn't want to go anyplace, even church, because it took effort.

In Sunday School on Sunday Sept 23, 2012 Pastor Mark discussed the ramifications and the emotional toll that long term illnesses have on a person's physical, emotional, social and spiritual well-being. He said often the afflicted person gets to the place where they are unable to even pray for themselves.

I didn't dare say a word because my own emotions were so fragile that I knew I would begin crying if I even opened my mouth. I was crying inside and begging God to just help me get through another day. I listened as they were describing me 'to a T.' Arne knew how I was struggling and just kept his arm around my chair and occasionally would pat my shoulder in reassurance. I don't know what I would have done without my husband's strength and prayers for me.

Church began and Pastor Jonathan asked for those who wanted prayer to come forward. Arne slid his arm around my waist and pulled me toward him as he whispered in my ear,
"We are going up for prayer."

When Pastor asked why we were there, I explained that I had a Mayo Clinic appointment coming up because my ear was in bad shape.

He said, *"You are STILL having trouble with that ear?"*

Then he touched my arm and said, *"Oh, BJ, I sense that you are discouraged today."*

That was all it took. I lost it in front of everyone and began just sobbing uncontrollably, my entire body shaking. Arne just held me tightly as Pastor anointed me with oil as he and Jennifer laid hands on me and pastor prayed,

"Dear Father, you see my Sister's discouragement. Give her the grace that is necessary to get through this trial. Flood her heart with the joy of the Lord, which is her strength, and bring this trial to an end."

He then prayed for the doctors at Mayo. Immediately I felt as if someone had unzipped a body bag and I peeked out to a bit of sunshine. The depression lifted and a joy began flooding my heart like I had always had before. I went back to my seat knowing I was once again going to make it. Nothing changed in my physical condition, but I knew in my heart God had answered my prayer EXACTLY:

1. Discouragement to be gone.
2. GRACE and Peace.
3. JOY of THE LORD, which truly is my strength.

I knew beyond a shadow of a doubt that God would see me through whatever was ahead. I was at peace. And I knew I would have the energy and strength to fulfill our obligations at RV Convention. That had been a concern of mine as the time approached for us to depart.

My personal devotions and time with Jesus were the only thing that kept me sane. I have caught a tiny glimpse of a different perspective – one that showed how fleeting life is, how hollow things of earth are, how shallow and empty are the goals on which we place such importance. The only important thing is my relationship and time with Him. I need daily forgiveness and I need to be constantly in touch with Jesus. Jesus must be number one. All pride, self-importance and ego must be crucified. Jesus must increase – I must decrease. I am at God's Mercy. I can't do this alone.

"Help me, Jesus, to be obedient and faithful to you."

"No weapon formed against me shall prosper and every tongue that shall rise against me in judgment shall be condemned. This is the heritage of the servants of the Lord and their righteousness is of me, saith the Lord." Isaiah 54:17

My time with Jesus today opened my eyes to see something more clearly. Patience is more than endurance and waiting. It is faith and trust in action. My Lord has stretched me this past year, and is still stretching me. I have not asked why – the rain falls on the just and unjust alike, but I had become impatient – the opposite of faith and trust. I must fling myself into the arms of Jesus, having confidence He doesn't make mistakes – EVER! There are reasons known only to Him "why".

Mine is to trust He knows what He is doing. He has the plan and hasn't shown it to me. Mine is to walk confidently with Him, knowing I can face <u>anything</u> without wavering. He is awake all night so let Him do the worrying. I must ask for His wisdom and guidance, then leave it to Him. I must rejoice IN Him, WITH Him, THROUGH Him, and enjoy the beauty and marvels of life. I must not become burdened with problems. They belong to You, O Lord! Allow discipline to move me into Your power!

The Awesome Power of God

We left for our RV Maps Convention in Carlinville, Illinois the following day. My energy wasn't much better, but I was happy inside and every day I just felt stronger inside and had a little more energy daily. I could handle anything as long as I kept the grace and joy in my heart that only God could give. It was energizing being with our RV Maps Family, who had been loving me and praying for me for over 2 years now.

On Sunday morning, September 30th, Rev. Schneider, District Superintendent of Illinois was our speaker. He basically encouraged us that God was our supply for everything: fuel for our rigs (RVs and trucks), provision for our finances, healing for our bodies, salvation for our souls. Everything we needed! Nothing was beyond God's ability to provide! At the end of the service he asked for anyone wanting prayer to step forward. I was the first one to the altar. I was there only a minute or two when I felt a lady's hand cover my left ear and warmth began to seep into my ear. The warmth turned into very, very, warm heat.

My left ear then began to get hot and this heat traveled down my neck in ripples to my collar bone and then just radiated hot heat back up into my left ear. It did not burn, but it was like turning up a heating pad on high and leaving it there. I became very quiet.

Only once before in my life had I experienced anything quite like this and that was on Dec. 27, 1970 when my parents placed their hands upon my shoulders and prayed for our 18-month-old son whom we had been told was "wasting away" from complications of rheumatoid arthritis. An electric shock had gone thru my body from the top of my head down through the tips of my toes and I knew my son, whom I was holding, had been healed. That healing was documented at Mayo Clinic in Rochester, MN and that boy became a star hockey player – important since the specialists had told us if he lived, he would be in a wheelchair by the time he was 9-years-old. That is a later chapter entirely.

There has never been a question in my mind that God does still heal today!

As I stood at the altar, feeling this amazing heat in my left ear, I asked the Lord what He wanted me to do.

He simply spoke into my heart, *"Praise me."*

So, for about 10-15 minutes I just raised my arms and praised my heavenly Father, Jesus and Holy Spirit in my prayer language. The power of the Holy Spirit was so strong on my body that I just trembled all over. Sometime during that time, Rev. Schneider laid hands on me and prayed a couple of times, I believe. I only remember what he prayed the one time:

"Father, you promised signs and wonders would follow the preaching of your Word, so I ask that you heal this sister right now in the Name of Jesus."

I continued praising until I realized no one else was standing at the altar and they probably wanted me to "be done" so everyone could be dismissed for Sunday Noon Dinner. RV Mappers like to eat and never miss a meal!

I turned to the gal behind me, a new 'RVer' that I had not previously met, Linda. I asked her if she felt what I felt.

She replied, *"Oh yes, I most certainly did."*

I never heard her pray out loud for me. She just kept her hand over my left ear the entire time I was praising until I finished. I knew God had touched me, but I really didn't know exactly what it meant. I felt in my heart that God had zapped the infection in my body, but I have always been very skeptical of Christians who "claim" things without medical proof – probably a carry-over of my medical background. However, I also knew the scriptures, and I <u>knew</u> God could do anything! What I did know beyond a shadow of a doubt was that I was soon going to be free of this nasty ear thing and I WAS going to be OK eventually. That knowledge lodged deep within my heart.

Later that afternoon as I was taking my Sunday afternoon nap, I again asked the Lord exactly what He wanted of me. He simply spoke to my heart saying,

"Rest in me. Just rest in me." I did.

However, I felt like this same gal should pray once again. I kept thinking about the scripture, ***Mark 8:22-25,*** where Jesus touched the blind man and he said he saw *"men walking as trees."* Jesus touched him again and he could see clearly.

She agreed and we decided to pray together privately, which we did the following Wed afternoon. Nothing unusual happened that day. Linda prayed. I told the Lord I accepted His healing and we sat quietly for a few minutes, neither of us speaking. She said she sometimes "gets pictures" when praying. This had happened to me in the past so I had no
difficulty accepting this.

Linda said the following:

"I saw you walking down a road that had rocks on it – not big boulders, but rocks, that if you stepped on them the wrong way, you could twist an ankle. But if you kept looking straight ahead and watched where you were going, you were fine."

She continued, *"This is rather new to me, but I think it means that there may be some discouraging times ahead, but if you keep your eyes on Jesus and just keep trusting Him, you will be just fine."*

I told Linda this was just a confirmation of what God had given me in my morning devotions that day. I have always felt that God is big enough to tell me something first, then confirm it through the Word of God – I wouldn't have accepted this if God hadn't directed me to *Psalms 91:5-7* in my morning devotions that day. It says,

"Do not be afraid of the terrors of the night, nor the arrow that flies in the day. Do not dread the disease that stalks in darkness, nor the disaster that strikes at midday. Though a thousand fall at your side, though ten thousand are dying around you, these evils will not touch you." Living Bible

The Lord urged me to <u>not</u> take my eyes off Him, but that I should walk in His power and truth, no matter what it looked like now because victory would be mine. I had even said to the Lord,

"Oh Father, I hope this doesn't mean there is more ahead. Please let this be over soon."

Arne and I left Maps Convention on Friday, arrived home later Friday PM, unpacked the RV and put it away, packed the car on Saturday, went to church Sunday and left for Mayo Clinic in Rochester, MN on Monday AM, arriving late Monday afternoon. My first appointment was Tuesday, October 9, 2012 – a hearing test.

~ FIVE ~

October 2012 Ear Surgery

My right ear was 100% in hearing and comprehension. My left ear was only 35% and I got almost every word incorrect in comprehension with the volume at the highest level. The doctor explained it was like listening to static on the radio, and turning the volume up would only make the static worse. I was not a candidate for a hearing aid and a cochlear implant would not work for me as the infection had damaged the cochlear too. We thanked him and left. I wasn't the least bit fazed – it was just a few rocks in my path. Now I understood what the *"picture of me walking on the road"* meant.

The next day we saw the head of the Otorhinolarynology (ear/nose/throat) Department, doctor and surgeon, Dr. B. We had faxed my brain MRI and all records from Bella Vista, Arkansas to Mayo Clinic previously. Dr. B. put an otoscope into my right ear and showed us how the inside of the ear was supposed to look. It had the eardrum covering the 3 little bones, perfect little sound conducting hairs all in place and the tissue pink and healthy. He then put the scope into my left ear and we saw on the TV screen what had happened in that ear. (Arne kidded me that nothing was there because I was a true blonde!)

The eardrum was **completely gone** and the three little bones (hammer/anvil/stirrup) were completely exposed. The bottom of the hammer was missing. And there were no little sound conducting hairs anywhere. All of this had been eaten away by the nasty infection that had raged war in my body. Dr. B. ordered a CT Scan to see exactly what was going on in my head.

The CT Scan showed NO INFECTION ANYWHERE AT ALL! That is so significant I cannot emphasize it enough. If the mastoid had infection, that would entail a mastoidectomy or at best scraping the mastoid and more complications. Infections could delay or inhibit any surgery to patch the eardrum. God had done the most important part of my recovery. He had zapped and healed my body of this massive infection that had been raging in my body for over a year. Nothing was able to eradicate it, although many different procedures had been tried. The "easy" part was left to the expertise of my gifted surgeon.

Dr. B. also told us it was *"a miracle"* (Mayo physicians do not use that word lightly) that I had not contracted other infections from the OUTSIDE, all of which would have gone directly to the inner ear and subsequently to my brain, causing extensive damage and probable death due to my ear being totally exposed, vulnerable and susceptible to the elements.

We had spent two months in June and July at the Royal Ranger Campground in Eagle Rock, MO getting ready for the 2012 Camporama where over 5,000 boys and girls camped and experienced an awesome time of camaraderie, events and spiritual growth. I drove our golf cart all around those dusty roads, doing laundry and assisting wherever I was needed, then brushing dirt and dust from my hair every evening.

Hairspray, insects and any number of things could have been my demise. BUT GOD HAD PROTECTED ME FROM OUTSIDE ELEMENTS for the entire previous year. And we didn't even KNOW I was in extreme danger from "outside elements."

"He shall give His angels charge over thee, to keep thee in all thy ways." "He shall call upon me and I will answer him. I

will be with him in trouble; I will deliver him and honor him."
Psalms 91:11, 15

Someone asked why I thought God had not just healed my ear completely. I have no idea! You will have to ask God that question for yourself, someday in heaven. However, I do know that God uses us in different ways and moves us around like Chessmen, if it is to His glory.

He is much more concerned about our spiritual condition than our physical condition. I know I held a nurse in my arms at Mayo and prayed with her during one of my appointments, after sharing all God had done for our family, my children and my daughter-in-law regarding God's amazing power, healing and love for us. She wept as she thanked me and said,

"We're not supposed to talk religion here at Mayo, but thank you so much for telling me all you did. It was exactly what I needed today. I have been struggling and I'm a Christian too, but I have been so discouraged. Thank you. I needed that so much today."

Arne shared with a woman in the waiting room one of those days as well and encouraged a discouraged lady with a loved one also at the clinic. God knows our needs and only Heaven will reveal the whys of what God does. I just know He doesn't make mistakes - **EVER!** I am content with that.

Dr. B. pushed me through the system and scheduled me first on the surgical list for the next day, Thursday, October 11, 2012 as an OUTPATIENT! Only God and Mayo Clinic could perform major surgery within the skull and send you on your way in the same day!! Praise God for the marvels of science.

At 5:45 AM the next morning I was being prepped for surgery. In the operating room, there were perhaps 15 or so personnel. Because I have had a double mastectomy, I am not supposed to have any blood drawn, IVs in my arms or blood pressure taken in either arms to prevent a possible painful condition known as Lymphodema, which is something that can happen anytime the remainder of my life. So, they put the IV in my ankle and Blood Pressure cuff on my calf. The only problem is I have tiny veins and they roll and blow out easily. Everyone was waiting as the nurse was painstakingly attempting to insert a "baby needle" into my vein. Three stabs in the right ankle, two in the left and still no success. It is not a pleasant experience, but quite inconsequential compared to what I had already gone through in the past. As she moved back to my right ankle, Dr. B., all garbed for surgery, took my hand and held it tightly between both of his and kept saying,

"You're doing fine, just fine."

He continued to hold and pat my hand with both of his until she finally got the IV into a vein on the seventh try. I didn't let go of Dr. B.'s hand because God had instructed me to pray for him – out loud – in the operating room before we began the surgery, but I didn't know how that was going to play out.

So, I continued holding Dr. B.'s hand and asked,

"May I pray for you before we begin?"

He replied, *"That would be fine."*

It got quiet in the operating room. Like ~ Real, <u>REAL</u> QUIET! You could have heard a pin drop. I then prayed as I knew I was supposed to:

"Dear Heavenly Father, Thank you for these professional and talented, medical personnel in this room. Thank you for their willingness to be here ministering to me at such an early hour. I pray that you will bless each person in this room today. Please bless their homes and their families in Jesus Name. Especially bless my Dr. B today. Give him wisdom, discernment, creative ideas, understanding, steady hands and nimble fingers to use the expertise with which you have gifted him. Help him to see and know exactly what needs to be done, in a timely manner, inside my ear. For Jesus, you know, and I know, and he knows that doctors can only cut and suture – only YOU can perform the healing. So, I entrust myself into the hands of these professionals through you today. I thank you. I trust you and I love you. In Jesus Name. Amen."

It was more than quiet. There was a <u>silent hush</u>. I looked up and said,

"Well, folks, let's get this show on the road." Everyone nervously laughed, and my lights went out.

We were told the surgery would be about 4 ½ hours because it was a delicate surgery. Dr. B. cut an incision behind my left ear, the length of the entire ear. He then peeled back a portion of the skull and took a dime size piece of my human tissue (temporalis fascia) from the inside of the muscle of my skull — my own tissue would become my new eardrum.

This human tissue is tough and thick, like leather, so they shave it very thin to create an eardrum. He then went into the inner ear, fashioning and shaping the new eardrum to fit exactly where it should be, as well as touching the remainder of the hammer, so the sound would vibrate correctly into the remainder of the ear. You cannot suture an eardrum.

He then packed the cavity behind my ear with six weeks of dissolvable fabric/tissue. Then he went from the outside of the ear and into the ear canal, packing it also with six weeks of dissolvable fabric tissue, securely sandwiching the new eardrum tissue in place.

This is much like taking a piece of wax paper and sandwiching it securely between 2 bricks. This process is called, "Tympanoplasty – Overlay Graft Technique." The amazing body God made for us will do the rest and the tissue will become my own new eardrum as it heals and will take on the properties of the eardrum in time. How amazing. We are wonderfully and fearfully made!

The surgery lasted just under 2 hours and I left the hospital at noon – completely coherent but a little loopy! And the pain was very tolerable. I didn't even take any pain meds until 6 pm that evening, just before our friends, and we played a card game together in the evening. Amazing? That's my God!! My head was bandaged like a big growth was protruding out of the side of my head and naturally, there was draining from the wounds, which was expected. Arne took a picture of me in the hospital and threatened to send it to our sons, who I just knew would post it on Face Book. I looked pathetic and mercifully he didn't send my pictures to anyone. God's working on my pride again.

We were back at Mayo the next morning (Friday 10/12/12) for the bandages to be removed and all I had was some ointment behind my ear and a cotton ball inside the ear canal. We went for lunch, shopped a bit for some necessities and the exhaustion of this entire ordeal finally hit me. I slept off and on for the next 8 hours while watching TV, including the Vice-Presidential debate of 2012.

We went back to Mayo on November 15th for a hearing test and final appointment. I had to be careful for the next couple of weeks as to lifting and bending over as my ear healed, but there was no need for anything further to be done. God was doing the most important part ~ healing my ear completely! Yes, we are fearfully and wonderfully made, indeed!

A side note here: The hearing test showed my right ear comprehension to be 100% functional. The comprehension in my L. ear was 35%. But the nerve ability to hear in the Left ear is 80% max, not 100%. The Audiologist said the maximum that my hearing could be restored would be 80% because 20% of the nerve was destroyed by the infection. They gave me no guarantees that I would be able to hear clearly at all in that ear. This didn't rock my boat. I KNEW I could already hear better, even with all the packing in my ear. But I reminded the Lord that He said,

"If your child asks for bread, do you give him a stone? If he asks for fish, do you give him a scorpion? Luke 11:11

God delights in giving His children GOOD gifts. He will finish what He has started in the healing of my ear and hearing. No problem for God.

"And I say unto you, Ask, and it shall be given you; seek, and ye shall find; knock, and is shall be opened unto you." Luke **11:9** The Greek language uses acrostics for emphasis and **A**sk/**S**eek/**K**nock spells **ASK.** This is a doubling up of our requests when we ask.

God's creative and restorative ability is awesome. I will be content with *whatever* God gives me, but I am asking for the very optimum best outcome! March 2013 was scheduled for my next return to Mayo Clinic.

A New Me

Hebrews 11 is known as the Faith Chapter in the Bible. What you see, feel and hear is not the final word.

"Faith is the substance of things hoped for, the evidence of things not seen."
Hebrews 11:1

"God has the final word. No one else does. He is our future and hope. God is love beyond what we can think or begin to comprehend. His love is unconditional and all encompassing. He is faithful. He is trustable. He is our Heavenly Father."

I enjoyed the holidays and felt like a new person. My joy was off the charts. I was seeing and hearing and feeling things as though I was born anew. It was magnificent! We were planning on doing some Maple Syrup collection with my husband's brother in Northern Minnesota. It was something we had been helping with for several years, a real labor of love and we incorporated my Mayo Clinic follow-up appointment into this trip to Minnesota. I had developed a sinus infection and my ears felt "clogged" from time to time, but the medication seemed to be helping.

My appointment on March 15, 2013 was awesome. The hearing in my left ear had gone from 20% to 80% and my word comprehension was unreal. The audiologist said I repeated back the words in rapid fire, almost as if I had them memorized. I only missed 2 words. But the biggest thing was I was no longer hearing as though a radio was static. The hearing was clear and concise, and my responses indicated such. God had done it once again.

The doctor said I could get a hearing aid if I felt I needed it, but he didn't think I would need one. I had mentioned to the doctor that I was slightly dizzy the day of my appointment and we both attributed this to my sinus infection. I didn't give it much thought as it wasn't terribly disturbing, but I found I needed to hold on to Arne's arm as we walked down the long Mayo Clinic hallways. They dismissed me with hugs. What a joy to have such caring doctors.

2013 One Final Test

We left for Detroit Lakes, Minnesota the next day and arrived during the beginning of what turned out to be the first of three blizzards over the next seven weeks. My dizziness accelerated until I was in bed almost constantly. I couldn't eat or get out of bed without the entire room swimming in circles. The nausea made food unappetizing. The wind outside blew and snow accumulated as the turmoil and fear accumulated in my heart. My thoughts went wild thinking something else was drastically wrong.

I called my personal friend and doctor in Bella Vista and Dr. Margaret told me what to purchase to help my vertigo and dizziness. She urged me to see a doctor if it didn't get better promptly, but had no idea what was causing all of this. I didn't have the flu, no temperature but I was miserable. We decided that if things didn't improve by the end of the week, we would go back to Mayo Clinic because something was obviously very wrong.

The Maple Syrup was not running because the temperature was too cold. We kept getting snow, snow, snow and more snow! I love snow. I had missed snow. I'm a Minnesota gal! But

I was trapped in a body that couldn't enjoy anything, couldn't do much except lay and feel very sorry for myself. And I wondered where God was. I wept out of sheer frustration. It was the biggest testing point of my life so far on this journey. I "felt" forsaken, but I KNEW differently.

Sometimes we just can't trust our feelings. They mock us, and our faith, way too many times.

If I did not believe God to be in control of my circumstances, with His loving, good purpose in mind for me, I could doubt and become bitter. God's character is holy, loving, forgiving and His Word PROMISES that His plans for me are for my good and for my welfare and He is ever true and faithful. Therefore, whatever befalls me must be sifted through the sovereignty of God's Hand in allowing it to happen.

"But when I am afraid, I will put my trust in you." Psalms 56:3

And I was fighting fear, big time.

God's good plan for my life is never frustrated by the magnitude of circumstances. Whatever or wherever I am, I must choose to believe it is a part of His overall plan for me. There are lessons to be learned, faith to be tested so I will grow stronger in my faith and in the end, understand fully His awesome faithfulness. Yet the flesh is weak and fear of circumstances is sometimes overwhelming. Still, in my heart I knew my God was faithful!

It was March 29, 2013 at 4:30 PM in the afternoon. I sobbed out to God like a little child, begging Him to please, please, please take this from me. I had never felt more helpless and more vulnerable than I did at that moment. I felt like a ragdoll, all limp and wasted. I needed to feel my Heavenly Father's arms around me, yet I just felt useless and alone. I laid on my pillow, exhausted from weeping but finally quiet and still. And then I heard that familiar whisper, of Jesus, saying to me,

"It is over. It is finished." It was so quiet I wasn't sure I had actually heard it, yet I knew I had.

I slept the remainder of that day and night and awoke the next morning, Saturday, and that dizziness was gone. It was an incredible feeling of relief. For the next five-weeks I took short morning walks in the woods or tried some cross country skiing, rode on the snowmobile with my hubby or just sat in the sun, all bundled up in snowmobile suit and boots. The afternoons were long nap times as I gradually regained the strength that had depleted my body for the last two years.

Unknown to me, my Heavenly Father knew I needed this "forced rest" in the beautiful wooded land of Northern Minnesota, even though we complained that we needed the warm weather for the maple sap to run. My precious brother-in-law and wife, Kurt and Andrea, housed us and loved on us as we shared their home together for seven weeks. It was a time of healing for my body, mind and spirit. And a beautiful time with them!

As I looked back, I realized it was on Good Friday that God healed my body completely. It WAS over! It WAS finished! Jesus had ALREADY purchased my healing on Calvary over 2000 years before. My heart was humbled. Why should He love me so?

Why should He love you so? Whatever has happened to you – God can forgive. Forgiveness brings us into God's eyes as pure and chaste. Purity is a matter of the heart, a heart in right relationship to our Lord. His love isn't changed or diminished by our wrongs. Forgiveness makes us clean in His sight. We are His Beloved, the light of His love – pure and undefiled – forgiven and clean as His New Bride.

Why should He love me so? Why should He love you so? He loves us because He created us. He loves us because He redeemed us on Calvary. He loves us because that is His very nature. And He loves us because we accept Him as our Savior and his blood covers all our sins. We are His children and He is our Father. A Father takes care of His children and loves them unconditionally.

"Thank you, Father, for your gift of Jesus and eternal life and for your Holy Spirit that lives within us every day for the remainder of our lives."

Yes, Jesus loves me. For the Bible tells me so, and He loves you too.

"And may your strength match the length of your days. There is none like the God of Jerusalem. He descends from the heavens in majestic splendor to help you. The eternal God is your refuge, and underneath are the everlasting arms." "He is your shield and helper. He is your excellent sword." Deuteronomy 33: 25-29

When you are weary and everything is going wrong – utter these words, *"When I am afraid, I will trust you, Jesus."* Then fall into His everlasting arms!

"Let everyone bless God and sing His praises, for He holds our lives in His hands. And He holds our feet to the path. You have purified us with fire, O Lord, like silver in a crucible. You captured us in your net and laid great burdens on our backs.

You sent troops to ride across our broken bodies. We went through fire and flood. <u>But in the end,</u> you brought us into wealth and great abundance." Psalms 66:8-12

On January 2011, I had told God I wanted everything He had for me. I wanted more of Him.

He spoke gently to my heart saying, *"I will make you shine."*

I hadn't remembered at the time that gold and silver become pure and shiny only through the smelting process. The raw ore is placed in a crucible, super heated over a very hot, intense fire until the ore melts and all the impurities are released. The Master Potter knows the gold/silver is pure when He can see His reflection in the gold or silver. It is a process. This has been a process. I have not particularly enjoyed the journey as it was extremely painful and torturous at times, but I would not exchange what I have gained through all of this, nor the closeness I have experienced with my Lord for anything in this world. And guess what? God was not finished with me yet.

It was time to leave Minnesota. We had no idea what was ahead.

~ SIX ~

2013 Fernando

Our neighbor of 13 years, Fernando, had been diagnosed with lung cancer two years prior in 2011. Fernando was a private and proud man from Mexico who had been in the United States for over 20 years. He was a hard worker, spoke perfect English and was a tax paying, law abiding citizen of 40 years old when he first purchased the house next door to us.

We became good friends and had him over many times for meals and helped him with any legal questions that came along. We grew to love him like a son and he confided in and trusted us. Arne became a mentor to him. He showed him how to do many useful things around his house, offering assistance or tools whenever it was needed. Fernando would often correct my Spanish pronunciation or usage and we laughed at my many mistakes. He was divorced but had two grown sons, one of whom was married with two little boys who gave their young grandfather great joy. His youngest son had gotten in with the wrong crowd and caused his father much sorrow, but he loved him so.

Many times, over the years we shared our faith with Fernando and always prayed for him before he would leave our home. This sometimes became daily as we noticed his fear of approaching death. The day came when Fernando fully surrendered his life to Christ and became an avid reader of the Bible. I noticed that he seemed to have quite a vast knowledge of the Word of God, but assumed his new relationship with Jesus had precipitated a hunger for the Bible. We suspected that he came over to our house for "no reason" many days of every week, just so we would pray for him and love on him.

When we returned home from Minnesota, Fernando had taken a turn for the worse and Hospice was called into the situation. Because there was no one who could stay with Fernando to help with his needs, particularly during the day, we became his primary care givers. His church, our church, neighbors and friends brought many meals, but I took care of his medicines and kept track of everything for him because I could write the Spanish names on the bottles for him and keep a detailed spreadsheet for him as to when and how much medicine he was supposed to have daily. He was taking 17 different regular medicines daily, plus oxygen treatments and hard drugs for the pain – all of which had to be monitored. He had a hospital bed in his living room and was hooked to oxygen with a long cord that permitted him to reach almost anywhere in his home.

I daily got up very early and checked on him many times throughout the day and night. The Hospice nurses came twice weekly, but I changed his pain patches and other medical necessities and interfaced with the various medical personnel. Fernando and I had many good times together of praying and talking about eternity and God's love during this precious time. I was at his home more than my own those eight weeks. Arne kept Fernando's yard cut and groomed and spent many hours talking with him also. Fernando loved Jesus and was clearly concerned about his sons. His father was deceased, his mother and brother lived in Mexico and we were trying to get permission for them to come to see Fernando before he passed away. We couldn't cut through the red tape and it was not to be.

The day came in July when Fernando needed to go into the hospice medical facility. We visited him often those last two weeks and the last time I spent time with him I told him we really needed to talk.

I knew he loved Jesus, but he was agitated much of the time and because I was granted permission to know his medical status, the doctor confirmed with me that, indeed, something was greatly bothering Fernando.

I sensed that he was very afraid and remembered he had once voiced his fear of suffocating to death. I gently broached the subject as Fernando lay with his eyes closed, too weak to keep eye contact.

I asked, *"Fernando, you know you are ready to meet Jesus, right?"*

He said, *"Yes, I know I am."*

I said, *"Fernando, dying is a precious thing to Jesus when one of His children come home to heaven. It is simply inhaling a breath of air on earth and exhaling that air in heaven. There is nothing to fear because it is a beautiful, peaceful experience for a child of God as he is ushered into the presence of Jesus. And the doctors will not let you struggle or choke to death. They are giving you medications now to make your breathing easier and you do not have to be afraid. There will be no panic. There will be no pain. They have promised me that. You will slip gently into the arms of Jesus."*

I told him how I had studied death and dying years before and I read of many who went to be with Jesus which the Bible confirmed that:

"blessed in the sight of the Lord is the death of his saints."
Psalms 16:15

Such a precious peace and presence of Jesus entered Fernando's room that day. I knew Jesus was cradling my dear friend tenderly. Fernando opened his eyes and with tears slowly rolling down his cheeks said,

"Thank you for telling me that. I have been so afraid of dying. I needed to hear that." He took a deep breath and his entire body relaxed as he closed his eyes once again in deep peace. Four days later Fernando went to be with Jesus, in his sleep, just as I had told him he would. He died peacefully in the arms of Jesus as he took his last breath on earth and inhaled his first breath in heaven. He was finally home.

Then the surprise came! Fernando's dear mother was able to come for the funeral. I have never met anyone so very tiny, frail, petite and crinkled, yet with such a steel gripped handshake. Her faith was of equal steel.

Also attending was a family of 4 children, a mother and father, who sat with the remainder of the family. I had never laid eyes on any of them. This father got up and told us that he was Fernando's out of wedlock son, who had only seen his father three times in his entire lifetime. He was a youth worker in an Assembly of God Church in Austin, TX and his entire family loved Jesus and had been praying for Fernando for years.

Fernando's "Mama" (we all called her that) spoke no English so I had to take over her care since I spoke some Spanish. She was staying at Fernando's house next door to me but Fernando's sons had all been born and raised in the United States and spoke only English. Come to find out Fernando's Mama, deceased father and entire family in Mexico were all very committed

Christians and Fernando had been raised in this Christian home which explained his vast knowledge of the Bible.

In Spanish, the first thing "Mama" asked me was, *"Do you know Jesus?"*

It seems God plopped Fernando down between two Assembly of God families who simply loved him to Jesus. And it was all because of a praying Mama in Mexico, who never had met her grandchildren or great grandchildren.

Oh, the faithfulness of a God who hears and cares about a Mama's cries for her children. Fernando knew Jesus 100%. We prayed together many, many times and it was a privilege to be a part of this beautiful story. God is faithful ~ always!! This Mama had been praying for her son for years. Mama hugged me and thanked me as I told her that Fernando was, for sure, with Jesus and his funeral was a celebration of praise – very loud with much audible praise from his Mama.

I marveled as for the next couple of days Mama and I shared prayers, singing praises to Jesus together in two different languages. It surely was not an accident that Fernando moved in right next to us 13 years prior and we were privileged to share the love of Jesus with him. A mother's prayers were answered. There is no distance in prayer – **ever**! And God never makes mistakes!

I could never have kept up the pace nor ministered to Fernando if God had not completely healed and restored my body while in Minnesota. What an awesome God we serve. He plans all our tomorrows, *if we let Him*! This same strength, healing and restoration would again become even more real in my life many years later, when I would need it more than any other time in my entire life. Yes, God, you ARE real!

~ SEVEN ~

Arne's Emergency Appendectomy

The Psalms are filled with verses that tell us how God preserves our lives; how he keeps us by His mighty power; how He protects us from danger that we don't even realize is there. How many times this has happened to us in our lifetime. One time stands out above all the rest: September 2013.

Arne has passed well over 250 kidney stones in our 54 years of married life. Mayo Clinic in Rochester, Minnesota did a study on why his body was producing the kidney stones and how to stop the production of them. They never resolved either issue. He has had many procedures including several Lithotripsy blasts, as well as major surgery to remove a stone that would not pass through his system. All of this has been excruciatingly painful and tiresome to say the least. He has developed a very high tolerance for pain, but it was never a piece of cake by any long shot.

He had been having back pain for several months and decided to request a CT Scan at the VA to see exactly what the stones were doing. This was the first time Arne had personally requested this.

The doctor came back and said, *"You have two small stones that you will pass without any trouble, but did you know that your appendix is _twice_ the normal size?"*

We had never heard that before. In checking previous CT Scans, the appendix appeared normal, so this was a relatively new phenomenon. The Doctor suggested we seek another opinion from someone more versed in this field. We decided to see our regular "outside" family doctor, who also happened to be a personal friend of many years, Dr. Margaret.

She studied the CT Scan and told us this was very strange and although rare, sometimes tumors can grow inside the appendix which can be very serious. Arne exhibited no fever, no appendix pain, and all his tests were normal with no symptoms of anything. She palpitated his appendix completely, without any reaction whatsoever. She said she wanted to send his CT Scans to a surgeon to review, and sent us home.

The next morning Arne awoke with pain in his side that was growing in intensity. Back to Dr. Margaret who promptly sent us to the Emergency Room. She called ahead and had them waiting for us when we arrived. Arne was rushed into an examination room. The surgeon checked him over, asking a myriad of questions. Arne wasn't in extreme pain, but he was uncomfortable. His threshold of pain from all the kidney stones over the years had conditioned him to be able to tolerate a great deal of pain.

It was decided that he must endure a colonoscopy to rule out any tumor that might later have to be removed, since the colon and appendix are connected rather closely. Arne stayed overnight in the hospital, drinking the nasty liquid which cleans out one's system. Not a fun night!

At 9:00 AM on Saturday Arne had the colonoscopy, which showed only two small polyps. Everything was normal. At 2:00 PM that same day they performed an appendectomy which revealed two good size tumors, in-tact, inside the appendix. These were cancerous and a very rare occurrence. This particular type of cancer is highly aggressive and is typically not found until after the tumor has burst, spewing deadly cancer into all nearby lymph nodes and throughout the body. The cancer is lethal and death occurs within a short span of time. The lymph nodes in Arne's body were clean and all tissue was healthy. They removed the entire thing laparoscopically.

Our family doctor, Dr. Margaret, followed us closely and had us meet with an Oncologist who told us,

"Arne would not be sitting here having this conversation if those two tumors had not been found as they were."

Arne had blood work every four months and a CT Scan annually to keep an eye on things. God went before us and made all the crooked paths straight. He protected Arne when we didn't even know anything was wrong. My loving Heavenly Father preserved the life of my devoted husband and gave us more years to share our love together and serve our Lord. We serve a great and powerful God.

How does serving Jesus make a difference, really?

Many do not understand why anyone would be devoted to and serve Jesus Christ. Life is not easy. Life is hard. Many difficulties face each of us every single day of our lives. Some have it more difficult than others. There are physical maladies; financial problems; marital differences; difficulties with children; job issues and the heart-rendering stories that are hurled at us daily in the news. We all have these. No one is immune from them. We live in a fallen world. Serving Jesus Christ doesn't insulate us from any of these problems.

BUT we never have to face a single issue alone. <u>Jesus is right by our side</u>, giving us the peace, guidance and all we need in this mixed up, broken world. He DOES give us what we need, just when we need it the most! He has promised to give us wisdom if we ask for it, plus peace and joy for every day.

He is my friend, confidant, Savior and coming King. How could I NOT love and serve someone who gave His life for me so I could be free from the guilt of sin, never walk alone and look forward to a heavenly home someday with him?

PS. Dr. J., Arne's surgeon, told Arne that she noticed he had previously had a splenectomy. He said she was correct and that he had ruptured his spleen, while sledding as an 11-year-old, and it had been removed.

The doctors had told Arne's parents that he probably would be sickly and would not live terribly long without a spleen. Dr. J. told Arne he had several little spleens that had grown back in place of the removed spleen and two were of fairly good size and fully functioning. This is a rare occurrence. God specializes in these rare occurrences!

Arne has been extremely healthy all his life, except for the kidney stones. Apparently, God had plans for Arne's life that didn't include early death from the lack of a spleen. What a great God we serve!

~ EIGHT ~

Invasive Eye Surgery

Wow ~ you have GOT to be kidding??! I had gone faithfully to my Ophthalmologist every four months for the last 6 years. I had faithfully put drops into my eyes to keep the pressure normal and prevent me from going blind. And now I am almost blind in my left eye? I was SO very tired of doctors and surgery, thank you very much!! I had four major surgeries in the last three years. Yet that is what I was hearing today (June 2014).

The conversation went like this:

"Your pressure is very good, but you are losing your peripheral vision now. We'll take another Visual Field test again next week to be sure, but you may have to see a specialist and surgery may be in order."

I was stunned. I queried, *"I thought you WERE a glaucoma specialist?"*

He simply replied, *"No."*

I was livid, confused and frightened. What had just happened? This man had been following my case for five years, ever since Dr. V., my original Glaucoma Specialist had left this clinic. I was told this present doctor was the glaucoma specialist for this clinic. As it turned out, there was NO glaucoma specialist any longer in this eye clinic.

Five years prior, in 2009, I was diagnosed with Open Angle Glaucoma, greater in the left eye than in the right eye. A young Christian glaucoma specialist, Dr. V., was practicing in this very well-known clinic in our area.

He took my hands in his, looked deep into my eyes and said, *"Mrs. Jacobson, I can't restore the sight you have already lost, but I promise you I will do everything in my power to help you retain the sight that you have left in your eyes. I will take care of you as if you were my own mother."*

He then asked to pray with Arne and me, and asked the Lord for wisdom and guidance and peace for us. It was a reassuring feeling.

By the time I was referred to Dr. V., I had already lost about 80 –85% of the upper vision in my left eye. I complained to my regular optometrist that my glasses felt "smudged," yet they were perfectly fine. After examining me thoroughly, he sent me to see Dr. V.

Glaucoma comes on very sneakily and one hardly notices it is occurring until damage is already done – my case exactly. I can best describe how it affected my ability to see: somewhat like wearing a ball cap with the visor pulled rather low on the forehead. There was almost a shadow blocking some of my vision, but it really didn't bother me that much because my right eye compensated and my vision tests were all 20-20 with glasses.

Because of the progression of this insidious disease, Dr. V. performed Selective laser trabeculosplasty within the next couple of months, on each of my eyes respectively, without complications. This was a rather painless office procedure that would arrest the glaucoma temporarily, but noted in my file,

"We may need to consider incisional surgery in her left eye."

I had been placed on a nightly ritual of Travatan Z eye drops, which I was cautioned to faithfully use, as these drops were to aid in lowering the intraocular pressures in the eyes. However, the intraocular pressures had continued to run in the high 20s so the trabeculosplasty along with the drops would hopefully keep my eyes from deteriorating any further.

I had undergone cataract surgery, yag capsulotomies, LASIK and radial keratomy in both eyes about 11 years prior so there was considerable scarring on my eye, which may or may not have led to my glaucoma problems now. There is no other history of glaucoma in our family.

In my visit to Dr. V. in March 2010, he placed in my records:

"Clearly she has a borderline intraocular pressure in the left eye.... I have recommended close observation and emphasized the importance of good compliance with Travatan Z. Incisional surgery may be warranted if she were to continue to progress."

Dr. V. was my doctor for 2 years, then left Bella Vista to open his own facility in another city. My last check up with Dr. V. was August 12, 2010. Dr. V. was no longer in my insurance plan and I asked who at the facility where I was currently being seen could take over my case. I was assigned to another doctor, whom I assumed was also a glaucoma specialist, and was told by the facility this replacement doctor was "very well versed in glaucoma issues."

I began seeing this new eye doctor in December 2010 and he seemed to think I was doing wonderfully. I thought I was in good hands. For the next 3 years, I continued to have regular vision tests and faithfully administered my eye drops, never missing a single time. I asked for print outs of my Field of Vision tests for the first year, but since there was no change and my new doctor seemed to be up on my case, I quit requesting them.

Now, after being told I was losing my peripheral vision too, I asked for a print out of all my records since beginning treatment. It took me literally less than 3 minutes to see that someone was NOT 'on the ball' with my eye care. Things had begun to get worse 2 years prior to now. I had questions and I wanted answers. I received a phone call from someone at this facility telling me my Field of Vision was the same as last week, but we would "wait and see" for 6-weeks and then have another Field of Vision test to be sure that it was, indeed, accurate.

We are only given one set of eyes. My print outs confirmed what I could plainly see and I knew I needed to see a specialist NOW – not in 6 weeks.

I looked in the phone book and found Dr. V.'s clinic. I called my insurance, which was now different, and found he was in my plan for sure. Furthermore, he had just opened a satellite office in my very own city, just 7 miles from my home in Bella Vista, Arkansas.

"God, are you GOOD, or what?"

I immediately went to his office in Bella Vista, and asked if I could be worked into the schedule. I brought my print outs with me and explained the importance of seeing the doctor as soon as possible. I was the last patient of the day, a wait that was well worth every single minute!

Dr. V. remembered me immediately and asked about our RV Maps work. You see, he had contributed to our gas fund while he treated me initially and we talked often about what we were doing and where we had been and were going next.

Since seeing him God had blessed him beyond belief, not without difficulties to be sure, but he had become well-known throughout the region, training other glaucoma specialists in his surgical techniques. People were coming from all over the United States for his care and skills. He was traveling to Iceland that very next week, at the invitation of the head of the FDA, to lecture other surgeons about his techniques.

I found out he was a very gifted surgeon with many awards to his credit. Yet he was only 42 years old, had a wife and 3 beautiful children and loved Jesus. He is also a gifted singer and songwriter, having cut two CDs, to his credit, which he gives out to his patients. I already had one of them. He is a humble, loving, caring physician who desires to help his patients achieve their very best.

He never told me these things – I found them out from his staff, the plaques on the wall and from my own investigation initially. Once again, God had gone ahead of me and planned each day before I even knew what I needed.

After a long afternoon of many tests Dr. V. told me what I already knew: I should have had the incisional surgery 2 years prior to now. I had, indeed, lost my peripheral vision in the left eye, leaving me with primarily central vision only. The right eye had also progressed some and would need surgery before too long, as well, unless God performed another miracle.

You know, we can choose to become bitter or better. It is always a choice. Yes, a mistake had occurred in the professional opinion of my doctor. I have no earthly understanding of why my 'other' doctor didn't choose to send me to a specialist as soon as he saw the deterioration from the eye tests. I certainly could see it the moment I viewed the printouts. But the damage was done. Only my Heavenly Father could restore my lost vision. I had no option but to forgive and simply trust the Lord one more time to keep me seeing what I needed to see. Surgery was scheduled for the following week.

The Big Day

June 17, 2014 was the Big Day. A TRABECULECTOMY was the order of the day. We arrived at the surgery center, checked in and settled to wait for the nurses to begin their preparations with me. We had brought along our iPad in order to check our emails and to keep us occupied until I was called into surgery.

I had noticed a six-minute U tube video showing the surgery of a trabeculectomy, but just had not taken the time to view it – until now. It was graphic, explicit and accurate. Probably **not** the wisest thing to view just before having it done! I barely finished watching the video when my turn arrived.

God promises a safe landing, but not necessarily a calm passage. I wondered what kind of seas I was embarking on this time. However, God's guidance and love in the past gives courage for the future. I was ready.

I don't remember anything from the time I was wheeled away until I was putting my flip-flops on and being helped into a wheelchair. I had no pain, but had a bandage over my left eye and just wanted to sleep. The remainder of that day I did exactly that!

It is amazing how easily the days can all run together following surgical procedures. sometimes. It's a good thing I keep some type of journal because the clutter of my mind prohibits me from remembering details that escape like little mice released from a cage.

My results looked great and my doctor was pleased with the healing that was taking place. Arne put several drops in my eyes, four times daily and at bedtime. Additionally, he had to tape a plastic eyepiece over my eye when I slept to prevent any bumping or touching of the eye. This little plastic eyepiece became a part of my body for the next 8 weeks. And no makeup for the duration of this journey!

OK ~ here we go again! More pride busting! Now, I'm 100% Scandinavian, naturally blonde and fair skinned. You cannot see my eyelashes and my eyebrows are almost non-existent because of the blonde color. I look in the mirror and see a very bland, colorless face looking back at me. I know many of us are too self-critical and I am no different. Every day, for as long as I can remember, I have "fixed my face" for the day! And I have envied the gals with the dark eyelashes and brows who look like they just stepped out of a beauty salon and need no makeup whatsoever. God truly has a sense of humor!

Thankfully over the years God has healed me of self-loathing, insecurity and the feelings that I had to be perfect all the time to be loved. He gave me a husband who validated me just as I was, no frills or extras needed. But I remember all too well the times of judging myself by how I looked, what I weighed, what I wore, how I behaved or how I thought others perceived me. When things were going smoothly and my performance seemed adequate, I found it easier to believe that I was loved and that God loved me too. But when I felt discouraged or inadequate, I would search inward to correct whatever was wrong.

To God we are made complete and absolutely perfect, lacking nothing. In HIS eyes we are exquisite just as we are! Who else's opinion really matters?!

"You are altogether beautiful my darling, beautiful in every way."
Song of Solomon 4:7

Introspection is good, but only if it is judged against the Word of God. Only Jesus can take away the inferior complexes that are imposed upon us in our society today. As you spend time with Jesus and begin to <u>really</u> know Him and know
how much He loves you – just the way you are – it is then that you begin to gain the confidence that only Jesus can give. No one can make you feel, think or be anything, <u>unless you allow it</u>.

"He made me get so angry." No, you allowed him to make you angry.

"She makes me feel so inferior." No, you allowed her to make you feel inferior.

"That picture made me think unhealthy thoughts." No, you allowed your mind to think those thoughts.

Jesus frees us to become <u>all</u> that He created us to be because He accepts and loves us. Thank you, Jesus, for your gift of love. Having an inferiority complex was a big problem for me in my younger days, but that is another chapter altogether. My Heavenly Father has continually given me the confidence through His Word and Love to make me know He loves me just the way I am, right now! And He will change anything that needs changing, if I allow Him. I was on my way to another stretching experience! With or without make up! Yes, God has, indeed, a sense of humor!

The Doctor clipped 2 stitches and immediately the eye pressure dropped from 17 to 2. It was amazing. Now I would be starting the waiting game. The remaining stitches felt like porcupine quills in my eyes. This too would pass. I kept getting the feeling that I still had not learned to be very patient.

My former pastor, Rev. O.E. told us this story:

A parishioner asked for prayer for patience. The Pastor began praying for tribulation to be heaped on the man. The man stopped the Pastor and said,

"Pastor, you are praying wrong. I asked you to pray for patience, not tribulation."
The Pastor just quoted the Bible, **"Tribulation works patience." Romans 5:3b**

I hope I learn that truth sooner than later!

Two days after the pressure went down, my vision became extremely cloudy, like I was looking through a piece of wax paper. I was concerned, but was told this would correct itself as the pressure rose to a higher number. Once again, I must trust my Lord and wait patiently.

After eight weeks into my recovery, my left eye was responding beautifully. My doctor was extremely pleased and my vision was getting clearer daily. I was excited about my tomorrows.

~ NINE ~

My Earlier Years

I was next to the youngest of five children and born in 1942. WWII was a turbulent time for everyone. In spite of the lean times for my family I never felt deprived. I was a very shy child who loved being at home by my mommy. They tell me that as soon as I was dressed up to go out someplace, I would become cranky and would fuss the entire time until we returned home. My mother told me it was so frustrating to her because I was such a happy and content child when at home. I still am today! I love being a wife and homemaker! I love my home! Give me a good book and a good cup of coffee, and I am a very happy camper. Interesting, since we travelled so much and were seldom home. God had taken care of that in me ~ but I still love being in my home!

I chattered like a magpie all the time and my Aunt said I sounded like peas rattling in a kettle. Apparently, my shyness didn't include my mouth because I never seemed to be at a loss for words and was always able to express my feelings openly – sometimes too openly. It was something my Heavenly Father had to work with me even into my young adulthood, and on...! I have all the verses in my Bible that refer to the tongue underlined in red with a note in the margin saying,

"This is for me," or *"Pay attention to this, Betts!"*

"A wise man holds his tongue. Only a fool blurts out everything he knows. That only leads to sorrow and trouble." *Proverbs 10:14*

"A man with good sense holds his tongue." Proverbs 11:12b

"Don't talk so much. You keep putting your foot in your mouth. Be sensible and turn off the flow." Proverbs 10:19

"Self-control means controlling the tongue. A quick retort can ruin everything." Proverbs 13:3

"A good man thinks before he speaks." Proverbs 15:28

"Work brings profit: talk brings poverty." Proverbs 14:23

Around the time I was in 7th grade I began getting tonsillitis, strep throat and such related illnesses on a frequent basis. I missed almost two months of school in my freshman year and finally in the 10th grade had my tonsils removed, which solved the problem.   I was hospitalized many times during that time and once I came very near to not making it. I do remember hallucinating and thinking everyone was trying to poison me and would refuse to swallow any pills. Obviously, I recovered and became an active teenager.

My school years were unremarkable. My parents gave us a loving home where Jesus was honored and loved. My mother taught me to sew and tried to teach me to cook, rather unsuccessfully. When I married, I knew how to make exactly 5 meals. Arne didn't know he would be saddled with the same 5 meals for several months as I learned to navigate the cooking skills.

I took many years of piano lessons and remember many recitals with Dairy Queen treats afterwards. I also played the drums and tenor saxophone in Junior and Senior High School respectively.

It was a happy childhood. I had good friends, but I wasn't the most popular girl by a long shot. We couldn't afford all the latest fashions and I learned to sew most of my clothes. I was tall and skinny and slightly bow-legged. My older brothers teased me mercilessly about having 'chicken legs'. I had the normal blemishes that many adolescents have. I had not learned to make my hair behave and the entire package, according to my brothers, was that of an ugly duckling. Especially since my baby sister, 4 years younger than me, was perfectly beautiful with long curly blond hair that stopped people in their tracks. I grew up truly feeling like that ugly duckling. So, I achieved.

Everything I did, I did to perfection. I excelled and took first place in every piano contest, brought home excellent grades and read voraciously. I also loved literature and speech and found them to be very motivating for me. I won every Bible reading and memorization contest in our church. As a Sophomore in High School I became the first Minnesota State Quiz Team Champion in our church denomination's Quiz Team Program on the Bible. I even beat out the largest Church Quiz Team in Minneapolis, Minnesota, Bloomington Assembly of God. This was significant since we only had 4 girls in our church's youth group and all of us were on the quiz team. Bloomington Youth Group had hundreds of young people to choose from who could compete on their team.

I loved every minute of it! I thrived on competition. However, I still felt ugly and inadequate. This poor self-image and self-loathing would follow me for years and would nearly destroy my marriage. Only our loving Heavenly Father would be able to heal a broken, misguided and untrue lie that I had embraced.

When I was in the 10th grade, I made a commitment in my heart to the Lord at the end of one of our Sunday morning church services. Our Pastor made a plea and I raised my hand in commitment to his plea.

What I heard was:

"How many of you, teens, will commit to not dating an unsaved person and trust God to bring you a Christian mate some day?"

I found out later that this plea was never made. It was entirely something else, but that is what **I heard** and that is what **my commitment** was that day! This commitment would save me from many heartaches, but didn't give me a lot of options for dating.

Our church was rather small. There were 5 young men in our youth group. Two of them were my brothers. With only three fellows and about 4 girls, well, the selection was limited! So, I really didn't date all that much. I was asked out by a couple of schoolmates, but I knew their lack of commitment to The Lord was not what I wanted to see in a husband.

When my older brother came home from Bible College to see his girlfriend, he often brought a classmate with him and I was left to do the entertaining of his friend. These guys were 4 years older than I, so that was mostly my frame of reference in dating. I had a crush on one of these young men, but he got married about a year after I had spent quite a bit of time with him in our home.

I won 3 small scholarships to North Central Bible College (now University)/McPhail School of Music in Minneapolis,

Minnesota: 1/Original Oratory; 1/Speech-Oral Recitation; and 1/Musical Presentation /Piano.

This netted me tuition for the first year and the first quarter into my second year. I became a full-time McPhail music student. I audited several Bible classes as well. NCBC was set up so students could take all their classes in the morning, leaving the afternoon and evenings for outside work, study and social opportunities.

I secured a job as a Counter Girl at Falconer's Dry Cleaners and Launders. I was paid well and it was only a six-block walk from my college. A couple of other male students from NCBC also worked there so it was an ideal situation with rides provided most of the time.

My brother's college buddy that I had fallen for 2-years prior had married, but his wife had left him almost immediately for another man and he was now divorced. We connected and began dating. We continued dating throughout the school year and into the summer. I moved into an apartment with two other close friends, but felt uneasy about continuing my course of study in music for the Fall Quarter of college. I really wrestled with what the future was to be and what God wanted from me.

As a pre-teen, I had felt perhaps the Lord wanted me to be a missionary and I was (and still am) deathly afraid of snakes. All I could imagine was going to Africa and that would probably mean grass huts and snakes. I realize now this was unreasonable, but it seemed very real to me for several years. I was willing to do anything, go anyplace and become anything The Lord wanted me to ~ except be a missionary to Africa. It got so bad that every time I knelt to pray all I could see in my mind was little grass huts. My brother's divorced buddy asked me to marry him, but I knew in my heart he wasn't for me. I did care for him, but not enough for marriage. I knew what true love really was from my early teen years.

Jerry / 1957

Jerry Lee was our pastor's son when I was just a young girl. My father was on the Church Board and his parents became fast friends to my parents. When they took other pastorates in various locations, we always visited them and our families took vacations together. Jerry and I grew up thinking we were cousins. We had a ball together and were close friends all throughout our growing up years.

Once at Lake Geneva Family Camp in Alexandria, MN he came bounding up to me and said,

"Hey, guess what? We aren't related."
"Come on, we sure are," I replied.

Our parents were standing together a bit of a distance away and Jerry said, *"Come on. I'll prove it."*

We went over to our parents and Jerry asked, *"Are we related?"*

Our parents just chuckled and said, *"No, wherever did you get that idea?"*

Jerry looked at me with a gleam in his eye and said, *"Want to go get a hamburger?"*

We were only 12 years old but from that day we planned our lives together. We talked about everything and planned the college we would attend together someday. It was an innocent but precious love that was growing into something very special. I wrote him many letters encouraging him to live for Jesus. He became a very popular 6'3" football player, handsome and well built. I worried about his popularity and prayed continuously for him. We just didn't call long distance in those days as it was expensive.

Jerry wasn't much of a letter writer, but I faithfully encouraged his walk with the Lord through my letters to him. Our times together were mostly at camps, family visits and vacations. Jerry had always talked about becoming a pastor, like his father, but on one of our last times together he asked me,

"What would you think of being a football coach's wife?"
I replied, *"I'm going to marry a preacher, Jerry."* Neither would come to fruition.

That summer between our 10th & 11th grade in high school, 1958, Jerry was hit by a drunk driver and died instantly.

When we heard it on the radio first, I refused to believe it. It wasn't until Jerry's father called us to confirm this devastating news that I knew it had to be true.

I had never ached so hard inside my heart than I did at that moment. I mourned all that long summer and cried myself to sleep nightly. I loved Jerry. I knew he loved me. It just didn't seem fair and it seemed like a bad dream.

My parents were concerned about me because I was so depressed and quiet. I lost a lot of weight. I walked in a fog of despair for several months and I really just wanted to go to heaven too, to be with Jesus and Jerry. One of my letters was in Jerry's billfold when he was killed and his father thanked me for all the letters of encouragement I had written to Jerry over the years. On the seat of Jerry's car was a booklet entitled,

"How can I know that I am a Christian." Jerry had been sharing Jesus with a friend. His funeral almost did me in as I felt my shattered world fall into pieces at my feet.

I questioned God many times. I won't know the whys until I get to heaven some-day myself, but I know many people came to know Jesus Christ as a result of Jerry's death. Perhaps he won more souls to Christ through his death than what he would have if he had lived. I have learned there are things we will never understand in this life. Ours is to trust the Lord Jesus Christ and hold on to His hand as He leads us through mazes beyond our comprehension. Jesus never makes mistakes – EVER! He is faithful and completely trustable.

Jerry's father went to the jail and shared Jesus with the man who had killed his son. He told him he forgave him and led him to a personal relationship with Jesus Christ, who forgave him, just as Rev. H. forgave him for the death of his own son. I will never forget that act of true Christian love and forgiveness. It left a permanent imprint on my life.

One night about 3 months after Jerry's death I had a dream. Jerry came to me and I could feel the warmth of his magnetic smile in my dream. He looked so happy and he was beaming with radiant peace and light.

He simply said, *"Don't cry for me anymore, Betty. I am happy here with Jesus."*

It was extremely real and I believe God allowed me to experience that dream to help me get on with what God had for my life. I never cried for Jerry again. I knew where he was and I knew he was safe in the arms of Jesus. My young heart began to heal.

So, when my brother's divorced buddy asked me to marry him several years later, I knew I did not have the same intense feelings for marriage as I did with Jerry, even though Jerry and I were so young. Few people know true love at 15 years of age but I had experienced an innocent love that went deeper than some ever have. I knew I could never be happy until I found that same love again someday. I said I was moving back home to work for a year, to decide what my future was to be. I wasn't ready to make any decisions of the magnitude that required such a commitment. I wanted another Jerry. Nothing less would do.

~ TEN ~

1962 Meeting Arne

Home to my parents I went. They had moved from my hometown, Fergus Falls, Minnesota to Rochester, Minnesota. I turned 20 years old that September. I worked in the office of Donaldson's Department Store and was thoroughly confused about the future. I shared my fears of going to Africa as a missionary with my pastor and told him I would do anything but that!

He wisely counseled me, helping me to see God wanted me willing to go ANYWHERE. I needed to be *"willing to be made willing"* to do whatever God asked. I wept at the altar of our church many times as I finally surrendered completely to the gentle voice of my Savior. I fully expected I would go back to North Central Bible College and take all the missionary courses to become a missionary to Africa.

A strange thing happened. The *"pull"* of becoming a missionary to Africa completely lifted and what I had felt as a *"calling"* was gone entirely. Now I was more confused than ever.

Back to my Pastor I went for counsel, clarification and understanding. Rev O.E. told me to remain open to The Lord.

He said, *"The Lord has something special for you to do and He wants you 100% committed to do <u>whatever</u> He asks. He wants your whole heart, nothing hidden, and then He will direct your paths."*

"Trust in the Lord with all your heart and lean not unto thine own understanding. In all of your ways acknowledge Him and He will direct your paths." Proverbs 3:5-6

I prayed for wisdom and direction and decided while I waited for God's direction, to become the coach for our Youth Group's Bible quiz team. I had a good background for it, having been the Minnesota State Bible Quiz Champion years before, and I loved the memorization of the Word of God. It was an ideal fit for me.

On that Rochester Assembly of God Quiz Team were two young boys in their mid-teens. They came from a family of 10 children and were funny, mischievous and adorable young teen boys. We hit it off incredibly well. They needed a ride home from quiz practice one night in October and I gave them a ride home. They lived in this lovely, older, historic home and asked if I would like to come in and see their home. I did. They showed me around, and sitting on the piano was a picture of this utterly handsome sailor in uniform. Wow, he was a knock out with a sexy smile that made my heart skip a beat.

I asked, *"Who is THAT?"*
He was their older brother, Arne, who was coming home at Christmas on leave from the Navy. I queried, *"I suppose he's married?"*

Nope ~ and these two cupids provided several pictures of their handsome brother for me to take home and moon over!

What I didn't know until much later was they, and their mother, had been writing Arne about this blonde from church that they wanted him to date when he came home on leave. Me! I began asking questions of mutual friends about this guy and got positive responses: neat in appearance, reliable, respectful and a man of integrity. Besides, I wasn't blind and he was very easy on the eyes!

However, he had a girlfriend who was telling everyone she was soon getting married to him. Arne's mother didn't approve of her for various reasons and knew she was not for her son. Of course, I found these things out much later, and that Arne had <u>no</u> intention of continuing a relationship with this gal.

It was a Sunday night, December 23, 1962. I played a Tenor Saxophone in the church orchestra which was located in the front of the auditorium. I didn't see Arne come in, but I knew he was being picked up by his parents from the bus station and would be coming to the church service with them. I was a bundle of nerves. How could this happen when I had not even met this guy??

Arne came in and slid into the pew next to one of his buddies at church. He looked up at the orchestra and asked, *"Who's the blonde chick in the orchestra?"* Al simply replied, *"I thought you would like her."*

But Al never told Arne my name, so he had no idea I was the same gal his mother and brothers had been hounding him about.

At the end of the service Arne and I were standing in the foyer and the teens were all whispering and giggling, yet no one was introducing us to each other. It became awkward so I walked over to him, introduced myself as his brother's quiz team coach and invited him to an ice-skating party I was hosting for our teen youth group the following week. We chatted a few minutes and Arne asked me if I would like to join him at his parent's home for some lunch (a common custom in our church group), like now! I turned to my mother, who was standing behind me and asked if that would be all right! She looked at me like I was an alien! I hadn't asked permission to do anything in several years, having lived away from home for over two years already. She offered a snickered smile and said it would be fine! I couldn't believe I was so nervous.

His parents had this big arm chair with claw arms that you sank into butt first! I had a fully lined black sheath dress, black nylons and high heels on and as I sank into the chair my dress slipped up to my thighs and my legs were long and exposed. Arne sat on the arm of the chair and thoroughly enjoyed the view and my discomfort. It was a full house with nine of the ten children present, plus a sister's boyfriend and me.

Arne's father asked the two teen boys to play the trumpet and trombone while I played the piano for some Christmas Carols. Any pianist knows how difficult most Christmas songs are and I struggled through the thrill of victory and the agony of defeat. I made more mistakes than I care to remember and felt mortified. I just wanted to get out of there as soon as possible.

We finally left and Arne asked if I minded if we took a spin down the main drag of our city. No problem. He didn't say one word and I determined I was tired of making small talk with guys, trying to make some kind of a good impression.

He didn't talk, so neither did I. We got within a couple blocks of my parent's home without one single word spoken between us. I thought I should say something. So, I remarked, *"Must be nice to be able to come home at Christmas."* *"Yeh,"* he replied in his New Jersey accent, *"except all my buddies are married now."*

(Hmmm.... lonely sailor home on leave??) Finally, we were in my parent's driveway. I thanked him for a nice evening and he walked me to the door saying, *"I'll call you tomorrow."* That was it! Some date! And I figured I would never hear from him again. Wrong!

I worked in the office of Donaldson's Department Store. It was December 24th and I was at the switchboard for the final hour of the day.

I answered, *"Merry Christmas Donaldson's."* No answer.
I repeated louder, *"Merry Christmas Donaldson's."* Still no answer.
I fairly shouted, *"Hello!"*
A sexy, low, *"Hi ya."*

My stomach did a double flip. What in the world was happening to me? Arne and I visited a couple of minutes and he asked how I got home from work. I answered that my father always picked me up. He asked if he could come and bring me home. Of course, I said yes, and instructed him to pick me up at the front door. The reason? My father was already on his way to pick me up at the back door. I met my father at the back door and sent him on his way and ran to the front door to see my knight in shining armor waiting to escort me home. Once again, very little conversation transpired between us. This guy was one quiet dude. Mysteriously quiet. Quiet waters run deep!

It was Christmas Eve and I knew my mother had her usual big Christmas dinner prepared and waiting, but I couldn't just say thanks and goodbye. So, I asked him into our home where Mom announced dinner to be in one half hour.

I invited Arne to a game of ping pong in our lower level. My brother was a Minnesota State Ping Pong Champion who taught me the art of ping pong on our dining room table. I regularly beat the guys at North Central Bible College when I attended and decided to pull out all the stops. We played three games and I won 2 out of 3 games. He was an excellent player. I tried to gain an advantage by flirting every time I served the ball. It was exhilarating and gratifying not to "let" this guy beat me. Arne was impressed and not intimidated by my wins – something that made points with me.

We said our goodbyes and he left, saying he would call me the next day. I honestly cannot remember what Christmas Eve was like that year. My mind was totally enthralled. Who can explain attraction? My mind came up with absolutely nothing to quantify my unusual feelings for this man I hardly knew. Could he be the one I had prayed for all my young years? This was happening way too fast and my mind was swirling and fuzzy!

Christmas Day came and went until 9 PM with no phone call. My family had been invited to some friend's home for the evening, but I didn't want to miss that all important phone call. For the very first time in my life, I laid on my bed and cried! About a guy who hadn't called as he said he would! Imagine that?! And I hardly knew this handsome stranger home on leave! Attraction and hormones are hard to figure out and more intelligent and degreed people than myself haven't been able to figure it out. I surely couldn't figure myself out this time.

At 9:30 PM Arne called. His father had just arrived home with the only vehicle available. Arne asked if he could come over for a while. You Bet! Uh huh! We sat in my parent's living room, Christmas Tree all decorated with twinkling colored lights, soft Christmas Music playing making the festive moment romantic beyond belief. We talked about everything. I found out how deeply this sailor felt about God, family, home, children, values and all of the important issues in life. I had always been guarded with my feelings in the past, except with Jerry, but I knew I was safe with Arne. His integrity and honesty came through loud and clear. I knew I didn't want to lose this one.

We dated every night of that week and on Saturday Night Dec.29th,1962, just six days after meeting him, Arne told me he wanted me to be his forever. I chirped, *"Right! Lonely Sailor home on leave? I'm not sure I buy that line."*

He replied with what truly summed up my phenomenal husband: *"You will learn in time that I only say what I mean, and I always mean what I say."*

He told me he loved me and would wait for my answer. I had known this guy exactly 6 days. It took me another 7 days to tell him I loved him: *"Yes, I would love to be your bride!"*

Arne came home for another 10-day leave in March when we were engaged. He came home in July when we were married. Did I have misgivings? Yes. We had only been together physically for 28 days, although he wrote twice weekly and called me every Thursday evening during those six months.

Arne had asked my father and mother for my hand in marriage, which impressed my father, BUT he grilled Arne about our future, how Arne would support me, treat me and where we would live.

Dad later said to me, *"This one's a keeper. Don't let him get away!"*

It was my father who often encouraged me when I would be apprehensive about hardly knowing my intended groom. Both of my parents reminded me of Arne's godly upbringing and character. I knew I cared deeply for him but those old feelings of inadequacy during my teen years kept me feeling uncertain.

I knew I didn't want to lose Arne, but I didn't want to make a mistake as I had seen some of my friends do. God would have to take care of those feelings of inadequacy in His time.

We were married in a beautiful church wedding on July 20, 1963. His two younger brothers were groomsmen and testimony to the part they played as matchmakers. We honeymooned in my cousin's lake cottage in Northern Minnesota for an entire week. It was heavenly with balmy days and moonlit nights. My mother had taught me to make five tasty meals. I proudly displayed my cooking abilities, but Arne didn't know he would be stuck with those five tasty meals for quite some time as I mastered the cookbooks which I had never touched before becoming married. I loved baking, but had no inclination toward cooking real food or meals. It became a necessity because contrary to the saying, *"We will live on love,"* that just doesn't work! It became a challenge that I determined to master!

~ ELEVEN ~

1963 Married Life

Arne was stationed in Charleston, South Carolina as a submarine sailor aboard the USS Odax SS484. We secured a tiny one-bedroom apartment within walking distance to the entrance of the Naval Base. This was a duplex with paper thin walls.

One night when Arne was out to sea, our neighbor was heaving his guts out next door. I was reading a book and hearing the retching as if in my own apartment. I, naively, knocked on the wall and offered Pepto Bismol to my overindulged neighbor. I'm sure they got more than one laugh out of that one ~ I was one very sheltered gal from the Midwest who thought she knew a lot about everything! Boy, was I in for a surprise!

Our new neighbor was a single gal. She had lots of male friends but it took me a long time to realize that the turnover was not just from new boyfriends. My hubby insisted I keep our door locked at all times and told me that in spite of what she said, she was conducting activities that were anything but innocent! I just couldn't believe such a sweet girl, who told me she loved God and "dated" lots of guys because she wanted to find just the right one, would be feeding me a line.

One cold evening this gal knocked on our door, saying her water heater was not working and would Arne please come and look at it. He said, *"OK"* and was gone just a couple of minutes. Once again, she knocked and asked for his help. He again lit the pilot light. The third time she knocked, Arne told me she was extinguishing it herself. I shamed him and said he had to help her.

He came back almost immediately. Boy, was I in for a surprise!! He told me when he came back that she wanted more than her pilot light lit!! She had tried to seduce him and he told her to *"quit extinguishing the pilot light as he was NOT interested!"*

I should have listened to my hubby the first time! I would learn through the years that my husband was filled with wisdom and common sense and I needed to listen with both ears!

We had a ball that first year even though we were as poor as church mice. Money does not bring happiness, but it sure helps keep the tummy full!

I finally landed a government job at the Naval Supply Center in Charleston, SC, which kept the refrigerator full! We found a good church and attended all services and had devotions nightly. But something was missing. Arne's prayers were always the same: *"Lord, thank you for my beautiful bride. Bless her please, and thank you for giving her to me."*

One night, Arne closed the Bible, looked at me and told me he had something he needed to tell me. He said he believed in God but did not have a personal relationship with Him. He smoked and drank when away from me, but would never do this in my presence. He said he had "tried" to be a Christian, but just couldn't seem to do it.

I wanted to die. The VERY thing I had not wanted was a mate who did not believe and practice the way I knew the Bible wanted us to be. That was why I had asked him so many questions about his faith before we were married.

I asked him every question except the most important one: *"Are you living for Jesus now? Are you a truly dedicated, committed Christian?"*

I never suspected anything less, but assumptions can be lethal. I felt my world was crushed and falling into shattered pieces of pain. I certainly did not want to bring children into a divided home without a father who led by example. This was the most important thing in my life and I was devastated.

Arne went out to sea the next morning. I called my parents and poured my heart out to them. My mother assured me they would be praying and reminded me that Arne had been raised the same way I had and he would make the right decision in time.

I prayed and cried the entire two weeks Arne was out to sea. I lost 12 pounds from fasting and praying. This was the most important foundation of our future. I had never wanted anything less than a home where Jesus was truly Lord of all. This may be difficult for some to understand. However, I had seen friends of mine, and people I had watched over the years and concluded that, the scripture that says, *"Be ye NOT unequally yoked together"* was given to us for a very good reason. It is a recipe for success at the most fundamental level.

The Bible was the cornerstone of my existence and I believed every word, literally. So, I prayed and placed Arne into the arms of my trusted Savior to work the miracle only HE could work.

Arne came home on a Saturday, two weeks later. My love overflowed to him as I trusted in Jesus to complete what I knew

He had started in my husband. We went to church as usual and in the Sunday night service we had two guest speakers who gave their testimony of how they had surrendered their lives to Christ.

At the conclusion of that service my hubby gave his life completely to Christ. I was overjoyed with thanksgiving and praise to my Heavenly Father. It was like a new beginning once again with God at the center of our home. Together we were growing more in love and learning how to please and walk in the ways of our Lord.

We loved the wondrous surf and ocean breezes that were so close to us in Charleston, South Carolina and spent many hours walking the beach together. We were blessed.

I discovered I was pregnant with our first child. I was so excited, but Arne was scheduled to get out of the Navy in August 1965 and our bundle was to arrive in November. We debated staying in the Navy, but decided to leave and go back to Rochester, Minnesota. With no job prospect, looking back, it seemed like a very risky decision and many friends thought we were crazy not to let the Navy pay for our baby!

Home we went: very pregnant, all our meager possessions packed into a 4x8 trailer pulled by our 1958 used, standard transmission Chevy. We were young, in love, crazy happy and trusting in a God who is real: to lead and guide our future. And guess what? We have never been disappointed! The Lord gave Arne loving favor in his job hunting and he was gainfully employed immediately.

He worked at this job for one month before being hired by IBM, whose insurance paid for our new arrival, a son. Arne would remain at IBM for his entire career of 30 years where God blessed him with promotion after promotion. God has been faithful in supplying our needs, and even wants, our entire lives. He can be trusted for every decision even when we make bad choices. He is there to pick us up and put us back on the right track. The Bible says,

"Commit your work to the Lord, then it will succeed. We should make plans, counting on God to direct us." Proverbs 16:3 & 9

Family Life

Bryan Arnold Jacobson arrived in November 1965. No two parents were ever more excited, and proud. Bryan was perfectly beautiful with wide shoulders and narrow hips just like his Daddy. We brought him home to our first little home on Golden Hill in Rochester, MN. It was a cute little two-bedroom home we purchased. We were on cloud nine. Life was wonderful.

Bryan's Diary of Little Things by Mom

I began this when Bry was nearly 18 months old after completing his 'Baby Book.' I made entries until his wedding day on August 14, 1987. I will take excerpts from it from time to time:

"Words cannot begin to tell you of the joy and pleasure you have added to our lives, Bryan. It is YOU who have truly made us a family now. We have spanked your little bottom and been hard on you sometimes, then loved you even harder. It is our desire to see you grow into a young man who loves Jesus as a

personal savior and friend. We want to be close enough to you, son, to guide you through difficult times and see you victorious in each of your successes and failures. For it takes both to become a man. We love you beyond words, Bryan. You are our little 'weed' and still just a precious little baby. May you become a father one day as your Daddy has been to you."

April 1967 (18 months old): *"You discovered Spring in Minnesota today! Your little legs slipped out from under you on Grandpa and Grandma Ohman's cement steps. We took you to the doctor but your little mashed, button nose wasn't broken, only bruised. So very puffy and black and blue your nose was. Your left eye is even a 'shiner'. Then your doggy, Tippy, was too playful and knocked you over and put scratches all over the left side of your face. My goodness, you look like you were in a fight and lost! Such a hard day."*

Next Day: *"This AM you ran into the garage door with your tyke bike and split your little lip. Blood was all over and how you cried. Then you fell off the couch and put a big black and blue knot in your forehead. Such a little guy with gigantic problems, you are!"*

My journal is full of fun, funny and adorable antics that all parents have the joy of experiencing. There were frustrations and we read lots of books to help us raise this precious child in the light of God's Word. It was a joy, really, for us because Bryan became all that we had hoped a little guy would be. He was easy to raise with such a tender heart wanting to please us.

In 1967 we visited Arne's sister and hubby in Nebraska. They took us to some friend's ranch where we were allowed to ride their cutting horses. My hubby tried to instruct me about this horse, but I pridefully answered that I had ridden horses many times and I could handle this one. I mounted the horse and without thinking leaned forward to grab the reins as my heels dug into his withers. Since this stallion had been trained to respond to heel pressures, he took off like a streak of lightning. I never got the reins. He galloped me down to the lake, turned on a dime and galloped me full speed back to the spectators where he abruptly stopped instantly, pummeling me into the air where I did a summersault and landed with a thud on my back. Mortified, but in pain, I lay there trying to catch my breath. I had fractured two vertebrae in my back. Fortunately, and thanks to my Heavenly Father, the two vertebrae were in-tact and not compound fractures, only simple fractures. Bed rest and careful lifting for six weeks and I was back in business. Once again, I should have listened to the advice of my hubby. I was stubbornly independent yet God had protected me from serious harm. I still had much to learn!

Bryan became a most obedient child, always wanting to please us in every way. People would comment on how well behaved he was and what a tender heart he had for others.

Eventually all we had to say to him was, *"Bryan you have disappointed us. That is unacceptable behavior. You must not do that again!"*

Big tears would well up in his little eyes and he would come into our arms and say he was sorry and sob like he had committed the worst of offenses. He was a joy to have around and was funny, inquisitive, sometimes impish but never malicious. He freely shared his toys with his cousins and friends and always wanted others to be happy too. He had a grateful heart even as a little guy. He loved books and loved having me read to him. When Arne and I would be reading in the evening, Bryan would curl up on the couch between us and 'read' the Reader's Digest, jabbering in his 18-month old language like he was truly reading to us. And he would sing, sing, sing. I taught him 'The Itsy, Bitsy Spider' complete with movements and he loved that song. His first song was *"Jesus loves me this I know, for the Bible tells me so."* In his baby words and gestures, he warmed our hearts and made our life full and complete. We couldn't have been happier. Our life was so full.

Excerpts from the Diary of little Things ~ Bryan

October 1967: *"We got a white Angora kitten today and named her 'Puff.' She's a snowy white ball of fur and love. Bryan, you just adore her. You try wrapping her up in your slippery little blanket but Puff just darts right out and you get so perturbed. You hug and kiss Puff and carry her all over. You cried when Mommy gave Puff a bath in the tub though. Puff liked it and purred so loudly. You squeal with delight as you pull a cord along the floor and Puff chases it. She is a good playmate."*

November 1967 2nd Birthday: *"Mommy and daddy gave you a rocking horse. We asked you to stay in your bedroom until we called you out. You came out into the living room, clapped your hands, put your hands on your cheeks and said, "Oohh, mine, mine." You looked so cute and you were so excited. Daddy picked you up and placed you on the rocking horse. After a couple minutes, you looked at us and said in your baby talk language, 'Tank ou mommy, tank ou daddy.' You just melted our hearts with your spontaneous affection and thankfulness. You are truly a gift from God."*

January 1968: *"Bryan, you asked Mommy to play the piano for you today and as you were singing, "Into my heart, come into my heart, Lord Jesus" you raised your little arms and closed your eyes in true sincerity and devotion. Such a precious, spontaneous little scene."*

"Bryan, you would be running and, all of a sudden, your little knees would turn inward and down you would go. My heart aches for you, my precious 3 ½ year-old-son, and I have asked God to give me this disease instead of you. You have been complaining about your knees hurting recently so we took you to our pediatrician, who also happens to be studying Juvenile Rheumatoid Arthritis. Both Dad and I have close relatives who have had severe Rheumatoid Arthritis, which is an inherited disease. Dr. O. suspects this might be the cause of your problems and has begun tests to determine if you are a victim of this disease."

We also did what we knew to do: have Bryan anointed with oil as the Pastor and Deacons of our church laid their hands upon our son and prayed in Jesus Name for healing of his little body. The Bible clearly states:

"Is anyone among you sick? He should call for the elders of the church and they should pray over him and pour a little oil upon him, calling on the Lord to heal him. And their prayer, if offered in faith, will heal him, for the Lord will make him well..."
James 5:14

God touched our little guy and he never had any further problems. After 8 months of tests and doctor visits, the tests were terminated without a conclusive diagnosis, other than the fact that Bryan had no further symptoms left in his body. We know Jesus healed our son and he never had another symptom of Rheumatoid Arthritis to this very day.

We were blessed with our second son in June 1969. He was beautiful and perfect in every way. We felt like we were living a story book life filled with continuous joy.

OUR SECOND SON – ANTON BUZ JACOBSON 1969

Diary of Little Things ~ Buz

"Buz, you are our own precious little monkey! You have made our family complete and we love you from the top of your soft blond curls to the bottom of your ticklish little toes. Bryan is delighted to have a brother and didn't miss a feeding for the entire first week. He did ask one day, rather unsurely, "Mommy, he really is a good baby……. isn't he?" Little precious Buz, you are a joy to hold and cuddle and already have given us much joy and contentment. It is our prayer that God will grant us the wisdom, patience and abundant love to raise you so that you will one day want Jesus as your own Lord and Savior. We want to always be close enough to you to give you security, yet far enough away to give you independence and room to blossom. As you read this, years later, I hope you will know that above all, we've given you our best, whether right or wrong. We have given you back to Jesus and we cherish the years ahead as together we enjoy each other. I love you, Son."

Buz began having multiple ear infections, fevers, strep throat and seemed to catch every "bug" that anyone around him had. He became listless and pale with a shallow appetite around 12 months of age. Our pediatrician was the same physician who had been our children's doctor since they were born, specializing in Juvenile Rheumatoid Arthritis (JRA). He began multiple tests to see what was going on in Buz's tiny body.

~TWELVE~

Juvenile Rheumatoid Arthritis

Rheumatoid Arthritis (RA) is an inflammatory, autoimmune disease characterized by pain, swelling, stiffness and reduced function of the joints. The exact cause is unknown but it is often hereditary. In a healthy person, the immune system acts like a bodyguard – keeping out or destroying foreign invaders like bacteria or viruses. But in autoimmune diseases like RA, the immune system mistakes the body's own cells for a foreign invader and causes inflammation of the lining of the joints. It is a chronic illness, which means it doesn't ever go away and usually progresses to joint damage. The inflamed joint lining invades and destroys nearby cartilage and bone. Muscles, ligaments and tendons that support the joint weaken. Crippling can occur in the case of a juvenile whose body is developing. Medications like aspirin, ibuprofen or naproxen can help relieve pain and reduce inflammation. Corticosteroids and analgesics are also used to manage symptoms associated with RA. Complications of Juvenile Rheumatoid Arthritis (JRA) can include:

- Wearing away or destruction of joints
- Slow rate of growth
- Uneven growth of an arm or leg
- Loss of vision or decreased vision
- Anemia
- Swelling around the heart (pericarditis)
- Chronic pain, disability and problems at school

There is no known prevention or cure for JRA.

September 1971: *"Buz, the Doctors say you definitely have Juvenile Rheumatoid Arthritis and are beginning to treat you. You have an enlarged spleen and affected lymph nodes throughout your body, constant temperature, rashes and a sedimentation rate that is doubled. Your immune system is compromised and very weak. My precious baby, I wish Mommy could take this from you and have it instead of you. But this isn't possible, so we are going to ask Jesus to heal you as He did your brother, Bryan, several years ago."*

"You must undergo blood work every 10 days and the nurses take a syringe-full from your little arm. They often cannot find your small veins because they roll. They have had to stick your tiny arms multiple times and dig around for your veins. We all have to hold you down until it is over. You cry so hard, my sweet, and my heart aches for you. I cry with you and hold you so tightly when it is all over. You have become terrified of people in white and only want Mommy. You scream in terror when someone in all white comes near you. Oh, dear Lord, please heal my baby. I can't stand to see him suffer."

The following weeks seemed like a nightmare. Buz seemed to get one thing right after another. His immune system was zero. He didn't rally or get stronger in-between bouts of illnesses and I was constantly in the doctor's office with him. Many weeks I saw the doctor every other day because Buz just was not improving and I was beside myself with worry. Everyone was praying. Arne and I took turns staying home from church because Buz would catch any sniffle that any child in the nursery had. We were exhausted from worry and concern.

December 1971: *"You haven't eaten much in 10 days and the Doctors say you are 'wasting away.' You have had a series of illnesses from cough, cold, ear infections, strep throat, tonsillitis, all ending with a virus that cannot be treated. Antibiotics don't work on viruses and all the previous medications are not working. You have been one very sick little guy. Dr. O. told me today that you were "wasting away." I looked Dr. O. in the eye and asked, 'Are you telling me my son is dying?' With a tear escaping from his eye, he said, 'We can only wait to see if his body is strong enough to get through this virus.' Buzzy, we have given you to Jesus."*

"Dr O. told us today that you may become our own little angel in heaven. Because of the Holidays, he told me to take you home and love you. If you don't begin eating by Monday they will put you into the hospital for intravenous feeding and hydration. We are trusting and believing God. HE knows best."

"I know whom I have believed, and am persuaded that He IS able to keep that which I've committed unto Him against that day." 2 Timothy 1:12b

December 26, Saturday night: *"My precious boy, tonight I held your hot little body and rocked you for most of the evening. As I laid you down in your bed, I asked Jesus to either take you home, or heal you. I will be prepared for whatever comes. I have a deep ache inside as I write this my darling little son. I am weeping, for a mother couldn't love her baby any more than I love you. I want you forever, but we have given you back to Jesus. I must keep trusting. I must keep trusting. I know I will have His peace soon."*

I must insert here what I went through to arrive at the above peace which culminated in my prayer of relinquishment. When

I laid Buz down in his crib and stroked his little wet curls that night I, all of a sudden, got very, very, VERY angry with God. My conversation with God, my Heavenly Father, went something like this:

"Thanks a lot God. I am SO angry with you. I've done everything right. I've served and loved you since I was six years old. I respected my parents and never caused them any worries. I followed your rules to the best of my ability. I never smoked, drank or slept around. I was a virgin for my husband. I've been a good wife and a good mother. I work in the church and sing for you. And this is the thanks I get? My baby is dying and you're doing nothing. Don't you care? I am so, so, SO angry and feel SO betrayed. What kind of a God are you? Where ARE you? Why don't you answer when so many have prayed? What do you want from me?"

I want to point something out which I will deal with in a later chapter. God's mercy does not depend on our goodness. He does not want our sacrifices and penance. He isn't looking for robots that obey every letter of the law as though that will win His blessings and acceptance (like the Pharisees). No. It is the truly humble, sincere person whose heart is soft and pliable and broken with a contrite heart of repentance. Our goodness is as filthy rags in God's sight.

"Create in me a clean heart, O God, and renew a right spirit in me. You don't want penance; if you did, how gladly I would do it! You aren't interested in offerings burned before you on the altar. It is a broken spirit you want – remorse and penitence. A broken and a contrite heart, O God, you will not ignore." Psalms 51:10, 16 & 17

My remodel inside was in the making and I will share that later. Yet God's mercy endures, even when we are arrogant and think we are deserving of what we want.

God can take our rantings and ravings. He can take our questioning Him. He knows us. He created us. He sees us. He hears and understands us, even when the heavens seem brass and no answers seem to come. I stood by my son's bed for a long time just letting my anger dissipate. Finally, I began to sob as I told my Savior I was sorry and although I didn't understand, I WOULD accept whatever HIS decision would be.

I remember saying, *"If you only gave us Buz to enjoy for 18 months, then thank you. I will accept your will. I just ask that you allow Buz NOT to suffer, and if he lives, I ask that you make him a healthy, happy, normal child - not crippled, in pain, nor confined to a wheelchair for the remainder of his life."*

A quiet calm settled over me and a deep peace surrounded me as though a warmed, soft blanket had been placed around my shoulders. It was a healing warmth that seeped throughout my entire body and soaked into my being for what seemed like hours, but was only several minutes. I knew the decision had been made in the heavens and I knew I could trust whatever was ahead. I went to bed and slept the entire night through. Something I had not done for months, always awakening and listening for my baby's raspy breathing. If I didn't hear his strangled breathing I would run into his room, afraid of what I might find. I had lived with a dread that I was trying hard to conceal, but this night I had settled it once and for all. I knew I could trust my Lord Jesus Christ completely. I slept like a baby all night long. God doesn't make mistakes – Ever!

A Day I Will NEVER Forget

December 27, 1971 Sunday, (the next day):

*"Today is a day I will never forget! Jesus has healed you, Buz! I hardly know where to begin. You awakened feverish as you have for 12 straight days. You were too weak to cry so you would only lie there, so white and listless. I stayed home with you from church and was rocking you in the living room when Grandpa and Grandma Ohman came over after Sunday School. They felt led to lay hands on you one more time and pray for Jesus to heal you. Buz, I felt something like an electric shock go through me from the top of my head right through my legs and feet and, Buzzy, I know Jesus healed you. I knew this must be the power of God. It was like I had touched a live electric outlet, yet it didn't hurt, it was just powerful! You ate lunch and supper and regurgitated it all up and your fever was **gone!** I felt impressed to not give you the 12- baby aspirin a day you had been taking to keep the salicylate level normal. I promised the Lord I wouldn't give you any more aspirin as long as your blood work was normal. I had criticized others for going off their medication without a doctor's permission and here I was doing the same thing. I felt so strongly it was what God wanted me to do yet I didn't even tell your daddy what I was doing because I was so afraid he would disagree. I had to trust Jesus all the way."*

I also asked God for a sign EVERY time I took Buz to the doctor that he really was healed. It was a step-at-a-time thing for me. The aspirin was to keep his body from becoming crippled and the next step was steroids. The salicylate level was the measurement of the amount of aspirin needed to regulate the crippling. He had been on as much as 16 baby aspirin a day and as little as 9 baby aspirin a day. I personally believe that when he vomited, he was expelling all that aspirin and poison from his body. There is no medical report to substantiate this, but that is my opinion.

January 1972: *"Your blood work was normal and the hemoglobin back to normal. Praise be to our Lord. I told your daddy about not giving you the aspirin and he said of course we would continue trusting Jesus. He was never in favor of all that aspirin in your body in the first place. We had you anointed with oil and prayed for by Pastor O. E. even though I knew you are already healed. The Bible says to do this, and so we did it in obedience to God's Word."*

March 1972: *"You have had chicken pox, ear infection, tonsillitis and strep throat, but NO flare up of arthritis. The doctors are amazed at your 'about face.' You have gained weight; your cheeks have turned rosy and you eat like a little pig. You are naughty and you never had enough energy before to be naughty so I'm most grateful. Your blood work is totally normal. Your spleen, nodes, glands and anemia and every symptom are all gone. Dr O. said to bring you back in 6 months for a check-up. You are healed. Praise God. He has worked a miracle in your body."*

September 1972: *"Doctors have dismissed you from the Clinic as well! Isn't God good to us? Praise Him!"*

October 1972: *"You've begun praying by yourself now at devotion time. It's priceless. You close your eyes tight and say under your breath while Dad is praying, 'Close eyes, close eyes!' Then when it is 'your turn,' you get your voice high pitched and jabber to Jesus so sincerely it's just almost too funny for words. Whatever you are praying to Him for, well, it is most sincere. I occasionally have to remind you to say 'amen'."*

December 1972: *"Oh you are some monkey! Your curiosity is something else. This AM as daddy was getting ready for work you took his glasses to him. He told you to put them back. You sure did! We finally found them 3 days later in Dad's good shoes in the closet. Poor daddy couldn't see to read the paper, watch TV or anything and oh was he upset with you. Then last night you emptied the box of fish food into the aquarium and two fish died. This afternoon while up at church, you went into Pastor Craig's office and proceeded to play "coffee." You had 8 cups sitting on his desk and had emptied the dry creamer all over the desk, floor and chairs. What a mess! You got your bottom warmed for that one, darling, and you looked quite contrite but oh how I chuckled inside at the sheer funniness of it all. We've had many laughs at your cute antics behind your back. We think you are a priceless, precious little pumpkin!"*

Christmas 1972: *"What a wonderful Christmas for you this year, Buz. You are now healthy and strong because Jesus has truly healed you and kept you well this entire year. It is so much fun to see your little eyes sparkle so bright with joy and happiness and it is so much fun to make you boys happy. God has blessed us with such precious sons. We love you, Pal."*

God restored our son's health and gave us a normal, inquisitive, sometimes naughty and mischievous little boy. His rosy cheeks became a trademark that follows him today even as an adult. Our God IS faithful.

Note: I asked Dr. O., Pediatrician and Juvenile Rheumatoid Arthritis specialist now, if he could explain what happened to our son.

Dr. O. said, *"Children have been known to burn arthritis out of their system over an extended period of time, but not in 3 months. I think you got yourself one of these miracles we hear about from time to time here at Mayo Clinic."*

We did, indeed! Buz has never been bothered by any symptoms at all his entire life. Early on during the diagnosis, Dr. O. said Buz would probably be in a wheelchair by the time he was 9 years old and we should prepare him for a desk type job as he got older. BOTH our boys were hockey players and were star defensemen on their teams that their father coached. BOTH boys snow skied, water skied and participated in many sports throughout their growing years. When God heals, he does a thorough job! They remain Rheumatoid Arthritis FREE to this very day.

~THIRTEEN~

Inner Healing

Because I had grown up with such an inferiority complex as to my outward appearance, and an older brother who consistently fed me messages of being the 'ugly duckling' of the family, I carried inside of me a determination to be self-sufficient and good at everything I did. If I achieved, others would HAVE to admire me. I wanted to be accepted, but didn't feel I had the necessary 'tools' to be accepted exactly as I was.

I wore a mask. Have you done that? It is an easy thing for any person, especially women, to do that today. We are constantly fed lies from the media, air brushed pictures of 'perfect' movie stars and perfectly shaped models who are sporting the latest, greatest, most up-to-date fashions that are absolutely a 'MUST' if one wants to be accepted and admired in our world today. Everything is coded by sex appeal in a tainted maze of unreal, fake salesmanship. And I bought into it. If I couldn't be what I thought was beautiful, then I would be perfect! I didn't realize this was my thinking process until my loving Heavenly Father got my attention with a rude awakening that changed my life.

I love to read. I came across an old book by Catherine Marshall entitled, _Beyond Ourselves._ At the end of the book she challenges us to: _"Ask God what you look like in His eyes."_ She gave examples of some who had done this and the phenomenal experiences that had followed – some not exactly winsome.

But I thought, *"I'm a good Christian. I go to church regularly and follow the teachings and laws of the Lord. I'm a good wife, a good mother, a great housekeeper ~ I don't think I have anything to fear by praying that prayer. I'm actually a very good person!"*

The Lord answered my prayer. He showed me how I looked like in HIS eyes - and it wasn't pretty. He showed me that I was selfish, self-centered, arrogant, self-righteous and filled with pride and jealousy.

He showed me that my ***"righteousness was as filthy rags."*** ***Isaiah 64:6***

What are filthy rags? I imagined smelly, garbage infested, putrefied, totally objectionable rags that had rotted and gave off a stench that offended the sensibilities of any nostril. And THAT is what I looked like in God's eyes <u>in my humanness</u>.

This was startling! It was shocking! It was horrifying! I was overcome with brokenness and felt small, humbled and broken. God left me in this condition for 3 weeks. I read the Bible but felt no comfort. I wept. I prayed. I felt sorry for myself. Finally I abandoned my preconceived ideas of what and how I felt a Christian should be and saw myself for what I was: a sincere person who was trying to be 'good enough' to gain God's favor.

Oh, I had accepted Him as Savior at a young age. Yes, I truly loved the Lord Jesus Christ. But I was trying to be someone I wasn't and was trying to be better in everything I attempted in the hopes that I would achieve love and acceptance in the process, both from man as well as God. I was trying to do it myself. Jesus said,

"Come unto me, all ye that labor and are heavy laden, and I will give you rest. Take my yoke upon you, and learn of me: for I am meek and lowly in heart: and ye shall find rest unto your souls. For my yoke is easy, and my burden is light."
Matthew 11:28-30

I didn't have to do it myself. I didn't need to strive to be perfect. Jesus showed me that He loved me – just the way I was, right then. He showed me that He loved me completely, unconditionally and, if I allowed Him, He would make me into the person He created me to be, developing all the potential He created within me. I abandoned myself into His loving care and a remarkable thing happened: I realized that if God loved me just the way I was, maybe Arne really loved me as much as he said he did.

You see, I was terribly insecure. Arne had to travel extensively with his job and was gone several nights a week. He traveled with both men and women and because I wasn't secure in my husband's love for me, I often allowed my mind to wander and imagine all kinds of scenarios of his being attracted to other women. I would quiz him repeatedly when he came home, asking what he did, where he went and with whom. He always called me every night and never gave me any reason to think he was being unfaithful to me. Yet I had this nagging sense of being unsure and was simply positive I couldn't be all he said I was to him. It was slowly driving me crazy. I constantly prayed and begged God for help and deliverance from this insane jealousy and insecurity. I was even modeling at the time at a fashionable department store, but that didn't give me what I needed to feel secure inside. I knew I was being unreasonable, yet I couldn't seem to keep from being sucked into a black hole of despondency. I believe if God hadn't intervened, I would have ruined our marriage with my jealousy and insecurity.

We had been married 7 years and Arne always would say, *"Babes, I love you so much. I love you with all my heart."* I would reply, *"Thanks hon, I love you too."*

But NEVER in 7 years of marriage had I EVER said, *"I know you do."* I guess I didn't think Arne knew my inner struggles of self-worth and my feelings of *"if I can just be a better wife, he'll love me more."*

Once I fully realized and accepted the unconditional love of Jesus, I was instantly freed of all the lies of inadequacy that Satan had fed me for years, <u>which I believed</u>. I now knew I was loved beyond words, and nothing would ever be able to steal that Love of God from me again.

"For I am persuaded, that neither death, nor life, nor angels, nor principalities, nor powers, nor things present, nor things to come, nor height, nor depth, nor any other creature, shall be able to separate ME from the love of God, which is in Christ Jesus our Lord." Romans 8:38 & 39

It was a miracle, a miracle that God can and will do for <u>anyone</u> who opens his heart, asks forgiveness, let go of self, and trusts the Heavenly Father to give the wisdom, guidance and love so desperately needed in each of us. If God loved me just the way I was and would faithfully stay by my side always, was it possible that Arne truly loved me the way he said he did? If I could trust God to love me with unconditional love, could it possibly be true that Arne really loved me as much as he said he did? That he really "adored" me like he said?

It was a Saturday morning and I was sitting on our bathroom counter watching Arne shave, face all lathered up with an old-fashioned brush and cup of shaving cream. It always fascinated me to watch him shave this way. Upon finishing he came over, took my face between his hands, kissed my nose, gently kissed me on my lips, looked deeply into my eyes and said, *"Babes, I love you so much. You are so precious to me."*

I looked deeply back into his eyes and replied, *"I know you do."* Looking startled, he pulled back a bit from me and said, *"What did you say?"*

I repeated, *"I know you do and I love you with all my heart too."*

Arne's eyes filled with tears that slowly trickled down his cheeks. He said, *"Oh Betts, I thought I would never hear you say that. I had resigned myself to the fact that I would probably never be able to convince you of how much I really loved you."*

That was the beginning of a deeper and more satisfying love; a love that could now grow and be nurtured into a thing of real beauty.

God wants us to be whole in body, mind, spirit and emotions. We short change ourselves when we buy into the lies that others and Satan impose on us.

"And be not conformed to this world: but be ye transformed by the renewing of your mind, that ye may prove that which is that good, and acceptable, and perfect, will of God." Romans 12:2

Our Lord Jesus Christ has made us individuals, not carbon copies of each other. The exceptional one is 'That Someone' who knows how to sing his own song, loud and clear. He is not just another clone of this modern world. So, stand up tall, sing your song clearly and be the person God created you to be. Thank Him for who you are and ask His Holy Spirit for the wisdom, guidance, creative ideas and knowledge to use all of the potential He created you to have.

"Call unto me, and I will answer thee, and show thee great and mighty things, which you know not." Jeremiah 33:3

"And ye shall seek me, and find me, when ye shall search for me with all your heart." Jeremiah 29:13

God doesn't make mistakes, Ever! He made you just the way you are too. He has only good plans for those who put their trust in Him.

"For I know the thoughts that I think toward you, says the Lord, thoughts of peace, and not of evil, to give you hope and a future." Jeremiah 29:11

Give yourself to this adventure of finding out what God has for you in all its fullness. It is through weakness and neediness that we learn to deepen our dependence on God.

"My grace is sufficient for thee: for my strength is made perfect in weakness…"
II Corinthians 12:9

"I will instruct thee and teach thee in the way which thou shalt go: I will guide thee with mine eyes." Psalms 32:8

I encourage you to read the Bible as much as you are able. The pages of this amazing book are filled with encouragement, love, and guidance. It is truly the road map to success in all you do.

I would like to add that deliverance from jealousy is something that also requires discipline of one's <u>thoughts</u>. I had *times of regression during my double mastectomy when I couldn't possibly imagine my husband still finding me attractive, yet I did know that he loved me unconditionally and I knew that his love hadn't changed just because of outward circumstances. The scripture that I have held on to for keeping my thought life in right order is:*

"For the weapons of our warfare are not carnal, but mighty through God to the pulling down of strongholds; Casting down _imaginations_, and every high thing that exalts itself against the knowledge of God and bringing into _captivity every thought_ to the obedience of God." II Corinthians 10:4 & 5

~FOURTEEN~

"Bryan's Diary of Little Things by Mom"

August 1971 (5 ½ yrs. old): *"Today was the most important event in your life. We had a singing group from Minneapolis at our church and at the altar call you asked Dad if you could go up. He said, yes, and then you asked him if he would come with you please. Dad helped you pray and you asked Jesus into your heart. You came back and sat by me and I asked you if you were happy. Through tears you nodded your head yes. You were so moved and I was so thankful that you had made this important step out of a heart filled with love and a desire to know and have Jesus in your heart. Also, a special privilege for your Daddy."*

March 1972: *"The other day you asked me who the Easter Bunny REALLY is. You said, 'Now tell the truth, Mom!' and you had the cutest, craftiest look on your beaming, knowing face. So, I confessed Mom and Dad were the Easter Bunnies. You exclaimed, 'I knew it, I knew it!' Then you asked if you could help hide Buz's goodies because we didn't want to tell him who the Easter Bunny is because 'he's still pretty little.' You are so precious, Bryan. Then you asked, 'Do you suppose you could hide some eggs and candy for me too, anyway?' And, of course, we did, Pal. Oh, how much we love you, Bryan."*

May, 1972: *"You made another commitment to Christ at the Lowell Lundstrom meeting at the Mayo Civic Auditorium. You were 6 ½ yrs. old and I believe this made an even greater impact on your life. I love you so, Bryan, and am so glad your heart is so tender before Jesus."*

Feb 1973: *"You had a freak accident with your snow skis. The ski tip broke right off one of the skis. Luckily your bindings released and you weren't hurt at all, although frightened. We are so thankful to our wonderful Jesus for keeping His Hands on you, pal. You could easily have been pierced by the jagged edge. You were afraid we would be upset with you, but it was an accident and we weren't at all upset, just worried about you. See, Pal, Mom and Dad understand, and you need <u>never</u> be afraid to tell us anything! We love you and are interested in how <u>you</u> feel about things too. You've been going up and down the chair lifts and T-bars without trouble and skiing the intermediate slopes very well. We're mighty proud of you! It's fun to ski with you, punkin!"*

April 1973: *"We bought a Tri-Hull boat and it's lovely. We've been fishing umpteen times and really had a lot of fun together with it. You and Buz seem to be the true fishermen, though, for you manage to hook all the fish! With your lines jiggling so much it's amazing you can even "snag'em." Must be some pretty fast fish, huh? It sure is fun to be together like this!"*

June 1973: (7 ½ yrs. old) *"You won a wristwatch for all the visitors you brought and all the memory work you did at Vacation Bible School. Bryan, Jesus has blessed you with a keen mind and an ability to learn."*

July 1973: *"We packed our gear in our boat and went to Indianhead Island at Crane Lake, on the Canadian border, for a long weekend campout. Uncle Marty is living with us for the summer, and he played his guitar as we sang together. It was so beautiful out away from everyone, except seaplanes and seagulls. The lake water was so clear and clean that we brushed our teeth in it. We had campfires and you and Buz explored and fished and Buz even water skied, standing on Dad's water skies with him. You've gotten to be quite a skier yourself, Bryan. You can even shift all your weight to one ski now. Pretty Brave for a 7 ½ year old!"*

August 27, 1973 *"You are a big second grader now. Seems impossible. Once again, we're attending John Marshall High School football games all together. You seem to enjoy school and I'm one of your room mothers this year, which seemed to please you a-lot. Bryan, lately we've been sharing more with each other and I love feeling so close to you. I love you so much and want you to grow up loving Jesus as I do.*

November 1973 (8th Birthday): *"We got you hockey skates and were you ever excited! You are growing so tall and into such a fine gentle boy, honest and trustworthy. I am so terribly proud of you."*

January 4, 1974 (Dad's Birthday): *"You finally got a chance to use those new hockey skates today. In the AM we went tobogganing and had a ball. After lunch we went to your school's outdoor rink and you literally amazed us by taking right off skating. You fell occasionally but even played hockey with Dad and me. We sure have had some fun times and have so many precious moments with you and Buz. We're so glad to be a happily married couple with two wonderful sons!"*

Fall 1974: *"Bryan the hockey player! We enrolled you in Hockey School and you're really doing terrific for a first timer. It's so much fun watching you boys chase the puck around like bees after honey. Surely am proud of you, hon."*

February 1975 (age 9): *"We spent 5 days and 6 nights skiing at Lutsen, MN with you, Buz, and Rusty (our dog). We stayed in the Elite Sea Villas, popped popcorn, made lemon pies in the fireplace and played 'Game of States,' remember?? What a lovely week of skiing. You and Buz just skied your little legs off and still had energy to spare. We loved skiing together on Bridge Run."*

March 1975: *"You won your first game in the hockey tournaments but lost on game 2. You have improved more than any other player on the team. We are bursting our buttons with pride."*

April 1976: *"Our first trip to Colorado skiing. How very beautiful and relaxing. Bry, you really had a ball skiing over all the moguls and even the expert slopes. You've become quite the hot dog!!"*

May 10, 1976: *"You had your first surgery and overnight stay in the hospital. You had 10 teeth pulled (braces next) so you'll really make out with the tooth fairy this time, eh? We cheered you up with a new baseball mitt. Surely do love you, pal."*

September 1978 (Almost 13): *"You are in love! Beth is your love and your eyes look like soft puppy dogs when you are with her. You are so concerned for her happiness and so gentle and tender hearted with her. You will make someone a very good hubby someday, son."*

1979: *"Graduation Banquet for seniors at church. You "double dated" with Dad and me and took Beth. You really looked sharp. We bought you a beige vest, slacks and new shirt. We took pictures with you and Beth. We were proud of you and your gentlemanly ways...except when you wore your glasses upside down during dinner! Guess you're still only 13, but big and lovable anyway. You nut!"*

1980: *"Each time we attend a school conference it is a joy for us. Your teachers have nothing but glowing things to say about your academic work, which is nearly all A's and B's, as well as you as a person. The principle is your home room teacher and really respects and enjoys you in his class. I have seen you blossom in Jesus this year through Bible Camps, personal devotions and the discipleship program you voluntarily entered. My prayers for the Holy Spirit to stabilize you spiritually are being answered right before my eyes. Praise God! Oh, you also shave now – peach fuzz, but you are growing up."*

September 1980: *"Besides playing hockey (Dad is your hockey coach), you decided to play football too. And guess what – you are the quarterback. And you're good! Dad and I have watched many games in the cold and rain, but it's really exciting and worth it. I liked the game last night when it was raining pitch forks and hammer handles at Mayo Field. We won with you running the ball like Fran Tarkington of the Vikings! We couldn't believe the moves and plays you engineered. You have become a 'star' for the present."*

Christmas 1980: *"This year we spent Christmas with just the four of us. We had Fondue, at your request, then listened to Dad read some poetry and readings, sang "The 12 Days of Christmas" as usual, and then Dad read the Christmas story from the Bible. Afterwards we piled into your Auntie Omie and hubby's "Punkin" and went looking at Christmas lights, another annual delight. Goodies followed and we exchanged our presents with each other. We are blessed with the love of family."*

Palm Sunday 1981 (age 15 ½): *"You portrayed John the Beloved in 'The Living Lord's Supper' presentation at our church. Dad portrayed Nathaniel. I was so proud of my men! Bryan, you are a natural actor. What a moving and convincing job you did. I can't begin to express the pride and joy I feel as I look at your 6-foot frame, seeing Jesus shine in you, and realize you are my beautiful son. How lucky I am. God has blessed me with you, and He has much in store ahead for you. You are Special! Your Loving Mother."*

Easter 1982 (age 16 ½): *"We performed the musical "The Witness" for Good Friday and Easter, again in church. You were part of the front cast, I played Peter's wife, Dad ran the sound and Buz did the spotlight. What a unique experience for all of us. Your father is an unusual man, full of genuine Jesus and His principles of Christian living. He is a quiet man, not nearly as verbal and social as your mom, nor you, but he is full of strength of character, steady and strong in his beliefs and God's abilities. He never seeks recognition or thanks. He is a true man of integrity!"*

Prom 1982: *"Your first Prom!" You wore a Navy Tux, white shirt with blue tipped ruffles and looked so handsome! Your date, Maureen, wore a light blue off the shoulder gown and she looked lovely. She is moving away in June and you are getting blue. But our family has influenced Maureen toward Jesus. She is not for you, forever, but has added a quality to your life in learning about relationships."*

In 1982 we lost 3 dear family members to cancer: Arne's father, our sister-in-law Janie, and my "other mother, friend," Liz W. It was a time of sorrow but because all knew Jesus as Savior, we have that wonderful knowing that we will see them again one day in heaven. How precious it is to know a Heavenly Father who can fill the voids and bring joy into sorrowful situations. Only He can do that, when no one else can.

Musicals became a great part of Bryan's life for the next several years. He had the lead role in "Oklahoma" and had to get a perm. He had a rich baritone voice and a superb stage presence. He had lead parts in other musicals and was asked to sing at Homecoming as well as his own commencement celebration for graduation. Our pride in our firstborn son just keeps growing. God has been so faithful to us as we trust in Him for our sons.

In between Bryan's 11th and 12th grades, Bryan joined the National Guard and went to boot camp at Fort Dix, NJ. He came back to finish his senior year in High School, then immediately went to Texas for advanced training.

"We are enormously overwhelmed with pride in you, Bry. But the thought of you going away, and leaving home is very hard to accept. So many memories flood my mind, but we have to let go, and we want what is best for your life. For the past 6 weeks, I have been fasting and praying on Mondays for our family and our needs; spiritually, financially and physically. I have lifted you before Jesus since you were a tiny baby, asking for wisdom, and beseeching God to keep you all your days. You learned early to tithe and God has blessed your faithfulness. You have also learned His way is the <u>only way</u> for real joy and true contentment. So, our job is almost complete. You are nearly a man, fully. And we are pleased, proud, and thankful to God for your life. I am continuing to pray that God will give you just the right wife. I have prayed this since you were in first grade. Your choices get better and better. We pray for your strength, emotions, feelings and your purity before God. So, we wait - and pray."

October 1983: *"During halftime of the last John Marshall Football Game of the year, you and several others dressed in "20's costumes" and did the "Charleston" accompanied by the school band. It was great and the crowd loved it. After halftime, you had your annual Harvest Festival Singing (5 Choir) activity at the Junior College."*

"Since Buz came with you, and you didn't know what to do with him (because the concert was in progress), you had him put your long black trench coat on and just stand beside you as though he were a part of the choir. You told him to say, "Watermelon, watermelon" and "smile lots."

"There stood Buz: flannel shirt, down vest, jacket AND black trench coat, cheeks flushed a brilliant red just sweltering! When the John Marshall Choir went up to sing, Buz crouched down behind a Bible College student and said, "I can't believe I'm doing this," which evoked many chuckles, indeed."

"Then, when the mass choir stood at the end, Buz had NO choice but to stand and join in. At first, he 'watermeloned' it but said he was saying 'watermelon' while everyone 'rested,' so tried to 'learn' the numbers and just sing. He got into it enough to 'really enjoy it.' He was dripping from perspiration, finally whispering, 'Bry, when is this done? I'm just cooking.' Bry, you and others around who knew the score, just lost it and howled at the preposterousness of it all, yet NO ONE caught on to your scheme."

"Mr. K. didn't notice, and Buz stood right beside you. Others who knew you in the audience didn't notice either. You pulled your charade off without a hitch. You are a couple of Turkeys! We laughed until we cried when you related the episode to us. We had remained at the game so missed the entire scenario! I loved it!!!"

April 1984: *"Only 6 weeks. to graduation, then off to Texas you go. I'm near tears as I am writing you this ~ remembering how excited I was when I knew I was pregnant with you. Then experiencing the thrill of a natural birth and hearing your first cry ~ holding you for the first time ~ the overwhelming protectiveness and pride in your little form! God gave us a miracle when He gave you to us, and now you are grown. So many years in between that last comma, yet the memories will last a lifetime."*

"My beautiful son, I love you. I wish and pray for you all the hopes, dreams, joys and blessings AND more, that have been your father's and mine to share. They <u>will</u> be IF you keep Jesus number one and follow His plan for every situation in your life. I continue to lift you up before Jesus. I guess I will so long as I have breath in my body, and I'm sure my final words to Jesus will be about you and Buz. Because, when it is all said and done, the ONLY thing that really matters to me besides Jesus, is my family and their relationship with my Lord. So, I will pray for you long after you have left our nest and established your own. I look ahead with great pride and joyful anticipation to all Christ has ahead for you! "Jesus, bless this my loving and obedient son, who has given us so many years of pleasure. And thank you for entrusting him into our care for these few years. I release him back to you now, asking for your blessing, wisdom, guidance, peace and joy to fill him and follow him from this day forth. He is yours. How I thank and bless your Name, Jesus. And I trust you to keep him YOURS for all eternity. In the precious name of Jesus, amen."

June 1984, Leaving for Advanced Training in National Guard:
"You flew out from Rochester. As we were standing in the garage, ready to leave, your father placed his hands on your shoulders and said some beautiful things, including how proud you had made us, and to remember whose name you bear. Then he said, "Bry, we release you to God now. You're a man and what you do from now on, you will not have to answer to us for, but to God." He told you we would always be there to encourage, listen and give advice, if needed, but basically that you are now a man and our task as parents was now complete. He assured you we would be praying for you, and would always

love you so very much. It was very emotional, and a very tender and precious moment to remember. I'm sure you will never forget that day."

July 1984: *"We motorcycled down to see you in Texas with our motorcycle buddies, Ger and Mary Henry. You were so surprised and pleased. It was over 100 degrees and we sweltered, even on the cycle. San Antonio is a beautiful place and we enjoyed our time with you. You weren't feeling well and looked so pale. I just wanted to pack you up in our trunk and bring you home. I hated to leave you! It was very hard on me, and I think not all that easy for you either! I know you are a man now, but you'll always be my little boy in some ways!"*

Bryan attended Rochester Community College for the next two years.

February 1985: *"We had tickets to Chanhassen Dinner Theater in Minneapolis, MN. The weather was bad so we called, but they said they never close. We traveled up to Minneapolis in a blizzard, and they <u>had</u> cancelled. Everything was shut down. We were at our motel in Bloomington and the four of us braved it and drove to Plymouth for a special dinner of Teppanyaki cooking. We had the entire restaurant to ourselves! The food was prepared right in front of us and it was tasty (and expensive). On the way back to our motel we got stuck 4 times, but you three men just picked up or pushed our little Volkswagen back onto the road each time, and we finally made it back to our motel. The snow was knee deep on the highways and the airport and everything was at a standstill. We were snowbound for 2 days and we had a ball ~ another memory!!"*

April 1985: *"We rescheduled Chanhassen Dinner Theater and went again on a Sunday afternoon. The dinner was divine and the play just great. Three quarters of the way through we had* to be evacuated to the basement because a tornado had touched down near-by and was heading our way. We spent 45 minutes tensely waiting in the lower level with some 700-800 other dinner theater guests as we could hear the roar of the winds and rain pass over. They resumed the play and we got home very late after yet another interesting and memorable time together. Life has not been dull for us!"

June 1985: *"Dad had surgery to remove a lump on his thyroid. He had lost 25 lbs. and had no energy. When they removed it, they found 3 large tumors the size of golf balls that were wrapping themselves around his windpipe. It was benign, praise God."*

July 1985: *"You spent 2 weeks at Camp Ripley and came home with the worst case of Poison Ivy the doctors had ever seen. You had it all over your legs, arms, face, neck, head/hair, inside your ears, chest and even near your eyes. I have been praying so hard for you because you are one miserable puppy!"*

September 1985: *"Your 2nd year at Rochester Community College, working at Menards and doing well. I love your dedication to Bible reading and prayer. Every morning you close your bedroom door and give God your first part of the day. I expect God to open your understanding of your subjects, to provide continually for your finances and to bless you later with a good job and wife. These blessings follow when Jesus is put first. I am very proud of you and you bless my heart many times with your tenderness to Him."*

April 1986: *"You did better than anyone as John the Beloved disciple in the "Living Lord's Supper" dramatization again. A friend from RCC, DeeDee Knutson came. She is a very sweet gal and was quite impressed."*

"The 'Grease' musical lead got laryngitis and you played the lead role at Rochester Civic Theater. What a fantastic job you did. You truly have a God given talent. It will be interesting seeing how God uses your life."

"You brought DeeDee to church with you (2nd date.) She raised her hand in the service for salvation and went forward to make a commitment to Jesus Christ. You went with her, and Dad and I joined you also. DeeDee is a precious young lady, sweet and sincere. We instantly liked her!"

May 1986: *"You also had the lead role in 'Guys & Dolls' at RCC and stole the show. DeeDee came and we met her mother."*

June 1986: *"We had a Conference on the Holy Spirit at church and one night, DeeDee went forward for healing of her knees (a painful degenerative disease), plus Asthma and a heart condition she has had since birth. The Holy Spirit was so strong on her that she shook as Jesus completely healed her of every disease. DeeDee just glowed. What an awesome God we serve!"*

September 1986: *"You went off to South Dakota State University in Brookings, SD. It was hard seeing you drive off in your 1976 Monza, all loaded to the roof. I realize you probably will not live at home ever again, and your room is so empty! I haven't been able to go in there yet to clean – it actually echoes! 'Course, a lot of 'junk' cleared out too-Ha! DeeDee comes over and we tan together as we are building a relationship with each other. Your father and I love her more and more."*

"You had a twice weekly Bible Study in our home with 5 of your friends, all last year. You would play your guitar, sing choruses and share Jesus with them. DeeDee was one of these. You asked the Lord to allow you to bring 2 souls to Him this year

and God helped you influence 5. Beautiful! You are exactly what I hoped my child would be spiritually: strong, gentle with wisdom, sensitive to other people's needs, but totally sold out to Jesus and committed to winning others to Christ. I pray you will remain 100% moldable in Jesus' Hands. I am thankful to the Lord for you, Bry. God is and will use you and many good things are in store for you as you continue to put the Lord first <u>always.</u> I love you my Big Son!"

NOTE from Bryan's Bible Study group

Scott became a Chaplain in the army; Mike and Amy married and are active in their church today, raising children to serve Jesus. Patty made a commitment to Christ but I do not know where she is today, and DeeDee married Bryan!

~FIFTEEN~

1985 Back Surgery

In 1985 we added a nice, large deck to our house, facing the back yard. The decking was on, but no railings at this point. I was standing on a plank of wood, extending from the new deck to the side cement steps, painting over puttied nail holes. I leaned back too far, lost my balance and began to fall backwards. As I felt myself falling, I pushed with all my might with my feet and said to myself, *"flex those knees baby!"*

I jumped backward over the open chain link fence, with an open spiked gate, landing 7 feet backward on an uphill slope. The bucket of paint was still in my hand.

The impact of my landing forced the oil-based paint from the bucket to slosh upward and back downward, all over my hair, face and body. There I stood: intact, humiliated, frustrated and shocked!

I could have been impaled on the open gate! There was lumber, with protruding nails, all over everywhere else. I landed the only possible place where I would not have been gravely injured. Thank you, Lord, for your protecting hand.

My hair got washed in turpentine and I felt lucky to be alive. I taught a CPR Class that night and all seemed well. I ached all over, but seemed to be OK otherwise. Three days later I couldn't move. This began a year long struggle of doctor appointments and constant pain. X-rays suggested all was well, but my body didn't agree. I would rest and be careful and my back would seem to improve. Suddenly, I would move wrong or sit too long or stand too long and my back would be killing me all over again. I was prayed for many times but never recovered completely. The nagging pain always existed.

Bryan was thriving at college, home every other weekend to see DeeDee, and us (for a few minutes)! We could clearly see this was probably going to be a permanent relationship. We had thought so almost from the day we met DeeDee. We could not have done better if we had hand-picked her for Bryan ourselves! She was growing in the Lord and we adored her. Maybe she would be the daughter we never had!

After falling down our basement stairs once and "almost" several other times because my left leg would "give out," the doctors decided to do more exploring. They decided on a then-new procedure (MRI) and immediately after, scheduled me for surgery. I had a Laminectomy of the 5th lumbar, herniated disc. Fragments had lodged into the spinal column and were embedded in the sciatic nerve of my spine. This had been grating into and against my backbone, causing my nerves to be shot, plus it was excruciatingly painful. They surgically removed the splinters, scraped the nerve, removed the disc and drilled the opening in the vertebrae larger for the nerve to pass through. There was a bulge in the 4th lumbar disc also, but they decided to leave it alone, feeling it was less dangerous to do anything with that right then. When I regained consciousness in the recovery room, I knew immediately that the surgery was successful. That excruciating, intense, searing pain was gone! Praise the Lord! I was so thankful for the expertise that God has given our many gifted doctors.

My recovery took almost 1 year physically. I could not lift anything heavier than a coffee cup for a very long time. It took almost 2 years for my nerves to heal. It was a time of learning to be careful and respect the body God had given me. It was a daily learning to trust God to restore every nerve ending which had been traumatized.

~SIXTEEN~

Bryan's Diary of Pretty BIG Things too!

December 22, 1986: *"You and DeeDee asked to spend some time with us discussing your future together. From **7:30 – 11:30 pm** you explained (with charts, graphs etc.) why, how, and where you would be able to make it as a married couple, still attending college. You wanted to be married in August of 1987. At **7:35 pm** Dad said he wasn't surprised and gave <u>his full blessing</u>. I rather anticipated this and DeeDee is a honey and a beautiful compliment to you. You were so cute. You had thoroughly worked out all the details and <u>were determined</u> to present them **in full**. Finally, at **11:30 pm** Dad convinced you we were behind you 100%. Dad took DeeDee in his arms and told her 'Now I'll have the daughter I have always hoped and waited for!'"*

"On December 23, 1986 you gave DeeDee her ring. Earlier in the day you asked her mom, Ginger, for DeeDee's hand in marriage."

"It seems strange to be coming to the end of this Diary of Little Things for you, as well as nearing the end of your time with us alone. Your "little" precious ways have turned into "big" precious ways and your loving ways and giving heart are now turning (as God intended) toward the one who will share and become the focus of your life and affection: DeeDee! We love her and will be gaining a beautiful daughter. I am adjusting to not being number one to you, but I'm not losing that very special

bond you and I share. I've cried a few tears and already feel "lonesome" in my heart. Yet because I have prayed for your future wife for many years, I believe in my heart that DeeDee will simply join our family and allow my love to encompass and include her. I pray she will grow to love me and find me to be a 'mom' and 'friend' who loves her. I pray God will bless her to be all God intends for her, you, and your life together. We are embarking on a new era – filled with changes, excitement and I'm sure, some difficulties. But our love, prayers and our united love of Jesus will find the proper foundation that will bring us through, strong, tall and united, in a firm family bond. Truly this is a God-given heritage few families share."

"My love for you is so very great, Bry. I respect you and am proud to be your mother. I am grateful for the wisdom and job God helped me to complete. You are truly God's man and your own person. God bless you, my beloved, firstborn son."

August 14, 1987, **Your Wedding Day**: *"It is 6:30 am and I am nursing a cup of coffee. Everything is ready. Today I turn you over completely to the comfort of another woman! As I headed this, "Your wedding day," I felt a great big lump arise in my chest and tears welled up in this mother's eyes. I have been happy for you - no, excited - as I've seen your anticipation of this day - maybe even anxious for you to be on your own. I relinquished you and sorrowed for your absence when you went away to South Dakota State University, but this AM I believe I do my final crying. I am remembering your baby ways, your adorable chubby legs, your innocent and trusting eyes of concern as you hovered over me when I broke my back from the fall from the horse in Nebraska. You were only 18 months old, but your love and tenderness as you stood over me, your chubby hand holding mine...so many, many years ago....it seems like forever. Time slips quietly and quickly away. Life is but a vapor and only what is done for Christ will last!"*

"The day will come when you and DeeDee will say your final farewells to us at our grave site and it will have gone by so quickly. I know it won't be long before I will be doing that with my parents. It happens so fast. So, cherish each moment, my precious son. Love your bride with every tenderness within your being and don't let anything mar your communication and commitment. You have seen your father and I love each other tenderly, but you have seen us be short and disrespectful too. I am sorry for that. I wish you even better than we have done. Each succeeding generation is supposed to give its best to its posterity. I believe we have given you the best we were able, in spite of some rough times. Now the Jacobson baton is passed to you, Bryan! It is for you to carry on the heritage of a godly home and perpetuate the love of Jesus, family and friends in even a better way. You and DeeDee will never again have to answer to us. You answer to God and to each other.'

*"The Word says, **"Submit yourselves one to another and so fulfill the law of Christ."***

"I charge you to do just that. Be the man of your home, Bryan. Your father was every bit that and I deeply respected him for exactly that! I am extremely independent, capable of running an army and taking charge of any situation (you know that)! However, I had no trouble ever submitting to your father's leadership. It's easy to submit to a husband when he leads under God, with love, and listens to his bride's wishes, thoughts and advice."

"You have a beautiful helpmate in DeeDee. We have grown to adore her and enfold her into our arms as our own daughter. You are both blessed, and this is the result of 21 years of prayer. You will go on loving us the same – you've just added DeeDee to your love list and moved everyone down a notch. Not so with

DeeDee. She is a normal woman who wants all of her husband's love and will sometimes be threatened even by his love for his parents and family. This love becomes 'secure' in time and finally settles into a comfortableness with his family. But, until this happens, there can be friction. I know. I went through it myself, but I thought I was the only one in the world so something must be wrong with me. It is normal! DeeDee and I talked about this, over brunch, after you were first engaged. you and I did also. I said all that to lead up to this: we give you total release and freedom to build your own togetherness from now on. No pressures to come for holidays or visits. You are always welcome but no obligations. We will pull back so you have the space you're going to need to develop your own identity together; to allow the room and freedom for God to make you one."

"We have never loved you more than we do today, son. Thank you for loving me, for proudly hugging me, even in front of your friends; for being respectful and helpful and so very thoughtful! You are precious (and yes, I am weeping) and I love you so very, very much!! We respect you and are so very proud of you. I believe God is going to use you in a unique way in your life. The one thing I will do: I will pray daily for you and DeeDee. I commit to that as I have been doing. Remember all He has done. He is your source and strength."

"So, God bless you, God go with you, and may God lead, guide and direct all the rest of your days. I will add a small postscript following tonight's wedding."

All my love, Your Mom of Little and Big things!

After everything was cleaned up and put away; while Dad was transporting gifts; Buz and I stayed to finish up and turn out the lights. Buz was exhausted and had laid down in the back pew. The church was empty and quiet and as I peeked over at him, his eyes were shut, big tears spilling down his cheeks. I touched his young shoulder and asked if he was ok. He just nodded, looked up at me and said, *"Mom, it's hard to lose a brother,"* He broke down and sobbed. I said nothing – just held his hand. After a few moments I said, *"Buz, you are so very special, and I love you so. I am very, very proud of you, son. You'll be ok – just be patient, hon, you haven't lost a brother, you've gained a sister."* I left him to himself for a few moments longer, shut off the lights and we finally went home. It was a perfect day.

PS 7:00 a.m. the next morning.
"Well...we made it! You are both coming over for Swedish Pancakes this A.M. before going on to your special honeymoon. Your request! The wedding was lovely – you have it on tape to remember forever!!"

~ SEVENTEEN ~

BUZ'S OLD TOES

In May 1983, we took our youngest son, Buz, to an Orthopedic Surgeon at Mayo Clinic. Buz had been complaining of his feet hurting. His toes would crack with a grinding sound. He was having excruciating pain. We had gone to Disneyworld in Florida the previous year and he was in pain the entire time. After many tests and x-rays, the surgeon said Buz had degenerating bone joints in his feet. He said the cartilage lining was all gone in his toes, which is most rare in a child. This usually is seen only in older people and doesn't generally begin to show itself until into the late 20's. The doctor said it may be a form of arthritis peculiar only to the big toe joints, which would require surgery. Or, it may be a crippling form of arthritis.

From "Buz's Diary of Little Things" by Mom:

May 1983 (age 13) *"Buz, you and I talked, and we are together agreeing for God to completely bring you through this with healing and victory. I believe Jesus healed you at 18 months old, from arthritis, and He will keep you until He takes you home someday. I will not accept anything less than victory! I don't think God healed you as a baby only to allow you to become crippled as a teen. Never! I think the devil is trying to attack our family. Jesus has already won and our healing was purchased on Calvary by Him. So – we are all claiming your healing and giving glory to God."*

May 1983: *"Dad surprised you by getting up and helping you with your paper route. You then treated him to pancakes at McDonalds. I gather you both rather 'pigged out' because neither of you were hungry at lunchtime! But you had a special time together. We love you, Buz. Your father can hardly bare to see you in this pain you are having. It just pulls his heart apart to think of your being any way unable to run, play and fully enjoy life. He got all teary eyed yesterday as we talked about it. But we must believe and trust. We must trust."*

May 16, 1983: *"Well, it seems the doctors aren't sure what your problem is. It is puzzling to them, but they feel it must be some form of arthritis. They have put you on anti-inflammatory drugs and Tylenol 3. Your toes have really given you lots of pain the last couple of days from all the punching, pulling and twisting plus the needles and dye inserted. I almost can't stand to see your pain, pal. I'm praying so hard for you, hon. I am believing Jesus is going to <u>completely</u> heal you. We are agreeing about it. You are so brave too and hardly voice a complaint. Do you know how much I love you and how proud I am of you? My heart swells with pride over the beautiful son you are!"*

May 25, 1983: *"I took you out of school the 5th & 6th hours and we went golfing. Boy, you were the envy of some of your classmates. We had a great time together. You did quite well too and are becoming quite the golfer. Your toes have not been bothering you with nearly as much pain. I believe either the Lord is healing you, or at least the medicine is helping. I don't want to just treat the symptoms though. I want God to heal the cause. <u>And He will</u>!!! I love you, Buz, so, so much."*

July 1983: *"Teen Camp at Lake Geneva Bible Camp. You seemed to be Mr. Popular and also took the Foosball Champion Award. You also enjoyed the spiritual challenge. We have seen a real maturing, a trying to please and become responsible this summer. Your attitude is much improved. We are so very proud of you. God is also healing your toes. You have less pain and trouble each day and are able to go golfing without severe pain now. Praise God."*

The night before the x-ray with dye, Buz prayed and told the Lord, it was ok if he would end up crippled, if that was God's will and as long as God would be with him every day. Quite a declaration of faith for a young teenager!

Fall 1983 (14 yrs.): *"Mayo did more x-ray with dye in your toes. I asked the x-ray technician what the results were, but he said the doctor would have to give us the results. I pressed for a hint and he said, "I don't know what all the fuss was about. This kid has more cartilage in his toes than the average bear."*

"Later the orthopedic surgeon told us he could find "nothing wrong" with your toes and your x-rays were normal. He said perhaps the initial x-rays were somehow mixed up. He dismissed you from Mayo care and you have been fine ever since."

*"What happened? I honestly don't know, but I believe God created new cartilage in your toes and healed you. Like the blind man in the Bible said, "**All I know is I was blind and now I see**." We don't always need to know all the answers ~ we just need to hold to His nail-scarred Hands. Thank you, Jesus."*

September 24, 1983 (My 42nd Birthday): *"You treated me to Peanut Butter and Chocolate Ice Cream. You made popcorn and babied me. You are such a cutie, Buz. I love you so much. You are so much fun to be around and you are so loving and sweet. I am blessed by you. I couldn't ask for a son more special than you! Our buttons burst because we are so proud of you."*

January 1984: *"JM Musical, 'Annie Get Your Gun.' Your brother, Bry, has the lead as Frank Butler and you have a speaking part too. You did a superb job and are definitely a natural with lots of potential for future musicals. It was such a delight sitting in the audience, seeing our two beautiful, handsome sons together, having fun and experiencing such a rich time together in their lives. We were filled with tremendous pride in you both, Buz. We are so pleased to see you maturing and developing a good and right set of values. Ohhhh, you did make the girl's hearts go pitty-pat....and you are only an 8th grader. Look out girls ~ the Lady Killer of Hearts is growing up! Slow down, Buz, you are growing up too rapidly, Pal."*

"You and Bry have been renting all the outstanding musical classics from the library and are hooked: South Pacific, Sound of Music, West Side Story. Great movies!"

May 1984: *"Your father treated you and Bryan to a fishing trip at the boundary waters in Canada along with Uncle Ev, Uncle Kurt and Ger Henry. It was a very special time with shared fun and hours of being with family. It was a pleasure to be able to treat you both to such a special time together. Dad caught an 18 lb. 42" Northern. You were all so excited when you came home, like little boys from a birthday party, excitedly leading me to the trunk of the car to show me your treasures!"*

June 1984: **Bryan's graduation Open House**. *"Everything was set up before we left for church and when we came home, we discovered Rusty, our poodle, had eaten ¼ of the chocolate sheet cake, cellophane and all. He had munched large chunks and we could see the teeth marks and paw prints. It was funny, really! You said that Rusty just wanted to help Bryan celebrate too! Poor Rusty suffered from that one all afternoon outside with diarrhea. He could have died from all that chocolate."*

July 1984: (15 yrs. old) *"We have been going to Lake Geneva Bible Camp all your life. We always bring our boat and take all your friends water skiing and have a lot of fun together. But it is spiritually enriching too. We are so pleased with your cooperative spirit and see real progress in our communication. I'm really enjoying the delightful young man you are becoming, Buz. My prayers are being answered."*

August 1984: *"I took you and a bunch of your friends to the water slide all day. As I was watching you, I remembered a few years ago when I had become so frustrated and angry with you and said some things I didn't mean. You have a way of pushing my buttons and God is teaching me patience with a capital 'P.' But I felt so badly for having hurt you and I talked with you again about it. You said, "Mom, it's under the blood. I know you didn't mean it, so please forget it." I think now I truly can. Oh, the beauty of Christ's forgiveness, allowing us to forgive and love one another. I love you so much my handsome young man, and I love the Jesus I see in you."*

September 1984: *"You are a big Freshman this year, and very popular. You are too handsome for your own good, you little Turkey! You are 6'1" and your personality has blossomed so that you are one neat young man, and we are enormously proud of you."*

February 1985: *"Today was talent day for school. You chose to sing a religious song, "All I needed to Say" by Michael W. Smith. Buz, you received the loudest applause of any student. You sat on a stool and sang just absolutely beautifully. I cannot tell you how swelled with pride and respect I was. I thank God for you."*

July 1985 Teen Camp (age 16): *"You came home so full of Jesus. How beautiful it is to see how you are growing and becoming all God created you to be. We pray every day for God's will for your life. You feel God has a special call on your life and we will be praying with you for real guidance and direction in the coming years."*

August 1985: *"You and Bry took our sailboat out and it got really stormy with 65 mph gusty winds! You were bouncing all over on Lake Pepin in Lake City and..... you were both frightened!! Bryan wanted to crank up the keel and ride it out. If you had done that, you would have capsized, and you knew it. You had the good sense to say, "No way" and threw out the anchor, took down the sails and rode out the storm. You have learned many valuable things from your father and God has given you lots of common sense. Once again we were so proud and thankful for God giving you to us."*

"You and Bryan sang a duet in church. It was just beautiful, and your voices blended perfectly. How our hearts swelled with pride in your beautiful Christian spirits. We love you both and are so thankful for your lives. You have brought us many fun and enjoyable moments. There have been trying times as you are learning to navigate the teen years, and sometimes we have made some big mistakes. But we have your best interest at heart. We want to do our part to help shape and mold you so that you will learn and develop all the potential God created within you. God surely gave you a beautiful voice, and it is just so precious to see your using it for Him. We are so proud of you, Buz."

September 1985: *"You are in 10th grade now/Senior High School. And popular. Too popular maybe. You and Joy were chosen to sing "The Search is Over" for Homecoming. At the school convocation you did not change the words "...if you give a damn, you'll know who I am." An electric shock and a momentary hushed disbelief went through the audience, even though they knew the words of the song. You, me and everyone else was disappointed. You came home and wept because you knew you blew it."*

"However, when you went to the Homecoming dance, sang the song and changed it to "...if you really care, you'll know who I am." There were a few remarks of surprise, but the King gave you a thumbs-up and they asked you to sing it again, which you did. Buz, that took courage to do that! We admired you and told you so. It's hard to be popular and keep a good testimony, but it can be done, and I pray God's Hands to keep you true to Him in these coming years ahead."

November/December 1985: *"You are in "Northern Lights," a small singing/dancing group from John Marshall. You are also in the Marching Band so really enjoy the football games all the more. Your grades are suffering because you neglect to study and often are late in turning in your assignments – this has been a problem all through your school years. You are such a charmer and so delightful to be around, but you frustrate the dickens out of this mother! You certainly keep me on my knees praying for you!"*

"I remember all too well one of the conferences with your teacher. She went on and on about how gentlemanly and polite you were, how charming and helpful in every way. Dad finally asked, "And what about his grades?" She replied, "Well, there's a bit of a problem there. He hasn't turned in anything yet this quarter. He has incompletes in everything." We would come home, sit down with you and lay the law down! You would turn into a dynamo and get all your assignments completed and bring home a "B" for that quarter! You could have been a straight "A" student if you had just gotten off your duff and gotten your papers in on time! So very frustrating, Son!!"

September 1986: *"Bryan left for SDSU and his room echoes hauntingly. Posters are all gone. I'm sure glad you're still here! I miss Bry, but I believe his leaving is hardest on you. Even though you tangled occasionally, you are still very close and there is a special bond between you two. I'm so glad for that. You are special, but you need extra love and encouragement from your brother. Someday, when we are gone, it will only be you and Bryan."*

November 1986: *"You purchased a 1979 GLC Mazda in terrific shape. You've been working at The Pizza Gardens and you are so excited. You actually got the car when I was in the hospital recovering from back surgery. Dad and I saw the car while on a motorcycle ride, and he felt it was perfect for you."*

"1986 has been a difficult year at our house. I was in so much pain most of the time. I couldn't clean the house like normally, so you became my #1 helper. You are a very special son, Buz. Many times, you have had to pitch in and do things for me when you least felt like it and without a thank you or appreciation from anyone. Your Father was worried and stressed about me and short with you. Your lot was not an easy one, but I have seen you grit your teeth and "take it," knowing you were being misunderstood and hurting inside. I admire and respect you, Buz. God is going to use you and bless you in a very special way. I dearly love you, my precious son. You are so very special to me. Truly a gift from God."

February 1987 (17 years): *"You played the part of the Butler in 'My Fair Lady' at John Marshall. You did a superb job! You stooped and shuffle-walked using a wavery, quivering voice and even bobbed your head like a very old man. You were a stand out! We could hardly believe what a good actor you were. We nearly burst our buttons. You loved it too. You're so cute!!"*

June 1987: *"You had a rather difficult year academically. You really didn't try and consequently blew it far enough into the year that you could not recover enough to get your "B" average – only a high "C." It is too bad because you really have it upstairs. I can sense you are discouraged. I am too! More prayer!"*

July 13, 1987: *"We went kite flying! It was so much fun. You suggested it and we had perfect, gusty winds. We went to the IBM field and played for 1 ½ hours. Neat! We laughed, and you had to help me get my kite going all the time. I watched you and my inward pride at the beautiful son you are nearly made me cry. You make me a very proud mom, Buz. Your strong body, clean and pure heart, your hopeful blue eyes, sparkling and twinkling with joy and delight, your blond hair, bleached by many hot hours on the church lawn mower all say what a terrific and special young man you are becoming. I love you more than you will ever, ever know!"*

Lake Geneva Family Camp 1987: *"I developed a virus and couldn't get to camp. You and Scott had the full run of our cabin. Dad motorcycled up to be sure you were ok and had enough money. He came home with $60.00 of your money to put back into your savings account! You, actually, had more than enough. I'm not sure what all happened but I believe you had a great time. You always were very frugal and quite the entrepreneur! You were on your honor, for sure."*

"You attended "Sonshine" and worked backstage, getting the opportunity to meet personally the singers like Carmen, White Heart, DeGarmo and Keith etc. You loved this exposure and opportunity. You were also resourceful and ambitious and because you worked the event, you didn't have to pay. You've become very innovative and enterprising!"

1987 Teen Camp: *"I am praying God will just unleash His Holy Spirit on you in a very dynamic way. My heart has been overwhelmed with pride and love as I've prayed and thought of you. I'm anxious for your return. I also miss you."*

"Your camp was great, and you came home so enthused and on fire for Jesus. Nothing thrills my heart more than to see your love flourishing for Him. Buz, you have so much on the ball and so much potential. It's going to be exciting just watching God move in your life and see His plans for you unfold as you submit to Him."

August 14, 1987: *"Bryan's wedding day. You are 18 now and were 'Best Man' and believe me, you were the best for the job! You ran your tush off for Bry all day long doing errands and were really tired by picture time. You sang 'Friends' and, oh Buz, we were so touched by you. It was just perfect and so beautiful. I cried the only time during the entire event when you sang. When you were finished, Dad wiped away the tears from his eyes too. Bryan and DeeDee were crying, using Bryan's handkerchief. Then when you returned to your place on the platform, Bryan turned and hugged you and you cried like a baby. Bryan whipped his hanky backwards to you and Pastor Shaw said smilingly, 'You gonna be alright, Buz?' Everyone laughed. It was such a tender moment. Your father and I are filled with gratefulness and pride over you. We love you so, so much."*

Monday, August 17, 1987: *"You returned the Tuxedos today. It is finally done. I'm just glad you're not going too, Buz. I do not think I could handle it. You were so tender and loving to me this morning, and hugged me so gently. I love you my beautiful son and I cherish your love and friendship. You recently said to me, 'Mom, I think I'm probably your best friend.' I believe you may be right. I know I feel so loved by you and my heart bursts today with joy in you. You are special. There are no words to describe how proud you make me feel."*

August 27, 1987: *"Your Grandpa Ohman, my father, has been in the hospital one week now at St Mary's Hospital here in Rochester, MN. His doctors are all Mayo Clinic doctors. He has a diseased heart muscle, plus arrhythmia. They are trying to regulate his heart. Grandma has been staying with us and she's doing very well. We've been having a ball in between visits to Grandpa. You went up last night and played 3-handed Rook with Grandpa and Grandma in his hospital room. It must have been a barn-burner as Grandpa was −200 in the hole. You and Grandma ganged up on him and set him good because he bid so high. Fun!"*

August 1987: *"We went clothes shopping and you got some neat and wild threads. You looked so cute and were so excited. I treated you to lunch after and we had a fun time. You are special to me, Buz. I treasure your tender heart. I am blessed having you for my son."*

September 1987: *"You are a senior in high school. It's hard to believe you have grown up so quickly. It seems like yesterday you waved from the bus stop, little lunch pail in your chubby little hands. You have given us so much joy, Buz, and it has really been fun to watch you grow, mature and become what you are today. We are so blessed having you for our son. You made Northern Lights singing group again this year. I knew you would, but you were not as confident. You are also still in the pizza business, this time delivering for Shakey's Pizza. Tips are good, which doesn't surprise me with your charm!"*

"You were chosen to sing for Homecoming. What an honor! Dad and I were able to attend Assembly at John Marshall to hear you sing. You are so beautiful, son, and your dad and I are

pleased at your becoming a man. We love you so much, Pal! Our littlest "weed" is nearly grown – doesn't seem possible. How we pray for God's Hand to rest heavily on your shoulders, Buz, so you will always accept and praise Him anyway, for all things - even adverse and sorrowful things - because God NEVER makes mistakes - EVER!"

"We don't always see and understand how good could possibly be in some things, but if we allow Him, He will make bitter become better. Some day we will understand and see the finished weaving has become a very perfect and beautiful work of art. Right now, we see only tangled cords and threads."

*"**Now we see through a glass darkly, but someday face to face.**" I Corinthians 13:12*

"One day we will know and understand. Today ours is to trust and take Jesus's Hand and let Him hold tightly to OUR hand....and go on. Remember, He knows the future. He knows what He is doing, and He NEVER makes mistakes. I love that beautiful Jesus, Buz, and I pray you will love Him too with all your being forever. I love you so, son, and want God's best for your life. He is the only answer."

October 1987: *"Dad and I went to Sanibel Island in Florida with Don and Beryl for two glorious weeks to celebrate our 25th wedding anniversary. It was wonderful in every way. While we were gone, you were in-charge of the house (and Rusty, our poodle) and on your honor, which we didn't even worry about. You decided to go visit your brother and DeeDee in SD over the weekend and asked our neighbor gal to watch and feed Rusty. She has been doing this for us for many years, so that was no problem. Apparently Rusty felt abandoned, first by me (he's really my baby), then by you. When you got back he had chewed up the new communication device and cord inside my new motorcycle helmet; got into a bag of photos I was separating and chewed and tore the bag all apart; got some of Dad's floppy disks from the computer desk, and there were teeth marks and holes on them; went to the top of the basement stairs and chewed all the carpet off the edge of the landing and chewed the bottom of the door as much as he could, leaving large gouges in the bottom of the door. Then he topped it off by saturating the rug at the bottom of the stairs. Do you think he was a bit upset, maybe??"*

"You were furious with him and he got a whipping from you. He had never done any of those things before and could always be trusted to be upstairs when we were away. I guess they call it separation anxiety. I called it being very, very, naughty, rebellious, and getting even!!"

"Because our carpet upstairs was practically new plush mauve carpeting, you called and asked us where the left-over mauve carpeting was. I said, "Why?" You wisely said you thought you might use a piece of it to lay on while you worked under your car."

"When we came home you told us the rest of the story. You had Floyd come over and put a new piece of carpet in place to repair what Rusty had done. Rusty had eaten the carpet all the way down to the wood floor. You couldn't even see a seam where the carpet was pieced because Floyd was an expert carpet layer. I was so mad at Rusty that I wouldn't let him lay beside me for almost 2 weeks and he had big tears marks on his fur from grieving. I was proud of you for having such ingenuity to get it fixed so we didn't take Rusty to the pound. I really wouldn't have done that, but it did cross my mind! All is forgiven for the poor, lonely pooch. Thank you for taking care of it all! You had a busy two weeks!!"

December 17, 1987: *"It was extremely icy and your car went through an intersection and hit a utility pole when you were delivering pizza. Going a little too fast maybe? It really smashed up your little Mazda good! We were most thankful that no one was injured. Cars can be replaced but beautiful sons can't! You were really upset. Earlier this week you had been cut from the musical. Dad and you talked to the school and you found out it was because you were so hard to work with. That was difficult for you to hear. Now the car. It has been a hard week for you, but Dad and I have assured you of our love. We just hope you look inside yourself and make good out of all of this. You and Dad are trying to salvage the car."*

Christmas Eve 1987: *"Dad, you and I, The Henry's, Jon and Jim all went caroling from 5:30 – 7:00 PM. It really was a fun time and you boys really got into the singing! We caroled at a nursing home plus several elderly people's homes from church, and a few others too. We surprised and brought joy to quite a number of people tonight! Back home we ate fondue with Bryan and DeeDee after Dad read the Christmas Story. We prayed for each other and opened our gifts. It was a perfect Christmas Eve."*

January 1988: *"Your Father and you have had a good time fixing your car. At one point, Dad told you to go start the car. You tried, then said, "Dad, a car needs a battery to start!" You both got a good laugh out of that. The car is looking quite decent, even without a bumper. It appears to have weathered the storm and runs great!"*

Dorian Festival at Luther College: *"You and five other students were chosen to perform at Dorian Festival. This was quite an honor, considering all the John Marshall High School students that are enrolled at JMHS. Each person is chosen to participate at the festival on talent exclusively. We are extremely proud of your God given talents, Buz, and we hope you will develop your talents and always serve Him."*

Prom 1988: *"Anna asked you to take her to the Prom. Her father is here at the Clinic for a special study from Norway and she has never attended an American Prom. You took her and Geoff and his date to a very nice restaurant, the Broadway Street Café. You almost had her believing in the 'American Tradition of Arm Wrestling' for the paycheck. In the end you picked up the tab, of course, but you had fun giving her a hard time. You all laughed and had a great time."*

Graduation 1988: *"You made it! Although I think you wondered if you would in English. We had a perfect day for an Open House for you, and I'm glad school is over and done with. I wonder if I can hack college stress with you now! We worry about your future and your grades with the lack of motivation you seem to have. We have given you over to God. He will have to do it!"*

July 20, 1988 **our 25th Wedding anniversary**: *"You got up at 5:30 AM, set a lovely table and made us scrambled eggs with green peppers and onions, toast, orange juice and grape juice, coffee and even lit the candles so we could eat by candlelight at 6:00 AM. Your card was just beautiful. Thank you for being so thoughtful on such a special day."*

August 1988: *"We went on a 2-week vacation to the West Coast. Bryan and DeeDee came with us in their own vehicle. We visited Mt Rushmore, Yellowstone National Park, Grand Tetons of Wyoming, Shoshone Falls in Idaho and many other beautiful sights. We visited Grandpa and Grandma Ohman in Klamath Falls, Oregon as well as visited my sister, brother and families who live nearby. Crater Lake is one of the 7 wonders of the world and it is gorgeous with its water of deep, royal blue shade. We had a wonderful picnic there with family. We took the 6-mile Old Stagecoach road (dirt) through the giant Redwoods. How very majestic and scenic! The ocean was beautiful, but we nearly froze. We ate prawn, oysters and just had a marvelous and memorable time. We played games with grandparents and ended with a Family Reunion at Lake of the Woods State Park in Oregon. Grandpa brought his boat, and everyone had a time of visiting and eating together. Bryan and DeeDee left to finish their vacation on their own, to celebrate their first anniversary. Our trip home included the John Day Dams in the Columbia Gorge where we watched the Salmon in their Salmon Ladders from the park observatory. We went through Hungry Horse Dam and then Glacier National Park. The Road to the Sun is quite the scenic (and a bit scary) ride. Many years later your father and I, along with motorcycle buddies, Ger and Mary Henry, would motorcycle this same route. Trust me, now, that is scary, for sure, on a cycle!!!! It was fun being with you through all the memorable times of sharing together. You have such a special way about you, and your insight into other people's emotions just blows me away. God has given you a great gift of discernment. I am trusting Him to guide all your future decisions."*

August 1988: *"You will be attending Rochester Community College in just a few days. Your days remaining at home are fast approaching. Soon you will be on your own...time has so quickly passed...but we have wonderful memories, pictures and a close family to help us look forward to the future. You have blossomed this year and are continuing to grow into a fine young man of whom we are intensely proud! So, God go with you as you enter still another season of your life. "*

"You are in Band, Jazz Ensemble, Choir and Barbershop Quartet plus your regular studies. You like college and have established a beautiful testimony as to your faith in God too.

Super! You will also be working at IBM as a student on weekends, and any extra time you can spare. This is a neat opportunity and we hear you are thought well of, work hard and getting along very well with everyone. Do you know how proud of you that makes us? We are blessed by you, and your example as our son! You goof up once in a while (don't we all??) and therefore you think you don't 'ever' do things right. But you surely do, and this is just one of many examples."

Thanksgiving Day, November 24, 1988: *"We left for Vera Cruz, Mexico with a team from our church to build a Bible Center under the Assembly of God Maps program. We left Rochester, MN at 4:30 PM on Turkey Day and traveled all night, spending 4 ½ hrs. in the Mexico City terminal, sleeping on the marble floor and freezing. Remember, everyone needed a rest room and we couldn't find anyone to ask as there wasn't a soul around? I went looking and found a janitor who spoke no English and I spoke no Spanish. I crossed my knees and acted like I needed a restroom. He got it and showed me where one was. I learned my first Spanish word! We were all very relieved!! Ha! We got to Vera Cruz, but our luggage was 2 days late, with missing shoes and a few other missing things but nothing really serious. Others lost cameras – not a good thing to pack in a suitcase! We are TIRED! It is Hot & Humid."*

"We unloaded cement blocks, mixed cement, tied steel, scored the block and worked our fannies off with the hot sand blowing in our eyes. On the way back to the motel I said we looked like American Migrant Workers because even our eyebrows were covered in sand and we were dirty, disheveled, stinky and tired. But we felt so accomplished! We all love the Mexican 'Helado' = ice cream. Wow is it yummy! And so refreshing!"

"The food was great, the services were fantastic, and we also showed the movie, in Spanish, 'The Cross and The Switchblade.' This is the true story of David Wilkerson who started Teen Challenges. Five people gave their hearts to Jesus. Our missionary, Glenn, conducted the service in Spanish and Carla Maroquin led the singing. Mexicans can sing us under the rug! Their beautiful singing, straight from their hearts, amplifies their love for Christ."

"The pastor's wife is trying to marry you off to one of the Mexican Senioritas! Your blond hair and fair looks make you quite an attraction, for sure."

"Gilberto had been barefoot and had a nasty cut in his foot. After first aiding it, you gave him your socks and shoes. He couldn't believe it - you had an extra pair of shoes in the bus. That night Gilberto asked Jesus into his heart. Neat!"

"Today we saw two little children breaking open a plastic garbage bag at the dump and eating from it. It was so heartbreaking. This is a common scene here. Many children appear to be homeless, living in the dump area. Jesus is their only hope. Many of their homes are just cardboard shanties. It makes us wish we could do more to help."

"These church people here have so little, yet are so happy, living contentedly and loving the Lord. You had wanted a leather bomber's jacket and had saved money for this. After the first service, you whispered in my ear that 'you could do without that jacket - there were more important things here to put our money into, like this offering and these beautiful people's lives.' So, we all dug deep and gave much of our spending money to a higher cause. I was very proud of you, Buz. We are falling in love with this lovely culture and these precious people."

"We finished the first floor of a three-story complex that will serve 250,000 people here who have no place of worship at all. More teams will follow us to complete the next phase. It has been an eye opening, yet wonderful experience. We will not quickly forget our Spanish brothers and sisters in Christ in Las Brisas, Mexico."

"We were able to visit several sights like, the Castillo de San Juan prison, where many Christians died for their faith trying to get religious freedom. Bonito Juan Juarez spent 2 years in this prison and finally won religious freedom for all. The Spanish Inquisition and Cortez rule was part of this prison complex where terrible torture and death occurred. We visited the pyramid ruins in Zampoala, the ocean, and did some shopping. You got quite a charge out of the Volkswagen police cars, and riding on that school bus to and from our hotel to the worksite was an experience in itself. We were scared half to death as vehicles were so close together you did not dare have your arm out the window as it just might get sheared off! We ended our tour at Bocca del Rio where 'The LaBamba' dancers and singers originated. What a memorable time we shared together."

February 1989 (20 yrs. old): "You are going to Florida for the Rochester Community College Band Tour. We're delighted you are able to go, as you have never gone on a school trip before and it really can be a wonderful time. You have such a neat personality, Buz. Your sense of humor is delightful, and your tenderness and thoughtfulness has just grown exponentially. I pray God will use these qualities to His glory in the future years. You are one special young man and I thank God for you, and the joy you have given us. When I remember how God spared your life as a baby and how He has healed you several times, I know God has something very special ahead for you, and I pray for your future."

September 1989: *"Your second year at Rochester Community College. You are again heavily involved in the music department and seem to be thriving. God is using you also. You helped one of your classmates get into counseling for past sexual abuse. God has given you a unique ability to counsel and help people see what their needs really are. It is going to be rewarding just watching what God is going to do with your life. God has given you amazing insight."*

February 1990: *"You were chosen to be Master of Ceremony for the RCC Snowball Coronation which was quite an honor! The school provided the Tuxedo and everything. What a fun experience for you."*

February 18, 1990: *"My mother died suddenly today. She was only 74. You, Buz, actually, took the phone call (it was a Sunday afternoon) from Auntie Donna. It was such a shock. It seems like a dream. Oh, how I hurt inside. I had my airline ticket already purchased to go out there just 4 days later for my father's 80th birthday. I had purchased my ticket in January and I told your father that 'I had an uneasy feeling that I would have to use my ticket early.' I just had a feeling something was going to happen to Mom, but I hoped I could see her again before God took her home. She wasn't sick, but had been doctoring for heart arrhythmia problems. God is still faithful though. She inhaled on earth and exhaled in heaven and did not suffer. Thank you, Jesus, for that blessing."*

"Mom was beautiful in death. She was like a grown china doll with her hair, nails and makeup so perfect. Her beautiful hands folded. Those hands loved, caressed and gave such love to all. She taught me to be a lady, and so many other things. She was a great lady who loved her Lord and Savior. Oh, I shall miss her so. My brother, Gordy, has turned his heart back to the Lord

through this. Mom must be rejoicing in heaven. Yes, God is faithful, always. He never makes mistakes – EVER."

~ EIGHTEEN ~

Buz Meets Vicki

Sept 1990: Buz attended Evangel Bible College in Springfield, MO. We talked often on the phone, questioning him about his studies and friendships but our son was more interested in the social life of college rather than truly buckling down and getting an education. Mr. Social, Buz. He was the gregarious life of the party and everyone's favorite guest. We learned too late that his grades were below par, or hardly passing at all in some instances. We had some "come to Jesus" discussions on the phone, but he eventually dropped a class or two, unfortunately not soon enough to get the money back. We were disappointed.

The Bible says to *"Train up a child in the way that he should go, and when he is old he will not depart from it." Prov.22:6* Unfortunately, it doesn't say HOW OLD. So, we prayed.

It is difficult being a parent. No instruction booklet comes tucked with each child at birth that tells how to best prepare this new little human life for the best results. We had read many books on parenting, enough to realize this one was a strong-willed child! This means he has enormous potential, but directing that potential and motivating that potential requires lots of prayer, elbow grease, tough love and creative thinking. Perhaps this is more daunting the older he gets and the more independent he becomes. We could not 'make' our beloved son 'want' to get the education we felt was so valuable.

Buz 's Diary of Little Things:

*"You were going through orientation for a position at the Assembly of God Headquarters in Springfield, MO. All orientation persons were being taken on a tour of the facility by this attractive, petite brunette. All names to accompany this guide were called, except yours. And that is how you met your future wife. Vicki came back after finishing with the group tour, asked a few questions and discovered you should have been a part of that group also. So, you got a **private tour** from this very pretty, young lady. And yes, you flirted and gave her a very bad time as she patiently took you on your own private tour."*

*"You brought Vicki home to Minnesota in June of 1993. We were attending Lake Geneva Family Camp in Alexandria, MN and had a cabin to sleep six persons. Since DeeDee was pregnant, they got the double bed in the middle of the room. The four double bunk beds were on either side of the double bed. We had room to hang our clothes, a couple of small tables and a window fan. The shower and bathroom facility was just a short walk away. It was close quarters and the guys would go shower after we got back so that we could dress for bed before they returned and then the reverse order in the morning. A cut above tent camping. Now ~ **we** were used to this. But Vicki wasn't a camper and here she was with an entirely unfamiliar family, in very close quarters, with little privacy!" This had to be quite a test for an unsuspecting, prim and proper New Englander.!"*

"One evening it began raining cats and dogs! It was a downpour for sure. We were all snuggled safely in our beds, fast asleep at 1:30 AM when someone began pounding on our cabin door, yelling that we had to come to the dining room basement or the auditorium immediately, because a tornado was only 30 miles away and coming fast. It was a huge one and we had to move fast! It had already touched down and caused damage in a neighboring city."

"Just what do you do when six people are in their bedclothes in one room? Arne said, 'Everybody up, face the wall and no peeking. Get dressed NOW!' We were out of that cabin in record time, bee-lining toward the basement dining room. There we huddled like sardines in a can, dripping wet, in various modes of dress with bed hair and eyes darting nervously around. Everyone began praying quietly. It was eerily quiet, except for the wind that howled overhead. We heard the roar, and then it was over. It had passed over our campground only to devour some fields beyond. The all clear was given and we sloshed through the muddy paths back to our cabins, dripping wet. This was the introduction my Daughter-in-law-to-be had on her first night with her future family. It didn't faze her, and we thought she must be one special gal. We were so right!"

~ NINETEEN ~

Final Surrender / RV Maps

Buz and Vicki were married on October 7, 1995 in Springfield, MO. Arne had taken early retirement from IBM at age 52, in August 1995. We had moved to Bella Vista, Arkansas just one week prior, on September 30, in time for Buz and Vicki's wedding, October 7, 1995. We were living in our RV trailer at the time. We would continue to be a part of the RV Maps ministry, living full time in our trailer for the next two full years. Although I missed having a home and a permanent place to be, those two years were full of adventure, closeness and an introduction into a ministry that has captured our hearts ever since. However, God had to do a work in me to mold me into a willing vessel for Him.

I fussed, whined and complained and was generally unwilling to give my full time to God. I wanted my way! I wanted to have fun, travel and have my husband completely to myself. I loved the Lord. That wasn't the issue. I just didn't love the idea of constantly living in a trailer park, giving all my free time to building churches or whatever. I guess my idea was donating a couple of weeks each summer and that would suffice. God had other plans and He gently nudged me onto the path He wanted for me. My heart has always been tender when I quietly stop and feel His presence and listen to what He is saying to me instead of ME doing all the talking and telling God how to do something according to MY wishes.

We had been in the RV Park at Bella Vista, Arkansas for a couple of months, getting adjusted to a new area, a new church and southern living. The Park had very comfortable facilities and we were parked directly across from the bathroom and laundry complex, which was most convenient for us. The showers were pristine and hot. This was ideal living for an RV couple.

Arne had read about an RV Maps project somewhere close by but had not been able to find any specifics. I was secretly hoping he wouldn't find out any information for a few months. I truly just wanted some alone time with my hubby after too many years of sharing his time with IBM, church, hockey and every other event. We had many fun times and fond memories, but I just wanted Arne to myself – for once! I had a very bad case of jealousy of his time due to so many "shared" years in the past. Arne was always loving, gentle and attentive, but I felt insecure in our new life and needed his time – or so I selfishly thought. I was thoroughly enjoying our leisurely breakfasts, our devotional times together and exploring the area we had now claimed as home.

One morning Arne was outside visiting with a man who was parking his RV right next to ours. I was busy baking bread in my bread maker and feeling so content, almost like playing house in this little home on wheels. I remember feeling so happy inside with my honey just a few feet away at any given moment. It was like heaven. Arne came bounding into our camper, all excited!

He said, *"You won't believe who moved in right next to us! It is the Coordinator of the RV Maps project in Rogers, the project I've been looking for."*

I feigned happiness and a smile as he again bounded out the door to secure the details of how we could get involved. I stood there dumbfounded.

I looked up to heaven and said, *"Thanks a lot God! Couldn't I have just one year without someone pulling my hubby away?"*

I was not a happy camper. I needed to have a little talk with Jesus for sure!

Not only did we become involved with this project, a Hispanic Church in Rogers, Arkansas, but my hubby insisted we move from the comfort of the RV Park and on to a big chunk of muddy, dirt ground with no laundry facilities or other creature comforts for RV dwellers. We would join other 'RVers' on site as we built this church from the ground up. I insisted our pipes would freeze. They did. I cried. I was miserable beyond belief. I missed my friends, my church, my son, his wife and 8-month old grandson who had been only 5 hours away and was now 17 hours away. Why had I agreed to this preposterous nomadic life? I was also angry...at everyone and everything. Yep, I was an unhappy wife and camper. (And a very selfish wife.)

There was a knock on my door. A beautiful, fashionable red head with a little girl was standing looking back at me. Her name was Kathleen and she was our Project Manager's daughter-in-law. She simply stopped by to welcome me. She and Dean lived in Bella Vista and Dean was helping on this project. Dean was an accomplished builder who had his own business of building homes in the area. Our RV still had frozen pipes and our "rig" was not even set up with the slides out. Never the less, I invited her in from the cold and proceeded to blubber out my frustrations and woes to an almost stranger. I had a bad case of self-pity. Kathleen took me in her arms and held me as I cried like a great big baby. Her genuine love and concern bonded me to her for years to come. I needed a friend and found a forever, loyal sister-friend in her that has lasted for years.

They fixed our frozen pipes and we finally got set up like a normal camper, complete with working water and the warmth of our home on wheels. I was still not happy.

That night at supper I told my hubby I was going back to Minnesota, with or without him. Arne had tears in his eyes as he told me that if I was really that unhappy, he would take me back home. I guess I expected Arne to give me a hard time, scold me or whatever, but I didn't expect him to acquiesce so easily. He proceeded to tell me that he loved me too much to see me this unhappy. I felt absolutely rotten!

By now all the other RV volunteers on this project had arrived and we were all meeting at the Pastor's home for a time of fellowship and getting acquainted. I told Arne I wanted to leave as soon as it was over. I didn't want to be here and I was determined I didn't want to get to know these people. Our rigs were already jammed together 6 feet apart like sardines in a can. I wasn't used to this close living thing at all! The RV Park had been spaced with breathing room between RVs – not like here at all. This was what a project was going to be like and I had better get used to it. Just another reason to want to leave.

We had coffee and bars and then they opened the meeting in prayer and suggested we sing a few choruses. The Project Manager knew I played the piano and said,

"BJ will play for us, won't you, BJ?"

I had wanted to be inconspicuous and here I was standing at a keyboard in front of everyone else sitting watching me play. God really had a sense of humor! I was mad at Him too!

I managed to get through the songs while God was gently using the words of each song to nudge my broken heart and rebellious spirit. Next came testimonies. The Pastor asked us to go around and tell our names, something about our reason for being here or something of interest to the others about our personal involvement with this ministry.

They went around the room and I was next to the last. The love and devotion to Our Lord, the difficulties and triumphs that were shared, the miracles of provision and protection to just get here were amazing. My heart began to bleed, and my defenses were dropping one by one. When it came to my turn, all I could mutter was my name and from where we had moved.

The meeting ended, and we scurried out the door. I put my arm around my husband's waist, pulled him close and began to cry – no sob. I asked him to forgive me for my selfishness and told him I knew all along this was his dream and our mission from God for retirement, but I had hated everything about it so far. I promised to ask God's help to adjust and would do my best to be the best wife and partner that I could be as long as he just loved me and encouraged me. We cried together as God cemented our call to the RV MAPS Ministry together.

Little did I know just how many precious people we would be privileged to know and how many churches, pastors, Teen Challenges and other areas of ministry we would be blessed to be able to work with and enjoy. Only eternity will tell what was done for Christ. And the prayer support was incredible. We had a group of over 500 couples instantly praying for one another's needs. This came to full fruition when I was diagnosed with breast cancer over 20 years later. God knew where He wanted us. He knew what was best for us. For me!! And yet I had kicked against the pricks as Saul, later Apostle Paul, had said.

Why do we think we know what is best? Why do we fight Almighty God? He has our very best interest at heart and He delights in giving us the most excellent gifts of all, along with His peace, love, joy and contentment. And He never makes mistakes – Ever!

My Surrender

I don't know where this life will take me....
I just know I have planted seeds.
It is God who tends the Garden,
It is the Holy Spirit who pleads.

I don't know where tomorrow will bring me...
It's enough jut to cling to His Hand,
And walk side by side with my Savior
Making His wish my command.

Precious Savior, Redeemer, My Friend
I adore you my Lover, My King.
I bow in your presence, I cling to your love,
I exalt you, Dear Jesus, My dove.

So until that Great Day when the clouds roll away,
And you come to take me ---Your Bride,
I'll walk by your side and there I'll abide
Through the dark, through the storms, through the night.
For your light leads me on and I stumble NO More,
There's no need for worry or fear.

I know now that Nothing 'er touches my life
That first doesn't go through Your Hands.
So, I trust you, My Jesus, I give you my all;
My love
My life
All my plans.

Written by BJ in October 1982

~ TWENTY ~

2001 Meniere's Disease

I woke up one morning in September of 2001 dizzy, nauseated and feeling completely horrible. I made an appointment with a doctor and managed to get to see him that day. He thought I had some sort of flu and my ears were being affected, although neither ear showed signs of having fluid in them. Home to bed I went. Over the next 6 weeks I visited the doctor's office four more times and he finally sent me to an ENT (ear nose throat) specialist. By now I was having sounds of a train rushing through my brain every time I moved my head in any direction. Music would be in one key in one ear and resound in the other ear in a different key. I could not get up off the couch without help as I was nauseously dizzy and couldn't walk a straight line. I was totally miserable. As I lay helplessly on our couch I cried out to my Heavenly Father for help and wisdom to know what to do and for help and comfort. I had no idea what was wrong with me. I knew I could not function like this much longer; it had now been over 2 months. Thoughts of the upcoming holidays were beyond my grasp. All I did was lie on the couch trying not to move.

After audiology tests and a thorough examination by the ENT, I was told I had *permanent nerve damage* to my left ear and had lost hearing completely in that ear. By now my condition had been diagnosed as Meniere's Disease and was told I could possibly lose my hearing in the other ear as well. Really encouraging diagnosis! I looked the doctor square in the eye and said,

"No, that is not going to happen. I have a Heavenly Father who is my Ultimate Physician and He will take care of me."

The doctor just looked at me and shrugged and said, *"Whatever."*

I continued to see him month after month, gradually getting better and better results, both in the audiology tests and his exam. I followed a low salt diet and did everything I was told to do to get better, which I did.

Two years went by until one day he told me he was dismissing me because there was no trace of a problem left in my ear. He said I was the *"best Meniere's patient he had ever treated."* My audiology test showed perfect hearing.

I asked him how that could be since it was supposed to have been *"permanent nerve damage?"*

He paused momentarily, then replied, *"Well I guess I could have diagnosed you incorrectly or the test was inaccurate."*

I then reminded him of what I had said to him on my very first visit two years prior. He put his hands up as in defense and said,

"A lot has happened since then in my life and I have come to believe you could have received a miracle here. You have no symptoms of Meniere's Disease."

He told me I needn't come back again unless I had further problems. I never saw him again and I never had another episode of Meniere's Disease.

How can one explain unexplainable happenings? There is no cure for Meniere's Disease and it can be very debilitating and can disrupt one's life unbelievably, or it can come and go for varying amounts of time for the duration of a person's life. Sometimes hearing loss occurs and sometimes it does not. However, how can an audiology test show *"permanent nerve damage and hearing loss"* one time and then gradually show improvement? The only thing different was I was being prayed for by many people and God had given me a deep knowing that it was going to be OK. I didn't know it would take two years, but I knew God had it all under control. Coincidence? I think not.

When we look around at all the mighty miracles our God does and see the power of His creation wherever we look, is it any wonder that it is a simple matter for our Big God to just blink an eye and heal a child of His? Or heal a hurting heart that has been broken in two by circumstances that they did not create? Or put His massive arms comfortingly around a lonely mother who has no idea where her wayward son or daughter is now? Or give peace when the turbulence of the waves of uncertainty threaten to swamp your life and upturn all your tomorrows?

"Whenever I am afraid, I will trust in God." Psalm 56:3

Trusting God's faithfulness dispels our fearfulness. He is all around us, circling us with a cocoon of golden light. He is always there but we become so involved with the pain we are going through that we fail to recognize His outstretched arms willing to help. Reach out to Him with all your concerns today. He is waiting for you. Just talk to Him like you would your dearest friend, because He wants to be just that to you!

"I am poor and needy, yet the Lord is thinking about me right now! O my God, you are my helper. You are my Savior. Come quickly and save me. Please don't delay."

Psalms 40:17

"Call unto me and I will answer you and show you great and mighty things which you don't know."
Jeremiah 33:3

Suffering and Sacrifice or True Joy?

Why do we suffer? Why are Christians expected to suffer? Are we REALLY expected to suffer? I thought Christians were supposed to be exempt from suffering?

"In this world you will have tribulation...." *John 16:33*

"...For He makes His sun to rise on the evil and the good, and sends rain on the just and on the unjust too." *Matthew 5:45*

Listen, suffering is something none of us wants. Yet it seems a fact of life. All through life. Why did Jesus say this? Jesus suffered on the cross for our sins, providing redemption through His precious blood for all sinners. The Christian story seems to revolve around suffering. There has to be more.....

There IS more: the entire Bible is filled with hope! Hope for every situation in life.

Jesus IS the hope of everything in this life and the next. He takes broken things and fashions something beautiful out of them. I have found that every time I have suffered physically, emotionally, spiritually or any kind of pain, God always turns it into good, **if** I allow Him. If we draw close to Him consistently during the good times, we are prepared for the hard times when they come. And they will come. But during the storm, He brings peace. He stills the winds and the waves that threaten to drown us and puts His arms firmly around us so we are never alone.

"Peace I leave with you, my peace I give unto you. Not as the world gives, give I unto you. Let not your heart be troubled, neither let it be afraid." John 14:27

Our Father also doesn't waste anything. EVER.

"Consider that our present sufferings are not worth comparing with the glory that will be revealed in us." Romans 8:18

He always grows us so we have a greater capacity for trusting Him as well as sharing our experiences with others to grow their faith. God is shaping us for what He created us to be: vessels of honor to show the beauty of His Son, Jesus. He is creating beauty out of the ashes of our humanness to radiate the brilliance of His Beloved Son, Jesus. He is making us like Jesus and preparing us for eternity with Him forever.

Are you struggling right now? Does it seem like there is no end in sight for your suffering? Take hope, my precious friend. Jesus IS that hope.

"...but be of good cheer; I have overcome the world." John 16:33

"Whatsoever you shall ask the Father in my name, he will give it you. Hitherto have you asked nothing in my name: ask, and ye shall receive that your joy may be full." John 16:23, 24

Does that mean I can 'get' anything I want? No. All the Bible must be taken into consideration. God's will, His words and our obedience to both.

What that does mean is that Jesus will come right beside you, if you ask Him to, and He will give you exactly what you need to have full peace and joy while He is still working on you to become all He created you to be. God will birth something beautiful in you, **if** you allow Him. It is your decision. God never overpowers the will of any human being. He wants our love and trust given freely. He wants to empower us, grow us to depend 100% on Him. That's when the joy and peace come. Even if the situation never changes. During times of pain, sorrow, death and disease, Our Lord brings rebirth, healing and light when we are trusting Him. He doesn't always perform miracles and healings on this earth to physical situations, but He has promised to give us peace, joy and love in our inner being every time we ask Him. He wants an intimate, trusting relationship with Him. We are to:

"enter into His gates with thanksgiving and into His courts with praise: be thankful unto Him, and bless His name." Psalms 100:4

"...in everything by prayer and supplication <u>*with*</u> <u>*thanksgiving*</u> *let your requests be made know unto God. And the peace of God, which passes all understanding, shall keep you hearts and minds through Christ Jesus." Philippians 4:6*

"But my God shall supply all your need according to his riches in glory by Christ Jesus." Philippians 4:19

"That you might walk worthy of the Lord unto all pleasing, being fruitful in every good work and increasing in the knowledge of God; Strengthened with all might, according to His glorious power, unto all patience and longsuffering with joyfulness; giving thanks unto the Father." Colossians 1:10–12

Dear friend, I know that suffering is painful. But our Lord Jesus Christ will strengthen you during this time and is even treasuring your tears by keeping them in a bottle.

"You have seen me tossing and turning through the night. You have collected all my tears and preserved them in your bottle. You have recorded every-one in your book." Ps. 56:8 (Living Bible)

He will bandage up your broken heart. He will guide you and give you the wisdom for each of your tomorrows. Take confidence in God's plan for your life and His promises for good.

"For I know the plans (thoughts) I have for you, says the Lord. They are plans for good and not for evil, to give you a future and a hope. In those days when you pray, I will listen. You will find me when you seek me, if you look for me in earnest." Jeremiah 29:11

"Many are the afflictions of the righteous: but the Lord delivers him out of them all." Psalms 34:19

"The good man does not escape all troubles – he has them too. But the Lord helps him in each and every one. God even protects him from accidents." Psalms 34:19, 20 Living Bible

"I have told you these things, so that in me you may have peace. In this world you will have trouble. But take heart. I have overcome the world." John 16:33

Prayer of relinquishment & submission:

"My Father, forgive me for my whining and unbelief. Come into my spirit right now and help me to lay all my burdens in your

lap. I give up my will and I surrender all my tomorrows into your hands. I choose to thank you for the situation I am in because I know nothing is too hard for you. You have promised to help me if I confess, repent and surrender my heart completely to you. I do that now. I choose to trust you. I choose to obey your Word and read it and make it a part of my daily life.

I choose to praise you in all things, because that is your will for me according to Your Word. I accept your peace, your strength and your joy. I ask for wisdom daily to become all you created me to be.

I thank you for your comforting Holy Spirit and I know you are working all things together for my good. Please renew my tired spirit and give me hope for each new day. I look toward the day when all the crooked paths are made straight by your return to take us to heaven with you. Until then, I am yours. In the precious name of Your Son, Jesus. Amen."

~ TWENTY-ONE ~

2004 Argentina

We were really excited about going again to Argentina to work with Martin and Charlotte Jacobson. Arne's younger brother and wife had been career missionaries for over 32 years in Argentina. We had made several other Mission trips in the past, but we were especially excited about this one.

On one of the previous trips to Argentina our bus driver, Aldo, became like a member of our group. He brought his little four-year-old daughter with him, and she became our little mascot whenever we were on the bus. I was learning Spanish and had a desire in my heart to win Aldo to the Lord. I had no idea how. He spoke no English and I spoke only a few words of Spanish. It was not to be on the initial trip, but I went back to the United States of America determined to pray for Aldo until our next missionary trip in four years. I enlisted the help of 30 ladies from my Bible Study to pray daily for Aldo's salvation.

By the time we were ready to return to Argentina in 2004, I had been studying Spanish for over four years and could read and converse enough to be understood as long as it was spoken very slowly. My most used phrase was, "Mas despachio, por favor." More slowly, please.

The Lord impressed on me to purchase a Spanish Bible to give to Aldo. I wrote, in Spanish, in the flyleaf of the Bible to him personally. I told him I had been praying for him to come to know Jesus as his personal Savior for four years, along with 30 other faithful ladies of prayer. I explained that knowing Jesus would be the most wonderful and fruitful thing he could ever do in his life; that Jesus would be his Savior, Friend, Counselor, Guide and give him eternal life in the end. I explained the message of salvation clearly and invited him to accept this wondrous gift from Jesus Christ.

I brought small gifts for his wife and little girl and prayed for just the right time to be able to talk personally with Aldo.

However, on the airplane down to Argentina, Arne contracted something on the airplane that gave him a raging high fever, followed by severe chills that shook the bed like an out of control washing machine. I piled all the blankets in the hotel room on him, and still he would be shivering. His teeth chattered so he could scarcely complete a full sentence.

And here we were, thousands of miles from our trusted doctors, in a foreign country, hardly able to speak the language. Going to the hospital was NOT an option as it was cleaner and safer to remain in the hotel where we were. We were in Southern Argentina in a place called Gaiman, Chubut, Argentina – very far from competent medical attention.

I went to the farmacia (Pharmacy) to get something that might help Arne. Just before leaving on this trip our Spanish Class had studied the course on medical phrases, words, asking questions and ordering necessities at a pharmacy. Coincidence? I don't believe so for a minute. God had it all planned.

I walked into the Pharmacy, knowing I would not need a prescription and asked if he had amoxicillin. He said yes and asked if I wanted one or two packages. I replied I wanted *dos (two) por favor*. That simple. And it was a fraction of the cost of amoxicillin in the United States. That was how it was.

I filled Arne full of the medicines but the same cycle would continue. The fever would break, then chills and unbelievable shaking. I stayed with Arne 3 days in a row, hoping he would begin to get better. We were to be in Argentina 14 days. It was going to be one very long, frightful 14 days.

About day five Arne began to feel better so we joined our group on the Bible School Van for our 1 ½ hour journey from the Hotel in Trelew, to the Bible School in Gaiman.

"Speed the Light" is a wonderful program in The Assemblies of God for the youth in our churches to provide transportation for missionaries all over the world. They had provided this wonderful 19-passenger van for the Bible School since our last visit 4 years prior. I was disappointed because Aldo and his bus were no longer needed. I wondered how I would be able to even see Aldo, let alone have the opportunity to talk with him and give him the Bible I had brought for him. I decided I would just have to leave the Bible in Martin's care and have him deliver it to Aldo after we were gone.

On the day Arne and I joined the rest of the team at the Bible School, who should appear but Aldo – all by himself in his big bus! He had heard the Americanos were at the Bible School and drove out to see us.

I was painting, along with another young man, Zak, from Kentucky, when in strode Aldo! God had answered my prayers. I gave him a huge hug and kissed him on both cheeks and we began conversing about his family – in Spanish. Zak had also been taking Spanish and was there to help when a correct word alluded me. God had it all planned.

After some time of visiting, I told Aldo I had something special for him. I ran and got my gifts, including the Bible. He thanked me profusely, but I told him to open the flyleaf and read what I had written. As he read, he began to weep, tears running down this well built, young Argentine man's face. He began to shake under the power of God's Holy Spirit as he read it completely through. He looked up and I told him I hoped he would give his heart completely to Jesus Christ. He nodded his head, grabbed me and hugged me for a long hug. I knew God was doing a work in his heart. My only regret was I never asked him if he wanted to pray <u>with</u> me. I prayed out loud FOR him but I never asked him to pray WITH me <u>himself</u>. I will always be sorry I did not do that. Yet I know God was working in his tender heart, and I believe he prayed in the quietness of his heart that day. I still pray for Aldo and I believe I will see him in Heaven someday.

Arne continued to be very sick, fluctuating between high fevers, profuse sweating, then tremendous chills and uncontrollable shaking. Out of the 14 days, he was only able to come to the Bible School a couple times. I had the hotel provide meals, ice and lots of water, but all we could do was pray. It was an extremely tense time of uncertainty. I hated leaving him alone during the day, but he mostly just slept and assured me he would be fine.

We left him with Martin's cell phone in case he needed us, and we called and checked on him often. I continued working with the team at the Bible College. The two weeks passed slowly as Arne would get better for a few hours or so, then return to the fever, chills, shaking routine he seemed to be on. I think the amoxicillin kept the infection/sickness he had from taking over his body completely. He had been strong and virulent but whatever was going on was sapping his strength and depleting his energy thoroughly.

We went to the airport to come back to the USA. Arne laid down on the seats and slept. He was excessively hot and mumbled words that were incoherent. I knew we might not even be allowed on the plane home because, it was obvious, he was very sick. He was burning up with fever. When the time came to go through customs, I woke him and told him to let me do the talking and just hug my back and look the other way. I told the customs gentleman how much we enjoyed his beautiful country and how gracious everyone was (in my broken Spanish), and flashed him my most engaging smile and distracted him from even looking at Arne. He simply stamped Arne's ticket and together we got on the plane.

We had the only row with an empty seat in the entire airplane in the last row by the Stewardess station. Another God thing! After we had been in the air a short while, Arne began shaking violently again. I asked for more blankets which the Stewardess brought. She also brought a huge bottle of water and said,

"Your husband is very sick. Make him drink all of this water to keep him hydrated."

She was very attentive and helpful for the 14-hours on the plane. We landed in Miami, Florida and I wondered how I was going to manage Arne and our luggage without the rest of the team, as they were now headed to Kentucky and we were headed for Arkansas.

We got to the correct terminal to wait for our connecting flight and I told the attendant I might need help. As it turned out I only had to worry about the two small carry-on bags. Arne was in the "better" stage of his fever/chills/shaking routine that his body was doing. We finally arrived at XNA in Arkansas at

3:00 AM after over 40 agonizing hours without sleep, only to discover our baggage did not arrive with us. At this point I really didn't care. I just wanted to get Arne home and to the doctor.

We fell into bed, exhausted, only to be awakened by the doorbell at 7:00AM. Our baggage had arrived and was being delivered. I groggily signed for it and we got ready to go to the VA for Arne to see a doctor. We went to the VA Emergency, where he was immediately admitted to the hospital, his temperature being 102. He actually felt considerably cooler than he had in days, so I often wondered exactly HOW high his temperature had gotten. Over the next 3-days they gave Arne multiple antibiotics and ran every test available trying to determine exactly what he had. His fever raged on. He was one sick puppy!

On Wednesday afternoon Arne's attending physician came into the room and asked to speak with me. He took me aside and told me they had tried every known test to determine what type of infection or disease he might have, as they had no clue what was wrong. They had sent samples to the CDC (Center for Disease Control) and were waiting for an answer. He explained that they had tried every antibiotic known to medicine, in multiple forms, and nothing could touch his infection or fever. He was preparing me for what seemed the inevitable – Arne just may not make it. I immediately called my church and told our pastor that unless there was a miracle, Arne may not be with us much longer.

That night in the Wednesday night service, our church bombarded heaven for healing for my hubby's body. You know, there is no distance in prayer with Jesus. At 9:00 PM that night Arne's fever broke, and he slept the night through. By Friday he was dismissed from the hospital, weak as a kitten, but over whatever was trying to destroy his body.

It would take almost a year to recover his strength, but he did recover completely. The CDC never could identify what it was that Arne had contracted. It was an "unknown" disease/virus/infection that he apparently caught on the airplane ride on the way to Argentina. But God knew. And nothing is too hard for Him.

All I know is that God once again protected Arne from early death. What an awesome Heavenly Father we have. Someday in heaven we will see the "rest of the story" and know exactly what He protected us from. Until then, I am content to just thank Him and praise Him for being my Lord and Savior, Father and coming King!

"The eyes of the Lord range throughout the earth to strengthen those whose hearts are fully committed to Him." *2Chronicles 16:9*

"The eyes of the Lord run to and fro throughout the whole earth, to show Himself strong in the behalf of them whose heart is perfect toward Him." *2 Chronicles 16:2*

This promise is for <u>every one</u> of us with <u>no</u> limitations. There is no expiration date and
no shelf life to the strength He promises. He watches over us like a mother protecting her young. He sees everything about us, our victories, struggles and failures and is ready to pick us up, dust us off and set us firmly on solid ground, the moment we turn to Him.

He even protects us from unseen dangers we will never know about until we see Him someday face to face. His eyes are ever watching over us, ready to show His masterful power on our behalf.

We need not be afraid of what is happening to us because God is in Control.

He controls the tides of the oceans and the wind in the trees. He flung the stars into space but notices when one tiny bird falls. He is the creator of the universe yet knows the number of hairs on your head. That is the kind of God we can trust.

And He never makes mistakes – EVER!

~ TWENTY-TWO ~

Arne's Thyroid Cancer / April 2004

In 1986 Arne had 3 golf ball size growths (tumors) in his left
Thyroid Gland. This was removed at Mayo Clinic in Rochester,
MN. They removed the left thyroid as well as the parathyroid
glands. They were benign.

In January 2004, he again had tumors in his right Thyroid
gland which were removed at Northwest Medical Center in
Bentonville, AR. Again, they were benign, and the doctor was
able to preserve one of the two parathyroid glands.

In April 2004 Arne had his routine CT scan for kidney stones
at the VA facility in Fayetteville, AR. Remember, he had passed
over 200 of those little suckers in our over 50 years of
marriage, so he was supposed to have regular check-ups to
keep an eye on his rock quarry. The technician had the
machine higher than normal which captured a large mass in his
chest. His doctor immediately referred him to a specialist for
follow up care. Surgery was necessary to remove the mass. It
was a large mass occupying a good chunk of his thorax, with
tentacles reaching out toward the remainder of his chest. It
needed to be removed immediately.

The surgery was completed, and all specimens were sent to
pathology. We came back for a consultation some days later
and were told that the mass itself was benign but there was
cancer at the end of one of the tentacles. However, thyroid
cancer in its early stages is one of the easier cancers to

eradicate. An appointment for a Nuclear Medicine Total Thyroid Ablation was set up. This is a routine procedure, but oh, so interesting to the patient!

On April 28, 2004 Arne arrived at the Nuclear Medicine Center Imaging Services. I was instructed to wait in the waiting area and told it would take just a few minutes. This is how Arne related to me his experience:

"This guy comes in all garbed in white with a head covering and face mask, long white and silver gloves, big white boots carrying a metal container. He looked like a fat snowman wearing a space suit. He explained he was giving me 2 radioactive pills that I was to take with a glass of water. He handed me a paper cup of water, opened the metal container and reached in with what looked like a long pair of tongs and retrieved 2 little pills in a cup that he handed to me. He told me to take them."

I thought, "You've got to be kidding! If you must be so completely protected that you come dressed like THAT, you can't seriously expect me to take these dangerous things?"

But he WAS very serious, and I took them and swallowed them in one gulp. Mission complete!"

This entire procedure took less than 10 minutes. How this works is quite remarkable. The Sodium Iodide Capsule 131 is radioactive iodine that is found in foods such as fish, and seaweed. This releases an electron which creates its therapeutic action. It is absorbed quickly by the stomach and intestines, then carried in the bloodstream to the thyroid, where it is taken up by the gland. Basically, it searches out only the thyroid cells and kills them. So, any stray cancerous thyroid cells left in Arne's body anyplace would be zapped into submission. Quite an extraordinary piece of medicine.

We were thankful that the CT scan was shot too high and the mass was discovered early enough to discover and remove the small thyroid cancer. One more potential disaster averted. Coincidence? I don't think so for one minute.

We continue to ask ourselves just how many of these "near disasters" have been short circuited because our heavenly Father watches over us constantly? Most people call this luck or good fortune or some such answer. I call it Mercy and Love. God loves us so much He goes to extreme lengths to give us what we need, just in time. He builds our faith with precept upon precept of multitudinous events in our lives that we take for granted. But His Word says:

"The steps of a righteous man (or woman) are ordered of the Lord." Psalms 37:23

I choose to believe that He loves me, my husband, my children and YOU! I am more than thankful for my wonderful Heavenly Father who cares so much for us. I am thankful for the gift of life no matter how difficult our path becomes because I know that God is with us right in the middle of every single one of our problems, to bring blessings into our lives no matter how painful the situation may be. Only eternity is going to reveal the many times God intervened on our behalf. The Bible says we are each assigned a guardian angel. I often think some of our angels must work overtime with some of us due to our own foolishness, but even then, God is there!

Thank you, Lord Jesus, that Arne has never had any problems with thyroid cancer, and for your intervention in another day in our lives. You are so very faithful to us. We praise your matchless, holy, powerful name!

"O God, your ways are holy. Where is there any other as mighty as you? You are the God of miracles and wonders. You still demonstrate your awesome power."
   Psalms 77:13 & 14

~ TWENTY-THREE ~

My friend, Sonja / June 2005

Sonja attended our church and they also lived just a few blocks from our home. We had also gotten them interested in RV Maps and they attended their first Convention with us. Shortly after the convention, Sonja discovered a lump on her thigh which turned out to be a cancerous tumor. For the next 5 years we prayed together, believing God was performing a miracle in her body. I had an overwhelming 'knowing' in my heart that God was, indeed, going to eradicate this entirely from her body. I rarely have such a deep certainty, but this was one of those times.

They attended Lake Geneva Bible Camp with us and we had many fun times together playing games and socializing. And many moments of prayer together too.

After about 4 years the doctors discovered that the cancer had metastasized and spread to Sonja's brain. For the next year I visited her often, sometimes helping her dress for her doctor appointments and other times just talking about the Lord.

One morning as I was stepping out of the shower, the Holy Spirit quietly spoke into my heart and said,

"Go and see Sonja."

I said, *"Yes, Lord, I am planning on doing that as soon as my hair is fixed and my makeup is on."*

The Holy Spirit persisted with, *"No, go see Sonja NOW. And take a notebook."*

Now, I don't regularly receive this type of clear-marching-orders, but I knew this was exactly what I was supposed to do – and NOW. So, I took off in the car and arrived at her door in 5 minutes. George's brother had been visiting from out of town and needed to be taken to the airport. Sonja really needed someone to be with her all the time, so I suggested George take his brother instead of paying big bucks for a cab for such a long distance. They immediately left the house. This would be the one and only time Sonja and I would have alone-time for the rest of her life. We had two long hours.

Abruptly, I heard myself asking,

"Sonja, we believe God is going to heal you, but if He doesn't, what would you want to say to your children, George, and everyone else if you could say anything you wanted to? What scriptures would you want read at your funeral? What songs would you like sung?" I had not intended to say anything of the sort when I came to their home. It just came out of my mouth. And I knew why the Holy Spirit nudged me to bring a notebook.

For the next two hours Sonja dictated to me, word for word, exactly what she wanted to say to her son, her pride in him, how she wanted to see him living for Jesus, and meet her in heaven someday. She dictated to her daughter how she hated to miss her someday wedding, her future successes, and grandbabies. She told her husband how she was grateful for his patience and love ~ and many personal, poignant thoughts for their ears only on that soon to arrive day. Sonja chose the special songs she wanted me to sing, the hymns and scriptures to be read out loud. She planned her funeral completely.

We finished as George came through the front door. I kissed her good-bye and left. On the way home, I wept, because I knew Sonja was going home to Jesus – and soon.

I asked God, *"Why would you give me such an overwhelming sense that you were going to heal Sonja if it wasn't true?"*

I was so perplexed and wondered if I had even heard God at all.

He replied ever so quietly in my heart, *"So you would be an encouragement to her."*

Sonja went into a coma the following week and remained that way for several weeks. I read to her, prayed over her, out loud, and still knew God COULD heal her, but I knew she was going home soon.

One afternoon, as I was sitting alone with Sonja, I knew it was time. I read the last chapter of the book I had been reading to her. I knew her spirit was there, even though she had made no noises or movements for several weeks. I believed she could hear me for I had read that a person in a coma often hears and understands conversation around them, even though there is no indication that they do hear or understand.

I took Sonja's hand in mine and said,

"Sonja, it is time. You can go home now. George will be OK, and I will continue to pray for Matthew and Jennifer. You will meet them in heaven someday too."

She let out a loud groan and moved her head from side to side. I then prayed for her children, grandchild and hubby, and for the peace of Jesus to invade her spirit and take her gently into the arms of Jesus. She exhaled, and a quiet peace covered and enveloped her.

When George returned home, I told him what I had done. He thanked me and wept. It was hard for him to see Sonja in this vegetative state. He sat by her bedside that evening and repeated to her that it was ok to go home. She went to be with Jesus within a few hours that evening.

I then told George of Sonja's and my conversation of several weeks prior and the notes I had taken. He asked that I share them at the funeral.

I shared every word Sonja said, verbatim. Her children wept at the beauty of the things Sonja shared so personally with them. Healing was being accomplished in many areas. It was the most poignant and precious time I could remember ever being privileged to share.

Sonja left a legacy and reminder of her love for her family. Thank you, Jesus, for giving me a chance to be obedient. What a loving God we serve. And He will speak to us if we will only listen for that still, small voice that we know.

~ TWENTY-FOUR ~

2010 The Dying Stranger

Over the years I have enjoyed gifting my neighbors with small loaves of banana bread, or my famous sugar cookies for special occasions like Christmas or Easter. Or, sometimes just because I enjoy baking and our waistlines wouldn't remain trim if we ingested all I loved to bake. This was one of those "just because" days. I had baked seven mini loaves of my mother's banana bread recipe. The loaves were warm and wrapped in foil and ready to deliver. It was a brisk November afternoon with sunshine winking at me through the bare trees.

One of my neighbors was away so I had one extra loaf of bread in my hand as I delivered to the last of my neighbors at home. My last neighbor asked me if I knew that the neighbor across the road from him was dying. I had never met her so knew nothing about her, but voiced my condolences. I didn't even know her name.

As I was beginning to go back home, the Holy Spirit whispered, *"Go give that bread to your dying neighbor."*

I thought, *"That's an excellent idea."*

I crossed the highway and rang the doorbell. A lady answered, and I asked if she was the lady of the house. She wasn't. She was a hospice worker attending Emma. I told her I would love for Emma to have the bread. The hospice worker explained that Emma was in a coma and dying and unable to eat the bread. I felt like an idiot. I apologized and began to leave when the hospice worker asked if I would like to see her. I began to say no, when I realized I was *supposed* to see her.

Suddenly, I was overcome with a breaking heart so filled with emotion I felt I was going to break down into sobs. I was led to Emma's hospital bed in the dining room.

Emma was pale, elderly and frail, with soft, pure-white hair brushed back from her forehead. Her eyes were closed peacefully. She looked like a sleeping china doll with porcelain, almost translucent skin. I asked if Emma had family with her. No, she was a widow who had only a niece who lived far away and Emma had no other family. She was alone.

I touched Emma's frail, wrinkled hand with my hand and brushed her hair back with my other hand and began to cry. I wept for her aloneness. I wept for her soul. And then I prayed out loud. I could hardly speak as my emotions overwhelmed me.

I began to pray, out loud,

"Dear Jesus. I don't know Emma personally, but you do. You made her, and she is about to enter eternity. I don't know if Emma has ever asked you into her heart to be her Lord and Savior. But Jesus, she is going to spend eternity somewhere and if she doesn't know you, I ask you to help her spirit pray now and ask you to come into her heart right now, to forgive her sins and make her ready to meet you very soon."

I prayed as I told her Jesus loved her and died for her sins and wanted her to spend all eternity with Him in heaven. I prayed more specifically and told her to pray the words after me with her spirit, as she could in her heart. I happened to open my eyes during my prayer to blow my nose and saw both her eyelids moving rapidly in an almost twitching sure-fire motion. I knew she was hearing me. I prayed peace into her spirit and asked Jesus to carry her into His loving arms. The rapid movement of her eyes stopped, and she returned to her peaceful, quiet state as I said amen.

I turned to the two hospice ladies, sobbing as though she were my very own mother and said,

"I don't know why I am so emotional. I don't even know Emma."

I told them to enjoy the Banana Bread and thanked them for their care over her. I sobbed the entire way home as I prayed Emma would come to know Jesus before she passed away.

I read in the paper that Emma died 5 days later. I hope to meet her in heaven someday. Only eternity will reveal what that was all about, but I have never been sorry I obeyed the prompting of the Holy Spirit that day. Perhaps that was Emma's last chance to spend eternity with Jesus.

~ TWENTY-FIVE ~

Arne's Heart 2010

In between our RV Maps projects, when we would be home in Bella Vista, Arne began building houses with Dean. All total over the years they built 15 different homes together. One of these was near Beaver Lake and it was closer and easier to place our RVs at the RV Park at Beaver, AR. That way the guys would not have to travel so far daily from the work site rather than going back and forth to their respective homes in Bella Vista.

This was an ideal situation for all of us, and especially for me because I love the water and am something of a 'water rat.' I can float on my back with my hands behind my neck and my feet crossed and have absolutely no water over me and remain that way for as long as I choose, with no motion needed whatsoever. I have been known to fall asleep while floating and Arne often keeps an eye on me, when I do this, so I don't just float away. That would be quite the sight! Floating in the water is totally relaxing to me. My mother had been exactly the same!

While lifting a very heavy pantry one day up a flight of stairs in the house they were building, Arne got a stabbing pain in his chest that sent him to his knees. It radiated down his shoulder into his arm. Dean asked him what the matter was, and Arne said he needed a minute. He waited a few minutes and was able to continue hauling the heavy pantry up the stairs to the next level. He said the pain was excruciating, but it did go away.

About an hour later they were carrying a very large bathroom vanity counter up the same flight of stairs when Arne again was hit with a pain that took his breath away and doubled him, again, to his knees. Dean wanted Arne to go immediately to the hospital. Arne refused, rested and seemed to regain his equilibrium for the remainder of the day, but was careful to do nothing more strenuous. Dean told Arne that he gave him one evening to tell me what happened or he, Dean, would tell BJ himself. Bless Dean!!

After supper that evening Arne said he wanted to take a bike ride around the RV park. He wanted to see if the chest pains were just a fluke. Of course, he didn't tell me that! He had not told me yet of the earlier incidents. As he pedaled around the park, he purposely exerted himself to see if he could bring about the same tightness and pain in the chest as before. Sure enough, he was gripped by a severe stabbing pain that lasted again for a rather short amount of time, yet was an extremely intensive pain. It was time to tell BJ!

After telling me the entire tale in detail, he agreed that I would make an appointment for him with a cardiovascular specialist and have all the tests to see what his heart muscle was doing. I made the appointment and we visited the CV doctor the following day. It happened to be a Friday, Arne had the EKG and Dr. P. said Arne had "failed his own stress test" so there was no need of doing another and scheduled a heart catheterization for the following Monday, October 23, 2003.

We had planned to go to a Benny Hinn evangelistic meeting in Springfield, MO that same Friday night and we followed through with our plans. We watched the proceedings with rapt attention as one person after another seemed to be receiving a personal healing. I had some questions about this ministry, but

I know God honors His Word and that He is entirely capable and does still heal today. I kept an open mind.

All of sudden Benny Hinn stopped praying for people and said,

"God is healing folks with heart problems right now. If that is you, step into the aisle and receive your healing from the Lord."

Arne says I elbowed him so hard he fell into the aisle, but into the aisle he went. I must admit it takes faith to do that because it seems out of the norm of things and the doubts of *"Am I crazy or just emotional?"* creep into one's thinking. But the Bible says we are to have the faith of a little child. A child looks with trusting eyes and just does it! So, we chose to just have that child-like faith and Do It!

Nothing explosive happened. Arne didn't feel any different nor did he feel any warmth or tingling or any kind of sensation that might suggest God had touched him. But in his heart, he believed God HAD done something.

Monday afternoon found us at the Northwest Medical center in Springdale, Arkansas for his 1:00 PM heart catheterization. In a cardiac catheterization, a long thin tube is inserted into an artery or vein and threaded through your blood vessels to your heart. This is used to diagnose and treat cardiovascular conditions and to see how well your heart is working.

Dr. P. came out about an hour later and told me everything was fine, and Arne did just great. He later told us in our follow up visit that Arne had the heart of a 40-year old and would never have heart problems at this rate.

He said, *"I hope my heart is that healthy when I am his age."* (Arne was 61)

He told us he never expected to see us in his office again! Arne's heartbeat is slow and steady...so slow that in future years when he needed hospitalization, the night nurses came running because Arne's heart rate had gotten down to 38 – 40 beats per minute, which is normal for him at rest. Dr. P. knew what he was talking about!

One could say this was all a coincidence. One could say there was nothing wrong in the first place and it was something else that caused the tight chest and severe pain through his chest and shoulder. Correctly so, that is possible. But God is so innately involved with our lives and gives us clues that often prevent trouble, that we choose to believe God touched and healed Arne at that meeting when Arne stepped into the aisle by faith and trusted God to do what God does best – take care of His kids!

We have no proof and only someday in heaven will we know the full story. But we chalk it up to just one more of God's amazing care and watchfulness over us. He is an awesome God and can do anything. Just think of the three Hebrew children being placed in a fire so hot the men who threw them in died from the heat. Yet Shadrach, Meshach and Abednego came out of that fire not even smelling of smoke. *(Daniel 3:12-27)*

I take the Bible literally and am a Bible person. I believe every single word. And the promises in this precious book tell me that God is no respecter of persons. He has no favorites. He loves each one of us totally, unconditionally, delightfully and without reservation. He will do for me what He did for the three Hebrew children. And He will do for YOU the very same.

"For whoever finds me finds life, and shall obtain favor of the Lord." Proverbs 8:35

"The fear (reverence) of the Lord is the beginning of wisdom: and knowing God results in every other kind of understanding. For by me thy days shall be multiplied, and the years of thy life shall be increased." Proverbs 9:10-11

~ TWENTY-SIX ~

2010 The Man on the Roof

Arne and I were out for our morning walk on the street behind us. It was already proving to be an unusually scorching day in mid-July. I was taking Spanish classes on a regular basis and as we approached a Hispanic man, by his car, I greeted to him in Spanish. He answered, looking down. I tried to engage him in conversation, but he reluctantly answered only briefly, without looking up and meeting our eyes. I had seen this subservient posture before and it broke my heart. We pressed the conversation issue by talking about the house he and another man were working on then. They were putting shingles on the roof of a newly constructed home.

We told Jose that we had helped build a Hispanic Church in near-by Rogers, AR and that we loved Jesus with all our hearts. He looked up THEN and began talking with enthusiasm, asking the name and location of the church. He was looking for a church home for his small family who was joining him from the West Coast in a few months, after being apart for several years as he was earning enough for them to join him. And he loved Jesus too. We had a delightful conversation, although in English!

As I said, it was a hot, humid day so I asked how their water supply was and discovered the water had not been turned on yet and they had only small bottles of water with them. I told them I would bring water back for them. We finished our walk and I loaded three, gallon jugs of ice water into the car and brought them back over to them.

I went back home, and the Holy Spirit just nudged my heart to bring some freshly baked banana bread, fruit, plates, napkins and forks over for them as a mid-morning snack. I did this, and Jose again asked about the Hispanic Church. I committed to go home and write down the address for him.

I called the Hispanic Pastor and gave him Jose's information and asked if he would keep an eye out for his appearance at church. I then wrote the name of the church, address, church service times and Pastor's name on a piece of paper and took it over to the work site. Jose met me on the ground and this is what he told me:

*"When you left, my partner (a Caucasian man) asked me why a Gringo would do this for a Hispanic stranger. I told him when God is **my** father and God is **her** father, that makes us brother and sister."*

He continued, *"I've been trying to talk to my partner for over a year about Jesus and God's love, but he always shut me up and wouldn't listen to anything I had to say. Today, because of what you did, he listened and asked questions. Thank you for being obedient to God's voice in your heart and giving me an open door to talk to him about Jesus and His love for him and his soul too."*

I never saw Jose again. They finished the roof that day. But I heard from the Pastor several years later that Jose and his family were regular attendees at this Hispanic Church.

We never know what our Great God has for us, just around the corner. What a joy to be a tiny little seed in God's great garden of love.

"But sanctify the Lord God in your hearts: and be ready always to give an answer to every man that asketh you a reason of the hope that is in you with meekness and fear. I Peter 3:15

"Quietly trust yourself to Christ your Lord and if anybody asks why you believe as you do, be ready to tell him, and do it in a gentle and respectful way." I Peter 3:15
Living Bible

I thank God for Jose's concern for his fellow worker, and for taking the open opportunity to tell his friend about Jesus. Only God knows the result of that day.

I am thankful for a tiny part in making that opportunity available to Jose. God works in mysterious ways, His wonders to perform!

~ TWENTY-SEVEN ~

Bryan's Colon Cancer

Bryan, our eldest son, now married and the father of two grown sons, was nearing retirement as a Lt. Colonel from the Army. He had just turned 50 years old which necessitated a required, mandatory physical, including that dreaded colonoscopy.

*(When I was leaving Mayo Clinic in 1995, I requested every test I thought I should have including a colonoscopy. My physician said he had never, in his entire career as a physician, had a patient **request** a colonoscopy before. It turned out I had 3 polyps: 1/pre-cancerous and 2/benign. Our God knows how to direct our paths!)*

Bryan's colonoscopy revealed five benign polyps and one invasive adenocarcinoma – cancer. God, of course, wasn't surprised by this diagnosis. He was already well aware of the situation.

In January 2016 Bryan had a laparoscopic transverse hemicolectomy – removal of 10-12 inches of his colon. Two days later the pathology report of the colon and the 11 lymph nodes came back clean. We rejoiced. This was Bryan's first major surgery and said he felt like a big, mac truck had run over his stomach. However, he was thanking His Heavenly Father for guiding and directing all his steps.

"The steps of a good man are directed by the Lord. He delights in each step he takes. If he falls, it isn't fatal, for the Lord holds him with his hand." Psalms 37:23,24

Now let me ask you: Was it coincidence that Bryan needed that Colonoscopy? He had NO symptoms of any potential problems. Was it coincidental that the Army required that medical test for his 50th birthday, which was just in time to catch a cancer diagnosis? I think not!!

Our God goes ahead of us and makes all the crooked paths straight. He has proven over and over in our lives how He has prevented tragedy by His divine direction and timing. No, it was no coincidence, and it was no accident that God was still taking care of our precious son. I just thank and praise the God we serve for always loving us so much that He takes the time to orchestrate our lives down to the smallest of details.

This could have been tragic in another year. In another year this could have been a death sentence or, at the least, a very serious situation with which to deal. But when God is involved, the ending is completely different. God wasn't finished with Bryan yet. He has other plans for the remainder of Bryan's life. And God is in charge! Besides, God never makes mistakes – EVER!

~ TWENTY-EIGHT ~

Arne/Exploratory Surgery January 29, 2016

The lights lit up like a Christmas tree. The PET scan showed Arne's abdomen and pelvic area full of cancer. The little lights that indicate cancer lit up Arne's insides like Silver Dollar City on steroids. OK, God, here we go again on another journey that is going to test our faith.

Arne was supposed to be closely followed since the removal of his appendix in September 2013 because of two highly aggressive cancerous tumors which were inside the appendix. He was to have regular CT scans and blood work. Our "outside" the Veteran's Administration oncologist was moonlighting at the VA and said he would follow up seeing Arne there, saving us several dollars. Unfortunately, the VA decided to release all moonlighting doctors and hire their own doctors. Arne's primary care physician retired about this same time frame, so a consultation was never done. The CT scans and blood work were regularly performed but not a follow up with a face to face consultation by a VA oncologist.

The previous September 2015 Arne had his regular CT scan and blood work but received no follow up appointment to see anyone about the results at that time either. We decided to pursue it ourselves and made an appointment with the VA Oncologist and was scheduled to see him in December.

This VA Oncologist doctor didn't even call Arne into a consultation room. He came out into the waiting room and said in broken English,

"You OK now and you go." He made a dismissing gesture flicking his fingers as if shooing a fly away.

Arne said, *"I would really like to know the results of the CT scan that was done."*

The doctor again made the shooing motion with his hands and said, *"You dismissed now. You all OK. No need you come back."*

He was difficult to understand in the first place and his English left much for which to be desired. Arne left.

I must say here that almost all previous care at this VA facility had been really top-notch. They have the most up-to-date diagnostic procedures plus a friendly, caring staff and most doctors have been thorough, listened attentively and explained everything concisely. This was truly an exception and quite a disappointing surprise to us.

We went online and printed the radiology report ourselves, so we could at least see what the doctor saw. It left questions in our minds. The conclusion basically said there were *"multiple nodules present in the mesenteric soft tissue area of the stomach/pelvic area."*

We decided we needed to have our original "outside" Oncologist have a look at the radiology report and find out what concerns there might be. We set up an appointment for early January 2016.

During this time-period we had 8 friends die unexpectedly and suddenly. All of them were younger than us except one. Attending these funerals was difficult and I sang at several of them besides.

That niggling thought tried to inch its way into my thinking: *"I hope Arne will not be the next one."*

We can trust the Lord with all our heart, but our human mind continues to wander in its own direction many times. I refused to go there. It took a determined effort to keep my trust and faith firmly planted in Jesus's garden of prayer. Fear is a nasty emotion that will always be used by Satan to try to discourage us and put us in a tizzy.

"You are of God, little children, and have overcome them: because greater is He that is in you, than he that is in the world." I John 4:4

We have the power of prayer to fight the fiery darts of the enemy. Satan wants to defeat us in every avenue of life and he will take every advantage to try to get inroads into a crack in our armor. That is why it is so important to have a daily time with Jesus. We must spend time in the Word of God, so we are equipped to stand firm without wavering. Do I always do that? No. We do our best with God's help. And we will get stronger as we flex our spiritual muscles in our personal times with Jesus.

Look at Joseph.

"So, it came to pass, when Joseph had come to his brothers, that they stripped Joseph of his tunic, the tunic of many colors that was on him. Then they took him and cast him into a pit. And the pit was empty; there was no water in it. And they sat down to eat a meal." Genesis 37:23-25

Joseph's story got worse before it got better. He was abandoned, enslaved, entrapped, and finally imprisoned. Yet he never gave up. He didn't get angry at God. He never lost his faith in God. Actually, he did very well. An Egyptian official promoted him to chief servant. The prison warden placed him over the inmates and Pharaoh elevated him to serve as the prime minister, the highest position in the land under the Pharaoh. He saved his family and the country from starvation.

"As for you, you meant evil against me, but God meant it for good in order to bring about this present result, to preserve many people alive." Genesis 50:20

However, tearstains flood this story. Heartache, sorrow, unknown circumstances and pain of every kind wrapped its fingers around Joseph. Still, he never gave up. He never threw in the towel. He never quit trusting The One who held his hand and put salve on his emotional and physical wounds. The very things intended to decimate and destroy Joseph turned out to strengthen him.

Sometimes we fear we won't make it through. We all fear. That is the humanness in us.

We ask, *"Will the sun ever shine again? Are we ever going to be healthy again? Will we smile again? Will we ever get out of this crushing financial pit we are in? Will my marriage ever get better? Will I ever be free of this pain?"*

You will. We knew we would get through this new trial also. There is a little plaque in our RV that reads,

"I am not afraid of tomorrow, for I have seen yesterday and I love today."

The words of the song 'Through it All,' by Andrae Crouch says it well:

"Through it all, through it all, I've learned to trust in Jesus, I've learned to trust in God. Through it all, yes, through it all, I've learned to depend upon His Word."

We finally saw Dr. S., the same young, talented and thorough oncologist we saw after Arne's appendix removal, several years prior. He quietly read the radiologist's report, then said he wanted Arne to have blood work and a CT scan immediately. They later called and said they had scheduled a barium PET scan also. This was performed on January19, 2016 with the following conclusion:

"Multiple soft tissue mesenteric nodules are seen in the abdomen and pelvis and although they are not hypermetabolic, are concerning for metastatic disease. There are additional soft tissue nodules seen in the mesentery of the left upper quadrant adjacent to loops of small bowel and the descending colon."

Because we had two more funerals, one in Minnesota, we had to postpone our follow up appointment and were not able to see Dr. S. until January 29, 2016. He showed us the PET scan results. A PET scan with barium will show any cancers in the body by lighting up the cancers as little lights on the scan. Arne's stomach and pelvic area looked like a completely lit up Christmas Tree. He appeared to be full of cancer.

However, something did not look right. First of all, these nodules have appeared in this area in every CT scan since 2008 – before his appendix cancer. They had not grown, so whatever they were, they were slow growing. On the other hand, this was the first PET scan that was performed, so perhaps these were cancerous all along and we just didn't know it.

Our doctor said he would be comfortable just waiting and having another PET scan in three months and watch it carefully since these were obviously very slow growing. Or we could go ahead and have an exploratory biopsy to find out exactly what we were dealing with. Metastatic disease simply means the original cancer may have spread to another part of the body. We decided to go ahead with the biopsy.

Before we got married, Arne's mother told me of a sledding accident that Arne had when he was about 11 years old, while living in New Paltz, New York. He hit a solid fence, ruptured his spleen, and almost died in the operating room. The doctors then believed a person could not live without a spleen and told Arne's parents that Arne might not live a long life. If he did live, he would not have enough fighting cells to make it should he ever get anything really serious such as cancer.

I was very conscious of this the many times Arne had anything physically wrong with him over the years. Yet he had been amazingly healthy, and we really believed that God had His hand on our lives and Arne would live as long as God decreed. Period. Still – this little fact circled my head like a vulture from time to time – this being one of them. That vulture was trying to land once again!

As I have said before, fear can be debilitating, and it takes extreme measures to keep fear from landing into our spirits. Every time a negative thought would flit across my mind, I would start praising the Lord out loud, thanking Him for everything He had ever done for me, my hubby and our family.

I would thank Him for Who He IS and thank Him for being my Father, for forgiving my sins, for preparing heaven for me someday. I simply thanked Him. This not only destroyed the fear temporarily, but it gave me a song in my heart and a joy that spread across my countenance.

Faith drives out fear. God doesn't promise that getting through trials will be quick, easy or painless. Remember Joseph. But God DOES promise to walk with us every step of the way. We never have to face anything alone. He is a God of abundance: mercy, grace, understanding, peace and love. He is all we ever need. I had to repeat this praise process many times a day, especially as the surgery was approaching.

We met with the surgeon, Dr. James I., a thorough young doctor with a firm handshake and an eye for detail. He, too, was perplexed by the PET scan. He assured us he would study the previous CT Scans, Arne's medical history, and thoroughly look at Arne's insides during this Exploratory Surgery. A biopsy of the nodules would tell the tale once and for all. Arne completed all his pre-op tests: EKG, chest x-ray, more blood work. Surgery was scheduled for February 19, 2016.

Again, Andrae Crouch's song resonated in my mind,

"If I never had a problem, I'd never know God could solve them and I'd never know what faith in my God can do."

On February 24 the biopsy came back Negative. There was NO cancer at all.

This is how the doctor explained it: He had studied Arne's previous medical history. When Arne had his appendix removed, that doctor noticed several spleens had grown back and a couple of them were quite large and operating fully.

Wow – no wonder Arne had been so healthy all these years. God obviously decided to just grow him back for what he needed. The doctor said that although they had seen this before, it was quite rare.

Also, when an organ of the body is ruptured, often little fragments of that organ may just float around inside, doing no harm. Or they may become embedded into other parts of fatty tissue. That is exactly what happened to Arne. They were called splenules and were in the fatty part of the omentum (stomach) just minding their own business!

Dr. I., *"We can now put this issue to bed once and for all."*

What a relief! It was like a 100 lb. bag of cement was lifted off my heart.

You know, it is always just like Satan to take some little thing and blow it way out of proportion. What Satan meant for evil, God turned to good! We were so very grateful and the stress of *"not knowing"* was finally gone. It was like: we can plan the rest of our lives now. The waiting was excruciating. God is never late. He's just not always early either!

It's almost like He was saying, *"Just how much will these kids of mine trust me now?"*

We grow through experiences like this, but I hope we don't have very many more for a good long time!

~ TWENTY-NINE ~

Arne / UTI / Septic – May 26, 2016

Our eldest son, LTC Bryan A. Jacobson, age 50, retired from the United States Army in Rapid City, SD. It was an emotional ceremony that included upper brass, his wife DeeDee, sons Paul and Timothy and parents Arne and Betts Jacobson. It was an occasion with heartfelt memories for sure. Bryan was highly honored and, Paul, his oldest son home on leave from the Army, was privileged to be able to present his father, Bryan, with his discharge papers, also called mustering out. This was quite an honor for SPC/Multimedia Illustrator Paul Jacobson, indeed. Youngest son, Timothy, was home from Bible College where he was studying to become a Missionary.

Following these festivities Bryan wanted us to join their family for a week of fishing and camping in South Dakota at Shaded Hill Reservoir, in Lemon, SD. This beautiful area is approximately 150 miles from any medical facility in any direction. We had been planning and looking forward to this for many months. It was a time to be cherished since we had not all been together for almost three years.

Bryan had made the reservations months prior but was only able to make it for 3 nights on the same site because of an upcoming fishing tournament. We would have to move to another site for the last night. This was a significant detail to the deadly following events.

I had noticed my hubby Arne had not been "looking right" for several weeks. He said he was fine, had no pain and had excuses for everything I questioned. I noticed he was shuffling his feet instead of picking them up and down when he walked. It was slight, but a change from his normal gate. When I mentioned it, he said he was simply tired or didn't have a good night's rest or it was the slippers he was wearing. He was slightly stooped over when he walked and again said his back was simply bothering him. He had slight tremors in his hands which had never been there before.

I suspected the beginning of Parkinson's Disease and made an appointment for him with our family doctor, Dr. Margaret, when we returned from our vacation. Others had spoken privately to me saying Arne didn't look good and wondered if he was working too hard since his exploratory surgery for cancer in February. Although Arne had not fully become his vibrant self after that exploratory, he said he was feeling stronger, although he seemed to have little energy or motivation to do much – a clear deviation from the past energetic, always hard-working husband of mine.

Approximately three weeks prior to this he mentioned there was blood in his urine. I asked if he had passed another kidney stone and he said he had, so we both dismissed this as one of the things that happened from time to time when passing a stone. He had now passed well over 250 kidney stones in our married life.

We got all set up with Bryan and DeeDee, Arne and I in the fold out camper and the boys in a tent nearby. We were having a ball. Arne joined in but was more quiet than normal. It was cold and rained the entire first day. We played games inside the camper and fixed our meals, had popcorn and snacks and it didn't matter as-long-as we were together. It was a precious time of sharing and loving each other as we laughed and talked together.

That night Arne couldn't get warm. We had down sleeping bags with extra blankets piled on top and even a heating blanket over him. He didn't feel feverish and said he was just exhausted. We had driven the 15 hours to their home in one day, something we hadn't done in years. The weather had been great, and the roads open so we just kept on driving. We thought perhaps that had taken too much out of Arne since he had done most of the driving. Little did I know I was missing valuable clues that could have made the difference between life and death.

The next three days we fished in perfect weather, getting rosy cheeks and sunburned noses. We caught our suppers of Walleye and Striped Bass. The Walleye were big and fun to reel in, giving us a run for our money!   Arne became less communicative and we all noticed he seemed distracted and almost dysfunctional at times. By Thursday we had all agreed we would pack up everything ready to leave the camp site, fish throughout the day and drive to Mobridge, SD which was about a 5-hour drive, camp there for the night and fish there the next day. We were heading toward Ellendale, N.D. where Bryan had taken a staff position at Trinity Bible College. They had purchased a home and wanted us to see the campus and their home before we headed back to our home in Bella Vista, Arkansas.

As I watched my husband walk to the outdoor bathroom, I was dying inside. Grandson Paul (22) came and put his arms around me and said, *"Oh Grandma, it's so hard to see Grandpa like this."*

He just held me and prayed for us. Arne was barely moving his shuffling feet and was stooped over, moving in slow motion as he proceeded to the bathroom. Something was grossly wrong.

DeeDee said, *"Mom, this is how my Sister Kari was just before she died. I think Dad is dying."*

While he was in the restroom, I called my Dr. Margaret back in Bella Vista. After hearing everything and asking many questions, she said to get Arne to the nearest medical facility for blood work immediately. We were at least 5 hours from Mobridge. It was nearly 6:00 PM already. We took off immediately.

As we drove, Arne began not making sense in what he was trying to say. He would sometimes look at me with a blank stare and would only answer a question with a yes or no, if he answered at all. I thought he was having a stroke. When we had stopped for supper earlier, Arne did not know what to do, barely took three bites of his hamburger and I had to take him by the hand to lead him where we were going. He didn't recognize our car afterwards as we approached it to leave. It was heartbreaking.

Words defied me in trying to describe the ache inside of me as I saw Arne deteriorate in front of my very eyes. He was dying in short segments. It had happened so quickly. How can one person go from being vibrant and alive to becoming an entirely different person in a week's time? But that is exactly what was going on, and I didn't know what was happening. It was a helpless feeling of fearful anxiety.

As we were travelling toward Mobridge, I began crying out earnestly to God. I guess I never stopped beseeching God on Arne's behalf and asking for wisdom. Arne was becoming agitated and saying one-word sentences.

"Slow!" He glared at me and was clearly very upset.

He raised his violently shaking hand toward me and said two words slowly spaced apart, *"Too.......fast."*

It was raining, and I guess he thought I was going too fast for conditions. I would tell him I was going only 60 mph and following Bryan, who was ahead of us, pulling the boat. He would lean forward as though looking for the boat. It unnerved me as he became more agitated.

We had to stop several times because Arne had to use the "pee jug." Bryan would try to help him, but Arne could not even get out of the car to stand up he was so weak and shaking uncontrollably. He was unable to control his bladder and wet himself more than once.

"Oh God ~ what is happening to my beautiful, precious husband?"

This became an agonizing nightmare ride that seemed to never end. I finally told the Lord,

"Father, if this is the end for Arne, please make it quick. He doesn't want to live in this condition and I don't want to see him suffer. If you are not going to heal him and he is not going to get better, then please take him home."

We had discussed on many occasions our final wishes regarding how we wanted to spend our end of life care. We both agreed we did not want anything to prolong our lives if there was little hope of recovery. Neither of us wanted to live hooked up to tubes and machines and we didn't want to be held captive in a bed the last years of our lives. We had both filled out a living will, but had not notarized it.

When our time came, we wanted nature to take its course and for our bodies to be freed to go and be with Jesus. We know we will live eternally with Christ and will reunite with our loved ones some day in heaven, so dying itself held no fear for either of us.

But the dying process is another story. That creates fear in everyone. And that fear was overtaking me at the thought of losing my best friend, my lover. Arne was my partner in the many of the adventures of our life. A panic began to inch up my insides like a snake slowly slithering its way up a tree. The cold fingers of icy fear almost paralyzed me as I thought of the "what if's" ahead.

Isn't it just like Satan to do that to us? He IS that slithering snake who comes to cast fear. He wants to kill and destroy every ounce of faith we have in our arsenal. The sails of my personal boat were being ripped and shredded and I could almost hear the sound of my spirit dying. I felt like a part of me was dying. All the dreams we had shared for the future were swirling down the drain at breakneck speed.

Arne had taken care of our finances and those thoughts began to overpower me. What would I do without him? How could I function without him? I didn't even know who to call for simple repairs on anything because Arne did everything. The panic rose inside me like regurgitating bile.

And then there was God!

A rainbow appeared on the left side of the highway with a mirrored reflection finishing on the opposite side of the highway. A full rainbow. I was driving in between!

I said, *"Oh God, I hope that is my sign that everything is going to be all right."*

I heard in my spirit that quiet whisper as God simply said to me,
"I have been teaching you to trust me. Now trust me."

God comes so gently, unforced, comforting and quietly whispers,
"I haven't abandoned you. I'm right here. Trust me. Let me be your strength."

I released all my pent-up tension, all my fears, my expectations and simply said,

"Yes Lord, I place Arne into your hands. The ball is in your court. I will walk through whatever is ahead and I will trust you – again. You have never left me. You are trustable. You are faithful. Give me faith for one step more."

A peace descended into my tortured heart like a ray of warm sunshine on a cold afternoon. I still didn't know what the future held, but I knew who held that future! My faith began to kick in. I knew I would make it because I wasn't alone.

God was right there with me. This was not a surprise to Him. He had the plan. The stillness of that sacred moment shrieked volumes. We were almost there.

"I am not afraid of tomorrow for I have seen yesterday and I love today."

Our God created within us a need to be satisfied by Him alone. And it is ours if we open our arms up pleadingly to heaven as a young child begs to be picked up and cuddled. He is there. He is here. As we open our arms and reach up to Him, He meets us and that liberating, fearful anguish is absorbed by Him as He gives us that extra strength that seems lost forever.

You may think you will never be the same – and you won't. For the God who created us also sustains us and transforms us into all He created us to be. He will grow and stretch you as you feel the weight of the deep, sharp piercing grief slowly dissipate. Each time as you enter this intimate cocoon of aloneness with God, you feel Him touching one more area of the depth of your pain. God does all of this and more for those who turn to Him.

He caresses us with a gentle breeze that refreshes and uplifts the troubled soul. He speaks softly in the depths of our spirit, where He has taken up residence. You find rest for your weary, tear stained heart that has been broken in two, and He begins to put it back together again with the glue of His compassionate voice. He tells you He loves you, and you know it's so. A glimmer of hope is birthed within you. I felt that glimmer of hope and a calm peace flowed over me and into my spirit. God had this. It was His. Mine was to trust. I was reminded that God never makes mistakes – Ever!

Bryan had already called ahead to the Mobridge Hospital telling them of the situation and asking them to meet us at the Emergency entrance.

As we arrived at the emergency entrance Arne raised his uncontrollable shaking hand and pointed to the word,

"EMERGENCY ENTRANCE." He looked at me and said, "You?"

I knew then his mind was at least working. I told him he was very sick, and we were at a hospital where we would get him help. By then Bryan had run to our car, opened the passenger side door and said,

"Dad, we are at a hospital because you are very, very sick. Are you going to cooperate?"

Arne nodded his head and said, "Yes."

He was helped into the waiting wheelchair and taken into the hospital. I parked and immediately followed.

Because we traveled a lot and might need medical care in a variety of places doing our RV Maps work, I had compiled a huge 3-ring binder for each of us with all our medical information in case of emergencies. It contained all vital information, medication information, vitamins we took, copies of all EKGs, hospitalizations and recent lab reports. I had never had a need for it before, but it was a god-send this time. Immediately they had all of Arne's medical information and all they had to do was copy it into their computer. It was comprehensive and up-to-date. The ER doctor said she had never, ever had anyone come in with such a thorough medical record of one's life going back nearly 50 years. It expedited the necessary care.

Arne was given an EKG, which was normal. The CT scan of his brain was normal. Thank you, Jesus, it was NOT a stroke. The blood work came back, and the story unfolded.

Arne had a "raging" (doctor's words) Urinary Tract Infection with a white cell count of 23,500. Normal is between 400 – 1000. He was dehydrated and had a 102.1 temperature. It was well after midnight when they finally got Arne settled into a room, IVs filling his body with life-saving fluids and antibiotics. I told my family to go set up camp and that I would stay at the hospital with their Dad. He was totally unresponsive now, but I knew he was in the care of expert medical personnel. Thank you, my Father!

His room had a couch, microwave, coffee maker and refrigerator. It was like a small apartment. The nurses brought me bedding, pillows, towels, soap and everything I needed to become as comfortable as possible. It was a sleepless night as nurses came checking on Arne every 15 - 30 minutes, changing whatever needed changing, taking vitals, drawing blood, checking his oxygen level and a host of other caring ministry duties. I would ask questions each time and they patiently explained everything they were doing. I was awake all night due to all the activity and my worrying about his condition. (This had *nothing* to do with my faith, but *everything* to do with my *humanness*.)

By the next morning Arne was much improved. He was restless and awake, but seemed to understand that he was in the hospital and very sick. His vitals were stable, and his white cell count was coming down slowly. The temperature fluctuated between 99.4 – 100.4 but he was improving. By the time the kids came back to the hospital, I knew Arne was going to make it, but had a long way to go before being released.

This was Friday morning, June 3, 2016. Timothy had gone back to college 2 days prior because he was traveling with a group for the summer, representing the college and had to leave with his group before we would be getting to Trinity Bible College. Paul had already been on leave for over a week and was scheduled to leave from the Minneapolis, MN airport at 4:00 AM on Sunday morning and Bryan and DeeDee had to travel there to get him to his airplane on time. The Army waits for no one!

They spent all morning with us at the hospital. Bryan pulled his chair up close to his father's head, gently pushing Arne's hair away from his forehead and talking slowly to him. Arne's mind was fuzzy, and it took concentration for him to think of the words he was trying to say, but his mind was working – just slowly.

Bryan tenderly fed Arne his lunch. Arne was shaking so violently he couldn't keep the food on the fork. We ended up laughing because he would get it so far, then quickly try to dump it into his mouth. Bryan's assistance helped get some nourishment into his dad's body. He had gotten so thin over the past week. The love and caring that radiated from Bryan to his father brought tears to my eyes. He loved his father with all his heart. He was also his best friend!

Bryan's idea of OUR retirement was to come and park our RV in their driveway for the summer! Of course, this was not what had happened, and Bryan was always wanting us to come more often and stay longer. They had remodeled their basement into a private suite with a bath just for us so all the noise of two naturally noisy boys and their instruments wouldn't drive us crazy. Even still, we were not able to be with them as much as we had hoped to be. The very thought of something happening to Arne was a devastating one to Bryan. Love poured out to Arne from DeeDee and Paul and it was hard for them to leave but leave they must.

Once they were assured Dad was going to be OK and I would be fully capable of handling it from here on out, they said their farewells. It was difficult to see their tearful goodbyes. But they loved and served the same wonderful, caring, faithful God that we did, and knew Arne was in HIS hands! I had emailed all our prayer chains and family members explaining the situation. I asked for immediate wisdom and direction for the doctors, plus healing and strength for Arne and me. Hundreds were praying, and I could *feel* their prayers.

I had been in contact with our Bella Vista doctor and she called me several times checking on Arne. She spoke with several of the attending physicians and concluded they were doing all the correct tests and Arne was being given excellent care. He was! This little hospital in Mobridge, SD was absolutely wonderful. Many of the nurses and doctors were Bible believing Christians who told me they were praying for us. Their encouragement and their constant care were beyond anything I had ever experienced in any hospital before. What a blessing they were to me during a tremendously anxious time. It was like we were with family who truly cared what was happening.

By Saturday Arne was 100% better. He was responding to all the medical care, his white cell count was coming down, the Pneumonia was coming under control and he was completely lucid and coherent.

His younger brother and wife, Kurt and Andrea Jacobson drove from Detroit Lakes, MN to Mobridge, SD to see Arne: a 5-hour drive. They arrived in the early afternoon and we had a delightful visit. Arne and Kurt discussed plans for our upcoming sibling reunion on Kurt's 80-acre country homestead. It was a beautiful time together.

We were also rejoicing in the complete turnaround in Arne's health. I was in constant contact with Bryan and family, as well as Buz and Vicki in Springfield, MO.

Buz had asked if I wanted him to come and be with me or drive us home. He is a college professor who teaches all summer and I knew I would be ok and encouraged him not to stop everything and come. I could tell Buz was torn not being there with us. He has always been so loving, caring and ready to assist in every situation. And he loved his father intensely. But I was doing well, and I knew Arne would be ok. I had the Lord! And prayers. Buz would come in a heartbeat if I needed him. We were well covered!

When Kurt leaned down to hug and kiss his brother good bye, Arne tried to say something, but couldn't get the words to cooperate. He hadn't had any difficulty all day but all of a sudden, he couldn't get a full sentence out.

He slowly said,
"I......know......what......I......want......to......say......but........ I..... can't....say.....it."

I instantly called for the nurse and a flurry of activity began. They had removed the oxygen and as soon as they put the oxygen back on him, Arne began to be able to talk. Within 30 minutes he was completely fine. His Pneumonia was still just enough to not allow his lungs to fully oxygenate his brain, so his speech was affected. It never happened again. Kurt and Andrea prayed their entire way home for Arne.

It was 1:30 AM on Saturday night (well, Sunday morning, technically) when I awoke to Arne moaning and begging the nurse to catheterize him immediately. He had been in pain for several hours but finally the pain was such that he couldn't stand it any longer and pushed the nurse's button for assistance. He explained his history of passing over 250 kidney stones and knew he needed a catheter NOW. He said it was the worst pain he had ever experienced.

The doctor was called, the orders were given, and the nurse put in the catheter. Instant relief as Arne's bladder expelled first 850 ml, then 650 ml and finally 700 ml of backed up urine. It was blackish red. No wonder he was in extreme pain. Obviously, he had a stone lodged somewhere obstructing the normal process God created for voiding.

The next morning, Sunday, another CT scan was done and a 12mm kidney stone was found lodged in the ureter. A urologist was consulted. It was decision time. Nothing could be done to be rid of the kidney stone until all infection was gone from Arne's body. It was determined that Arne's UTI infection was caused by E. coli and now they knew the source.

I had asked how he could have possibly gotten an E. coli infection? I knew that E. coli bacteria is sometimes found in food and water, but I've since learned it can also live as harmless inhabitants of the human lower intestine or may produce a toxin causing intestinal illness. The specialist believed his kidney stone was the cause of this entire litany of problems and this stone had been fermenting for a very long time.

Numerous more tests and we were confronted with a decision to make. Since the Mobridge Hospital was not equipped to do any lithotripsy procedures, Arne would have to be transferred to Aberdeen, SD where the necessary equipment was available. However, Arne could not have this procedure until he was completely free of all infection and the Pneumonia completely gone. The Pneumonia was almost gone, but his white cell count was still 12,500. He would have to be in the hospital in Aberdeen until he could have the needed surgery, or we could travel home to Arkansas and continue treatment there with our own urologist. Arne was stable enough for travel, although terribly, terribly weak. We opted to go home to Arkansas.

They dismissed Arne at 3:00 PM on Sunday afternoon complete with a prescription for antibiotics and with Arne still wearing a catheter. He had instructions to stop every hour and walk around to prevent blood clots and to oxygenate his lungs.

As I was packing the car for travel, the ER Doctor was leaving for the day. She stopped, rolled her window down and asked how the patient was. I told her about the kidney stone. Everyone in the entire hospital knew our story. There were only a few other patients in the hospital and like I said, we were like family there! She told me she was so glad Arne was going to be ok, and that in the ER that first night they all had doubts that he was going to make it. She said he was less than 24 hours away from death. Septic shock is a killer. I knew Arne was very sick, but I had no idea how close a shave with death he had come.

Remember our son could only get 3 nights at the original campground in Lemon, SD? Because we decided to travel on to Mobridge instead of moving to a different campsite in the same park at Shaded Hill Reservoir, we had averted Arne's possibly dying from Septic Shock. God knew all along what we needed. He put that urge into us to travel instead to Mobridge for our last night, placing us exactly where we needed to be to get the best available care in the area.

God always goes ahead and makes the crooked paths straight for His Children.

You ask, *"Why didn't God simply just prevent it in the first place? Why go to all the trouble to put you through such trauma if He IS a loving God?"*

I can only tell you the words of that afore mentioned song which answers it for me:

"...if I never had a problem, I'd never know God could solve it, and I'd never know what faith in my God can do."

I just know God's Word says we grow *"precept upon precept."* That means our faith grows stronger with each new experience. Someday we will know all the answers. Until then, we trust and walk by faith as our Heavenly Father walks beside us to guide, teach, inspire, protect and make all things possible. Who can ask for anything more? And God never makes mistake – Ever!

God Almighty wants a relationship with us. He wants a friendship with us. He wants us to know him – intimately.

In the Old Testament it speaks of Adam and Eve and it says, **"Adam KNEW Eve, and she conceived."**

The Hebrew word for "KNOW" is YADA. It means to know intimately. In this case it was a sexual union that brought forth a son. God wants us to be involved with Him in every intimate detail of our lives. He wants to walk with you, talk with you, counsel you, laugh and cry with you. He wants to know you and He wants you to know Him. He wants to help you with every aspect of your life. All your life. He wants to bring you to heaven to live with him forever. He wants to live within your heart now, until the day He takes you home to heaven.

Some months later Arne told me what happened that first night in the hospital when he was so deathly ill. He felt himself falling into a beautiful, deep, white, filmy type chasm. It was the most peaceful, heavenly, restful feeling. He suddenly realized he couldn't move any of his body parts and knew he was dying.

He cried out to the Lord and said, *"No Jesus, please not yet. Betts still needs me."*

Immediately he was back in his bed and fell into a deep sleep. God honored his prayer and preserved his life. Thank you, Jesus!

Most people walk in and out of your life, but close friends leave footprints in your heart. Jesus desires to be that best friend that leaves a permanent imprint in your heart. The one who knows everything about you – all the minute details of your life. He knows all your hidden thoughts, good and bad.

When you are with someone you trust implicitly and completely, you feel free to be yourself. No pretenses, no masks. This is one of the joys of true friendship. This is the friendship and relationship Jesus desires to have with you. It is a gift from God. A God who knows you and loves you unconditionally.

Oh, the inexplicable release in one's spirit when all the veils are lifted, and we look into the face of the one who loves so completely. That is pure friendship and true unadulterated love. It is complete oneness. Jesus *gives* that to us. That is what He wants *from* us. He died for us to give us that kind of wondrous relationship with Him.

"You don't want penance, if you did, how gladly I would do it! You aren't interested in offerings burned before you on the altar. It is a broken spirit you want – remorse and penitence. A broken and a contrite heart, O God, you will not ignore...You deserve honesty from the heart; yes, utter sincerity and truthfulness. Oh, give me this wisdom...Create in me a new, clean heart, O God, filled with clean thoughts and right desires...What I want from you is your true thanks; I want your promises fulfilled.

I want you to trust me in your times of trouble, so I can rescue you, and you can give me glory." Psalms 49 – 51 excerpted verses.

We traveled to Ellendale and spent the night with Bryan in an apartment on the campus where he was staying until DeeDee could join him and they could move into their home. We went to bed immediately after supper and slept soundly for the first time in weeks. No temperatures to take, no blood to be drawn, no lights to awaken us, although all the above was necessary! We both awoke refreshed.

Because Arne was very weak, Bryan simply took us on a 15-minute car tour of the campus and their purchased home next door to the college. We didn't go into their house but viewed it from the car. There was an RV Maps couple working at the college there and we recognized their rig. I stopped the car near where I thought I could find Gerald K. and went looking for him inside. Upon finding him, he gave me a huge hug and told me how they had been praying for us constantly. He came out to the car and took Arne's hand and prayed the most heartfelt prayer one could pray. It was loaded with power and I felt like he was representing all our RV Maps family members at that moment. Oh, the wonderful power of loving prayer that transcends status, gender, race, color, religion or anything that could stand in the way of love. We left feeling lifted-up and encouraged for sure!

We drove 550 miles that day, arriving at Mound City, Missouri in late afternoon. The gal at the motel counter was so very understanding and helpful. The manager was beyond helpful and went above and beyond to make our stay comfortable and to see everything was more than alright. They told us to sleep-in the next morning, not to worry about breakfast because they would see that we got breakfast whenever we got up. There was no hurry regarding check out time and they insisted we park our car in the handicap parking space right at the entrance. I could just feel loving favor coming our way from them and everyone we encountered. God was giving us that loving favor and guiding our steps home.

At one point as I was driving, I told Arne that on his tombstone it would say, *"She drove me to my death!"*

He always did all the driving. I read most of the time so didn't really even navigate for him unless he asked or needed it, which was rarely ever. I also have Glaucoma in both eyes and am 85% blind in my left eye. I needed a stronger glasses prescription for my right eye, so consequently I really could not see far enough ahead to discern which lane I needed to be in for route changes. Furthermore, we came across two very busy construction zones with detours. I was totally unused to this. I knew how picky Arne was about driving skills as he had once been a Driver's Education Training Instructor. I could tell Arne was definitely improving mentally because he never once closed his eyes for a nap the entire way home. I think I was terrifying him with my driving!!

Now, I'm actually a decent driver, thanks to my perfectionist husband, but with him in the car, knowing he watched every time I got too close to the fog line, didn't slow down quickly enough coming to a stop light behind another car, going too fast or any other number of infractions, well, as every woman knows, this only exacerbates the situation! He also had to be my navigator and tell me which lane to get into since I couldn't see far enough ahead to read the signs clearly myself. It was nerve wracking!

We finally stopped at a rest area to have a *"Come to Jesus"* meeting about driving and direction giving!

When he would say, *"Hon, get into the next right lane,"* I took the next right lane – never mind that it was going to another state! The wrong direction! He meant the right lane straight ahead.

Once we straightened out our voice commands and I told my sweet hubby to *"get over it"* when I'm driving because, **that's the reason**, all along, **why**, I had wanted to share the driving. I'm not used to driving and I needed that experience!

Things went more smoothly thereafter. We agreed that from now on I will have 50/50 responsibility for driving – even through big, busy cities. Even when we take the truck and pull our RV (that remains to be seen – ha!). We actually made it home safely without incidence and in record time. Imagine that!

My competent Dr. Margaret had already alerted the Urologist of Arne's condition and made arrangement for us to get in to see him just as soon as we were able. We saw Dr. A on June 10th and he took the necessary cultures, changed the catheter and said to continue the antibiotics until the right ureteroscopy with laser lithotripsy could be performed to get rid of the 12-mm stone stuck in Arne's ureter.

Many tests later a pre-op was scheduled for June 21st with surgery for the next afternoon. All infection was gone, and Arne's white cell count was in the normal range. There was no sign of pneumonia or anything else that would prohibit the surgery. We were anxious to get the show on the road.

A cystoscope is a thin tube with a camera and light on the end. This would also have a laser which would break up the stone so it could be flushed out of his body. This would be the first laser lithotripsy Arne had experienced although he had endured 4 other ultra sound lithotripsy surgeries in the past for other kidney stones lodged in various parts of the kidney. The ultra sound lithotripsy broke up the stones but they had to be passed through the penis as they exited the body before – always a painful experience. This laser lithotripsy sounded much more appealing. It would be just an overnight stay in the hospital. We were excited about finally getting this done!

Dr. A said the stone was deeply impacted and completely surrounded by the ureter and was very difficult to extract but he got it all. Arne came home from the hospital the next day with yet another catheter and a stent to assist the draining and removal of all the debris from the kidney stone. We were on the homeward stretch. So, we thought!

We had a follow up appointment to remove the stent and catheter the following week. It was Wednesday, June 29th, and Arne woke up with pain. His appointment was for 2:00 PM in the afternoon but Dr. A told us to come right in. He removed the stent but left the catheter in place and explained the pain was from the stent.

We left the doctor's office at 9:00 AM and pulled into the garage at 9:35 AM. I was still doing all the driving and got out of the car, leaned into the passenger's side and asked Arne to please hand me our water bottles from the holders. He gave me a blank look. I repeated my request and he picked up a small clutch bag I had beside him and handed it to me. I pointed to the water bottles and he then handed them to me. I instantly knew something was wrong.

I told him to unbuckle his seat belt and he didn't know how. Just that quick! I had to do it for him. He shuffled into the house and sat down in a chair. I instantly called Dr. Margaret and she agreed I needed to get Arne into the ER immediately. She called ahead and alerted them that we were on our way.

His temperature in the ER was 101.4 but he was alert enough to give his name, date and year. Tests and more tests determined that he, indeed, had another UTI. Four hours later he was in a hospital room and when asked his name, he did not know it. He was already getting septic. I never knew urinary tract infections could develop so quickly but this time, at least, I knew what to expect.

I moved into his room for the next four days. His temperature rose to102.9 and he was incoherent and was being treated with a variety of antibiotics since they had not gotten the cultures back to decipher exactly what the infection was this time. He was, again, septic. Until they isolate the exact infection, they give many different kinds of antibiotics to cover every possible situation.

By the next day Arne was improved, but still very, very sick once again. He was too weak to be able to even adjust his body higher in the hospital bed. It took two of us to slide him up so his feet were not pushing against the bottom rail of the bed. I constantly was giving him sips of water. He didn't know who Dr. A was when he came in to see him at the end of his day. I again sent out emails requesting prayer.

Another day went by as Arne slowly began to eat a little. He had no appetite and although he was in no pain, he was miserable with the catheter still in his body. His cognitive abilities began returning but he was still unable to sit up by himself. His body was more weakened than I had ever seen him. Prayer, prayer and more prayer. I knew in my heart he was going to be alright, but this was taking its toll and I, too, was becoming thoroughly depleted. We both needed a touch from the Master.

Finally, the culture came back. He had a pseudomonces aeruginosa infection. The doctor treating Arne in the hospital, Dr. R. said this was a rather rare infection. It wasn't uncommon, however not seen often. Apparently, this is a type of bacteria seen sometimes after surgeries and often related to using a catheter. They gave Arne the exact antibiotic necessary to stamp out this infection and we, again, waited.

The next morning at 7:00 AM, I suggested Arne try to sit up on the edge of his bed for his breakfast. I helped him as he desperately tried to pull himself up, then try to continue to remain in a sitting position. He kept falling backwards. His strength was completely gone. I eventually got him balanced such that he would not tip over backwards and he ate his breakfast sitting up. After breakfast, I helped him stand and while shaking profusely and hanging unto his IV stand, he was able to walk the few steps into the bathroom. He wanted to wash up but after brushing his teeth and using the washcloth to wash his face, he was literally swaying some and said he had to get back into bed shortly. I quickly sponged off his back and chest and assisted him back into bed. He promptly fell sound asleep and slept the remainder of the morning, waking only when a nurse came in for something.

At noon he awoke, looked at me and said, *"Hon, I feel normal! I think the Lord has touched my body."*

A walker had been brought in for his use since, it appeared, we would be needing to take one home with us.

However, Arne sat up in bed, unassisted, hesitated a little, then swung both legs over the railing and unto the floor. I stood open mouthed gaping at him as he stood up and said,

"I think I want to take a walk."

I mean to tell you it was a total turnaround! He grabbed his IV pole and headed toward the door. I told him if he fell, I'd kill him! He took off down the long hall, me at his side, and when he reached the end with all the windows, he just stood there and said,

"What a beautiful view!"

He was quite a sight carrying his own purse (catheter bag) and holding on to the IV pole, with eyes bright, shining mischievously. He looked better than I had seen him in weeks! Back to his room we went at quite a brisk clip. I just thanked the Lord. I knew God had done it again. When Dr. R came in later that day he was amazed at Arne's quick turnaround and said just that. He had told us Arne would be in the hospital for quite some time because his white cell-count this time had been 25,500 and it was taking longer for him to respond to the medication.

Arne just continued to improve dramatically. One of his brothers, Martin (& Charlotte) Jacobson, is a missionary to the Patagonia in Argentina. They were home on furlough and were planning to visit Arne on Saturday, July 2. Up until this time no visitors had been permitted because Arne was so very sick. Buz and Vicki were also coming. Buz had come to be with his father several days prior, bringing filet mignon and grilling it for us. He kept in contact constantly by phone. One of our Hispanic Pastors, his wife and daughter also stopped by for a visit. We ended up having a roomful of visitors for several hours on Saturday and Arne was outgoing, laughing and being his normal cheerful self with energy he had not displayed at all until God touched his body. We had an absolutely delightful visit with our precious family. Arne was tired when everyone left but he was feeling really good and was a happy camper!

"Jesus, you are so awesome to us. We love how you take care of us and give us exactly what we need, exactly when we need it. Thank you so much for your continuous encouragement."

Dr. R came in and was taken back at how well Arne was doing. No need for a walker for this patient! After losing 15-lbs throughout the past month, Arne's appetite seemed to have returned also. He said Arne could go home the next day. All infection was completely gone. We were elated. Dr. R said to remain on the prescribed antibiotic until after the next surgery was complete. Arne's prostate was enlarged, and he would need another procedure as soon as possible to be free of the catheter. Dr. R made his recommendations to Dr. A and our Dr. Margaret concurred completely.

The following week, on July 8th, Arne had a transurethral resection of benign prostate – TURP for short. This is commonly called a 'Rotor Router' surgery by many men. It is a routine surgery and again just an overnight stay. Because of all the complications Arne seemed to have been having, I decided to spend the night in the hospital as well. Because he was not experiencing any problems, and everything went as clock work, we both had a wonderful night's sleep with few interruptions. The catheter was finally gone! Yeh! He had that apparatus for 5 very long weeks, sometimes leaking and wearing Depends for men to keep things tidy. All he had to do now was to be able to empty his bladder, leaving only 100ml of urine in his bladder at the most. Then we would be free to go home.

We ordered our meals for the day as his bladder and prostate began to wake up from the surgery. Each time he visited the restroom, it was measured, and a nurse would use an ultrasound machine to see how much urine was left in his bladder (each ultrasound treatment was $100.00/ouch). As morning turned into noon with little progress, we began being afraid that Arne might have to go home with a catheter once again. So, we prayed. Yep, God cares about things like catheters too. Finally, at about 3:30 PM Arne reached the magic number, well, close enough said Dr. R and we were told we could be dismissed. We had already ordered our supper so we decided to stay for supper, watch a movie on TV then leave. After all we would be charged for it anyway. This way I didn't have to worry about supper either! Mercy hospital food is the best. If Arne kept this up, I would gain 50 lbs. for sure! We left the hospital at 6:00 PM and came home rested and fed. It was a good day and Arne was feeling really great. He was weaker than normal, of course, but remarkably, really good. God is so faithful!

"That is why we never give up. Though our bodies are dying, our inner strength in the Lord is growing every day. These troubles and sufferings of ours are, after all, quite small and won't last very long. Yet this short time of distress will result in God's richest blessing upon us forever and ever. So, we don't look at what we can see right now, the troubles all around us, but we look forward to the joys in heaven which we have not yet seen. The trouble will soon be over, the joy to come will last forever."
II Corinthians 4:16-18.

Thankfulness (even for bad situations) frees me from resentment and frees God's hands to work His will in it. The Bible tells us to,

"Always give thanks for everything to our God and Father in the name of our Lord Jesus Christ." **Ephesians 5:20**

Not an easy thing to do. But when I totally and completely trust my Heavenly Father, and realize that I am no longer in control of my life because <u>He is</u>; then I AM able to thank Him for <u>everything</u> because I know He loves me more than anyone will ever be able to love me, and because He has my best interest at heart. He has written MY name upon the palms of His hands. He delights in me. I know many of the verses in the Bible by heart, and I know I can trust Jesus 100%, yet I am just as human as you are.

Fear is a natural reaction placed into our minds to protect us from potential harm. However, it sometimes humanly reacts to stimuli that we have no control over. It really has nothing to do with our faith. It has everything to do with simply being human. Yet God is teaching us to react first with praise to Him because He is in control! This does not happen overnight. It has been a lifetime process for me. And I have not yet arrived. I am better at turning to praise than I was 5 yrs. ago and hope I will be quicker to turn to my Jesus with praise 5 yrs. from now, than today. He will continue to grow us until the day He calls us home. He walks with us and He talks with us, and He tells us we are His own as He tenderly leads us forward into greater experiences with Him.

"I want to remind you that your strength must come from the Lord's mighty power within you. Put on the whole armor of God so that you will be able to stand safe against all strategies and tricks of Satan." Ephesians 6:10-11 Living Bible

~ THIRTY ~

2016 Personal Thoughts from BJ

When I was young, I had such child-like faith. I had not been exposed to the horrible things that adults impose on children. I didn't know about the atrocities of war and hunger. I never knew about the pathetic things one human being could inflict on another human being. My childhood was a protected childhood of innocence and love. I never knew such bad things could happen to good people. I was shielded.

But I grew up. We live in a broken, fallen world full of sin and evil and debauchery. It is getting worse. No one can listen to the news without hearing of riots, terrorism, looting, murders and unbelievable ugliness visited upon our cities and neighborhoods. We are not even protected from evil and violence in the house of God. It is unsafe to walk the streets alone of almost any major city in these United States of America, especially at night.

When I was a girl we played outdoors until dark. Our parents didn't have to sit and watch us. Our doors weren't locked. We walked home alone after dark without fear. We enjoyed all the outdoor games of 'Hide and Seek,' 'Captain May I,' caught fire flies and laid on the grass counting the stars and naming the constellations – all in peace and quietness without a single thought to harm. Our children today have no idea what simple pleasures we cherish from our childhood days. We entertained ourselves by climbing trees, playing neighborhood baseball in the vacant lot 6 blocks away, or making snow angels and having snowball fights, yes, blocks from our house! Many a time we walked the 10 blocks home from the ice-skating rink, after dark, with the snow gently falling, glistening like diamonds in the street lights, and felt the vibrant thrill of just being young and full of life. Completely without fear.

Yes, things have changed. We grew up and reality took hold. Our lives began to unfold yet we were still full of hopes and dreams. Then the difficult times came. Sometimes they came one after another just like those snowflakes of years ago. And they still come. But they aren't as glistening diamonds anymore. You sometimes feel like you are being bombarded and buried alive. You feel lost and alone and God seems far away. You feel like you are being suffocated, left to die alone in misery. I am told God loves me but the darkness and terrible emptiness in my soul is overwhelming. Where are you God?

The Bible says He will not allow us to be tested beyond what we can endure.

"There hath no temptation taken you but such as is common to man; but God is faithful, who will not suffer you to be tempted above that ye are able; but will with the temptation also make a way to escape, that ye may be able to bear it."
I Corinthians 10:13 KJV

"But remember this – the wrong desires that come into your life aren't anything new and different. Many others have faced exactly the same problems before you. And no temptation is irresistible. You can trust God to keep the temptation from becoming so strong that you can't stand up against it, for he has promised this and will do what he says. He will show you how to escape temptation's power so that you can bear up patiently against it." I Corinthians 10:13 Living Bible

So why are we tested in the first place? This is so hard to grasp for most of us. We don't like being tested. We don't like trials. We don't like temptation. We don't like pain.

God says that with temptation He will always provide a way of escape, if we turn to Him. He is strengthening us for each next step in the future, as we learn to trust Him completely. It may look desolate, but His plan is to help us grow strong.

When the winds blow, the roots of trees go deeper. When the waters along a river begin to dry up, the roots of the trees along the banks go deeper. God wants us to go deeper in Him. He wants to make us unshakeable, unsinkable. It is part of His Plan for me. It is a part of His Plan for you. However, you never have to go through these struggles alone. He is right there beside you to give you wisdom, strength, guidance and hope. He will never leave you defenseless. The presence and will of God are inescapable. Even in death, He is there with us. We don't make the decisions, He does. And Jesus NEVER makes mistakes!

"Yea though I walk through the valley of the shadow of death, I will fear no evil, for thou art with me; thy rod and staff they comfort me." Psalms 23:4

Did you know the shepherd used the rod to guide and direct his sheep for correction of their direction and path? The staff was used to pull a sheep away from some dangerous cliff or injury. And even in death He tells us to fear no evil because He is with us – always!

One of these days a sickness may come that may take your life. Sometimes God gives the ultimate healing – promotion to heaven. For the Christian, this is marvelous and freeing from the pain, cares and difficulties of life. For those left to mourn their loved one, it becomes a lonely, longing time of sorrow. Again, the Bible has the answer.

We don't sorrow as those with no hope. When we and our loved ones know Jesus, there is hope of eternity in heaven together forever. We will see them again. We will be together once again for ever and ever. There we will never be parted again.

"But I would not have you to be ignorant, brethren, concerning them which are asleep (dead), that you sorrow not, even as others which have no hope. For if we believe that Jesus died and rose again, even so them also which sleep (are dead) in Jesus will God bring with him. For this we say unto you by the word of the Lord, that we which are alive and remain unto the coming of the Lord shall not prevent them which are asleep (dead)."

"For the Lord himself shall descend from heaven with a shout, with the voice of the archangel, and with the trump of God: and the dead in Christ shall rise first: Then we which are alive and remain shall be caught up together with them in the clouds, to meet the Lord in the air: and so shall we <u>*ever*</u> *be with the Lord. Wherefore comfort one another with these words."*
I Thessalonians 4:13-18

Recently I fell and badly bruised my kneecap and tore some ligaments in my opposite shoulder. It was a painful experience that lasted many months with chiropractic appointments and physical therapy. At first, I wasn't even able to pull up my own panties due to the pain. I could not stand up without help and felt enormously helpless. I was confined to ice packs on the knee only to switch to heat packs on the shoulder and then reversing the process. I couldn't get a comfortable night's sleep and became very depressed. The bills were coming in from

Arne's previous hospital stays and we were financially strapped just when we had it all planned out how we would be debt free with savings for our future and another car. Arne was slowly improving from his medical problems so I had to carry the heavy end of household duties and yard work. It was Autumn with leaves galore.

I have not had very many bouts of depression in my lifetime, but the ones I have had have been demoralizing, hopeless, leaving me falling into a black abyss of aloneness. It is a sinking feeling of no longer caring. Yes, I felt sorry for myself too. We had had enough, and I just wanted to be normal again, be happy inside and have hope for tomorrow. Yet everywhere I turned it seemed something was trying to steal my joy. I wanted it back!

Have you been there? We've all experienced that ache when something we've hoped for doesn't quite work out. It is exacerbated when we are also not well or experiencing pain.

"Hope deferred makes the heart sick.." Proverbs 13:12

Every situation and circumstance that we hope for is going to fall apart, go away or not materialize, and will dissipate eventually. Because life is not fair and bad things do happen to good people. When that occurs, we fall to our foundation.

What is your foundation?

What is your deeper hope?

Hope can break your heart. The hope Jesus offers is the only strong, reliable, faithful, sure hope there is when the bottom falls out of our lives. Not because He is a sugar daddy who will fulfill all our wishes. He is our hope of the future, no matter what happens. Hope is faith waiting for tomorrow. Faith is believing our commitment to Christ and His commitment to us. It is a commitment of our wills. It is getting the belief from our minds down into our hearts where hope is collecting.

I knew the scriptures. I had memorized many of them, yet that black draping of despair hovered over me like an eclipse blocking out the sun. I begged God to please deliver me. Yet each day seemed to suck me deeper until I didn't feel like or want to do anything but sleep. I wasn't sleeping well due to my pain and my mental equilibrium was bringing me lower and lower. I knew only one way to get out from under this miserable existence: God's Word.

You see, because of many doctor appointments, commitments, coming holidays and other family members going through extremely difficult medical conditions plus the upheaval in our political world with nothing but squabbling talking heads, I had neglected my Bible reading and personal time with Jesus. I let the cares and troubles of this world, my world, come crashing over me, drowning out my joy as I allowed my time to be robbed of the most important of all – loving and thanking my Heavenly Father for who He is and His care for me, His little girl.

I have had Jesus in my heart since I was 6 years old. He is my Savior and coming King. But I am just as human as you are. I am not a super Christian. There is no such thing! All of us experience the same tests and trials – just in different circumstances. We are all living our lives toward one eternal end: heaven someday. God is preparing us for that journey. He shapes us to become all He has created us to be for His glory and honor. He wants us to encourage others to love and serve Him also. My responsibility is to *allow* Him to do that shaping, *keep close* to His Word and remain in *close friendship* with Him.

When I deviate from that path, He gets my attention one way or another and brings me back to the path He has chosen for me. Sometimes that means I can get pretty miserable.

I would love to tell you I'm never despondent, depressed or sad anymore. It would be a lie. As I said above: "Every situation and circumstance that we hope for is going to fall apart, go away or not materialize and will dissipate eventually." Because life is not fair and bad things do happen to good people. When that occurs, we fall to our foundation.

I finally gave up and cried, *"God I cannot do this anymore. I can't worry about my husband's health anymore. I can't obsess about how we are going to pay all these medical bills. I can't worry about the future anymore. I give up. It is your problem and I turn it completely over to you."*

I fell head first to my foundation – again!

That is the answer: Our foundation! My foundation IS in Jesus. I spun my wheels and did nothing but dig a big hole of despair. However, I knew where to go – back to my foundation. I immersed myself back into God's Word, taking time to read, pray and listen for that gentle, quiet voice of the Holy Spirit. I began praising. I thanked and praised God for everything I could think of. Because I knew that Satan could not remain tempting me to wallow in self-pity when I am thanking and praising God. He wants nothing to do with the praises of God and he will leave us as we praise the Lord. You see, God inhabits the praises of his people. And God delights in the praises of His children.

"O God my Strength! I will sing your praises, for you are my place of safety. My God is changeless in his love for me and he will come and help me." Psalms 59:9

"But as for me, I will sing each morning about your power and mercy. For you have been my high tower of refuge, a place of safety in the day of my distress. O my Strength, to you I sing my praises; for you are my high tower of safety, my God of mercy." Psalms 59:16

"Give your burdens to the Lord. He will carry them. He will not permit the godly to slip or fall." Psalms 55:22

"But true praise is a worthy sacrifice; this really honors me. Those who walk my paths will receive salvation from the Lord." Psalms 50:23

"I want you to trust me in your times of trouble, so I can rescue you, and you can give me glory." Psalms 50:15

Did my circumstances change? No. My knee would take a long time to heal. It was getting better, but I had to be very careful of my activities. My shoulder was very painful and physical therapy was painful. But progress was being made. I disliked taking so much time for recovery and the physical therapy it involved.

I would much rather have a quick fix, but that wasn't about to happen. I am thankful for physical therapists. I am thankful for doctors who care and take the time to listen. I thank God for precious friends who pray with you. I am thankful for all God has brought me through. It all could have been so much more serious. Most of all I thank my loving Heavenly Father for never leaving nor forsaking me no matter how much I neglect him. He is always right here, by my side. He loves me and wants me to draw closer and closer to him.

He is interested in every little thing that happens in my life. And He wants me to trust Him with all my tomorrows. Best of all, I know my sins are forgiven, my name is written in the Lamb's Book of Life, a place in heaven is being prepared for me and Jesus is with me now, no matter what happens in my life.

I want to make it very clear that this Christian Life is not something that we live with anticipation to perfection. We don't *'attain'* a certain status that makes us impervious to discouragement. We will constantly need to trust and lean on Jesus all the days of our lives until He takes us home to heaven someday. It is a walk of faith. It is a walk of conscious determination to follow God's ways completely. It is a walk of obedience and thorough trust in God Almighty. It is a walk of joy and peace when we place our fleshly human hand into the nail scarred hand of the One who has all of life to give us.

If you have never asked Jesus Christ into your heart and life, to forgive your sins and make you into the person He created you to be, I invite you to pray this prayer. He will become your Savior, Lord and Coming King also.

"Jesus, I believe you are the Son of God. I believe you died on the cross for my sins and I ask you to please forgive me for every wrong and sin I have ever committed. Please come into my heart to live forever as my Savior and Lord. Show me how to live for you. Give me a love for your Word so I can become all you created me to become. I want to love you and live with you forever in heaven someday. And I want you to be my closest friend. Thank you for saving my soul. I believe your Word that says you will come into my heart if I ask you. Thank you for loving me and coming into my heart right now. In Jesus Name. Amen."

"For if you tell others with your own mouth that Jesus Christ is your Lord, and believe in your own heart that God has raised him from the dead, you will be saved. For it is by believing in his heart that a man becomes right with God; and with his

mouth he tells others of his faith, confirming his salvation. For the scriptures tell us that no one who believes in Christ will ever be disappointed. " **Romans 10:9-11** *Living Bible*

"Behold, I am standing at the door and I am constantly knocking. If anyone hears me calling him and opens the door, I will come in and fellowship with him and he with me." **Rev. 3:20** *Living Bible*

~ THIRTY- ONE ~

December 2016 Another UTI

Dec 14, 2016 Arne had another cystoscopy in the urologist's office to see if everything was alright. Arne was still having some issues with voiding and the urologist wanted to be sure all was well since the TURP surgery (Prostate) in July.

I asked if perhaps Arne should be on antibiotics before this procedure was done.

The urologist said, *"No, that is not necessary. No one ever gets a UTI from this procedure. Well, at least it is very rare."*

I expressed my concern because of Arne's history of urinary tract infections and the fact that it had only been a couple of months since he almost died from one of those. The urologist assured me there was nothing to worry about. The procedure went as scheduled at 1:00 PM and home we went.

The next day, Dec 15, at 5:00 PM I noticed Arne just sitting on the couch, looking at his knees. The TV was not on and the couch leg-rest was not up.

I said, *"Put your feet up, Hon!"* He lifted his feet up and just held them there.

I said, *"Are you messing with me?"*

He said, *"No, you said to put my feet up, so I did."*

I just knew! I asked him to get up and walk for me. He shuffled his feet again. I took his temperature and it was 100.1 – it was time for another trip to the hospital.

I called my Doctor friend, Dr. Margaret, and told her what I was doing. She completely agreed and called ahead to the Emergency Room to tell them to get Arne right in and not to keep him waiting in the waiting room because time was of the essence here because a UTI was in progress.

Sure enough, his white count was 18,000 and rising. But he wasn't septic yet. How I praise and thank my Heavenly Father for His wisdom and for the good doctor He had brought into our lives so many years before, Dr. Margaret.

Another Septic condition was averted by quick diagnosis. Arne spent the next 5 days in the hospital getting rid of yet another infection of the urinary track system. This was just 12 hours after the cystoscopy. We needed to have a talk with our Urologist.

During the next three weeks I had such a peace and joy in my heart. I realized I truly had given my worries completely over to God. These were HIS problems. Not mine. He was in charge – not me! It was absolutely freeing, and my joy had returned. I had no idea how we were going to pay yet another hospital co-pay. We had accumulated over $9,000 in medical expenses. Our deductible was $5,800 that we were responsible for and the insurance took over after that. This was eating our saving away very quickly. Our plans for the future simply went out the window. God was in charge. I still had peace. I didn't take back my fussing and worrying about how this was all going to pan out.

We would take it one step at a time and trust Him. Christmas was just a few days away!

It was a quiet, low key Christmas with our son, Buz and wife in Springfield, MO. We shared Fondue on Christmas Eve and each of us told of our most memorable Christmas, good or bad. It was a reminiscing of God's faithfulness to our family all our lives. We had so many miracles to thank the Lord for and so many times of God's rescuing us from potential problems and danger. What a mighty God we serve! Why ever do we doubt!?!

"Let the morning bring me word of your unfailing love, for I have placed my trust in you. Show me the way I should go for to you I entrust my life." Psalms 143:8 NIV

"The steadfast love of the Lord never ceases; his mercies never come to an end. They are new every morning. Great is your faithfulness." Lamentations 3:22-23

"Weeping may last through the night, but joy comes in the morning." Psalms 30:5

It is good to proclaim your unfailing love in the morning, your faithfulness in the evening." Psalms 92:2

God wants you to know that He cares for you. He is cheering for you, and He has a plan for your life. No matter what our circumstances, God's Word has a promise of hope.

"But as for me, I will hope continually and will praise you yet more and more."
Psalms 71:14

"My soul waits in silence for God only; from Him is my salvation. He only is my rock and my salvation, my stronghold. I shall not be greatly shaken."
Psalms 62:1 *NASB*

God wants to develop our faith in Him. When we trust God for simple answers to prayer, our faith increases. The more we read and study His Word, the more aware we are of His ability. He wants us to bring all our decisions and cares to Him. We also learn that if we ask Him to show us what we should do, He does. He speaks to us through His Word. Then as we soak up the Scripture, we begin to internalize His truth in our heart.

We tell Him our needs, and He responds, by giving us insight and wisdom. Whatever He calls us to do, He will also confirm in His Word and equip us to do it. He opens a door and we step through. He opens another door and once again we trust Him because we have learned He is faithful all of the time – not just once in a while – all of the time!

Our words are so important also. Speak words of life. Speak words of faith. Each word we speak either waters the seed or destroys the seed. So, hide the Word of God in your heart and speak life.

~ THIRTY -TWO ~

January 2017 Confronting the Urologist

In January we saw Arne's urologist. We discussed Arne's fragile immune system and the importance of antibiotics and the need to listen to what a patient and his/her spouse says. We KNOW our own bodies. Arne's UTI track record cannot be ignored ever again. I worked at Mayo Clinic for 5 ½ years, grading the Internal Medicine Residents on their performance. I don't know of a surgeon alive who likes being "advised" by a non-surgical peon. Arne's urologist was no different. We came to an agreeable end. Since he is now VERY aware of how closely we are watching everything that is done, and he has agreed to consult other physicians involved, we left his office satisfied we could have confidence in his continued care of Arne and that he would "hear" us in the future. I will not gamble my husband's physical well-being ever again – second opinions are often required for a valid reason. We would be consulting another urologist in the very near future.

I want to add here that you should never be afraid to question your physician's decisions. With all the hoopla going on about healthcare and the expense of it, remember: it is your dollar you are spending. YOU are the patient that will suffer the consequences of the decisions made regarding your medical care. Be informed. Look things up on the internet and know all the possible reactions to the medication, and the interaction all the supplements and other prescribed medications may have on each other. It could be a matter of life or death someday. I know. Because it happened to us. It is our responsibility to manage our own health. Become knowledgeable about the food you eat and its correspondence to your physical and mental well-being. Don't be afraid to try new foods, new recipes. Let life be an adventure – in every avenue of your life.

~ THIRTY -THREE ~

January 2017 An Unexpected Miracle

It was a Wednesday night, January 18, 2017. Church had just concluded, and I was picking up my purse and jacket to leave. Arne was in charge of the sound that evening so had not come down from the sound booth yet. A couple came to me and asked how things were going. I told them I had been approved for a much better insurance plan, but Arne had been denied. His care would primarily come from the VA and our Medicare Advantage Plan. We hoped to be able to switch Arne to a better insurance plan in the future.

They said, *"The Lord told us several months ago that we are to pay for your medical expenses."*

I just stood and looked at them, speechless. I told them we couldn't let them do that. They INSISTED and said God had told them this several months prior but they were just waiting for God to say *"NOW."*

I told them Arne and I really needed to talk and pray about this. The lady said, *"So that's a yes?"*

We came home absolutely dumbfounded. This seemed like a dream, or something we had read about someone else. It was just overwhelming. We had never had anything like this ever happen to us. We were talking about a lot of money. We had been generous to others on several occasions in our lifetime, but not to this extent!

God owns the cattle on a thousand hills and He just sold a couple of them and had blessed this couple beyond measure. They wanted to bless us. Our devotions the next morning had this in it:

"God loves to give His children good gifts. Our job is to accept His gifts with thankful hearts."

This beautiful, giving couple did just what they proposed. They paid our medical expenses in full and wanted any future outstanding medical bills not yet processed.

Now for the background of what was becoming a financial crisis. We had opted for the IBM insurance coverage when Arne took his retirement package years before. It was excellent and covered everything for <u>both</u> of us together for a mere $66.40 per month. It was the best insurance offered on the market at that time.

When Obama Care came into being, IBM sent us a letter stating they were no longer going to be offering insurance coverage for us (retirees) and we would have to seek other insurance coverage, outside of IBM.

I searched for an insurance broker, asked many questions and couldn't seem to find the answers I needed, so I turned to the "Medicare And You" official U.S. government Medicare handbook that comes annually to a retiree's home. I read every word - twice. I thought I fully understood the concept and felt confident in what I was reading. My understanding was that Medicare was the Primary Insurer and the Insurance we chose would become the Secondary insurance, leaving any balance for us to pay, depending on the plan we chose.

There were many plans available at varying costs. But the cheapest premiums with the extra benefits seemed to be the Medicare Advantage Plans. So, I chose the best of the Medicare Advantage Plans. They are GREAT – as long as you don't have any major illnesses or surgeries. I thought these Medicare Advantage Plans were SECONDARY plans as I understood the system. I couldn't have been more wrong.

Because I needed physical therapy for a shoulder and knee injury, I signed up at a local Rehabilitation Center. The therapist asked if I had Medicare and I answered I did. I then showed him my Medicare Advantage Plan card. He looked it up and said I had not accessed my regular Medicare in over three years. He then explained that with a Medicare Advantage Plan, *THEY* become my Primary Insurance and *I* become the Secondary.

The difference in out of pocket costs is enormous if you have a major illness. I also found out that to get back into the regular Medicare system I would have to apply to an underwriter insurance company who could deny me for whatever reason they chose. The window to get this accomplished was from January 1 – February 14 of any given year. It was almost January now!

I was devastated, but that explained why we were getting so many bills from all of Arne's clinic visits and the first hospital stay in Mobridge, S.D. I became a nervous wreck and lay awake worrying many nights. Here I was, in pain from injuries myself, plus trying to care for a husband who had almost died twice already and was in a very weakened physical condition and we were without good medical coverage. The co-pays would only escalate unless I did something.

It was already December and we couldn't endure another year of more hospital bills like those which I knew had accumulated already. Should either of us need hospitalization in the coming year it would ruin us financially. It was all I could think about. I stressed!

And I prayed like I had never prayed. I prayed for deliverance. I prayed for favor. I prayed for a financial miracle, I prayed for wisdom. I prayed! I was exhausted physically, mentally and spiritually.

I finally gave up and told God He would have to work it all out because I just didn't see a way out. I dumped it into His lap. Only then did I have peace. I had spun my wheels just digging holes! When would I learn?

I had contacted Blue Cross and Blue Shield and spoke with a supervisor in Florida who told me I was one of hundreds of thousands of retirees who had made the same miscalculation with their insurance, going with an Advantage Plan. She advised me what to do and I made application for both Arne and I to switch from our Medicare Advantage Plan to Blue Cross and Blue Shield. The insurance company called for all our medical records and accepted me, but turned Arne down due to his medical problems.

It was the very next day, in church, that our dear friends offered to pay our outstanding medical expenses. They paid close to $2,000.00 expenses from the first hospitalization expenses and said to give them the remaining ones from Mercy Hospital when we were billed. It was now January and we had not been billed for $4-5,000 in outstanding bills to-date. We even went to the business office and had been told to just be patient because we would hear from them eventually.

As Paul Harvey used to say: "Now for the REST of the story."

Months went by without receiving a single piece of correspondence from Mercy Hospital. My new insurance took over my care. Arne had to remain with the same Medicare Advantage Plan until we could try again the following Fall to get him into a plan with better coverage. Yes, it would cost more, but the premiums were less than the out of pocket expenses so far! We waited. And we waited some more. Finally, nine months later we received an official letter from Mercy's Financial Assistance Program that stated the following:

"This year, Mercy's Financial Assistance Program helped you, or someone in your household, pay for health care services received at Mercy. On January 1, 2018, that program will change. Please read on to see if your care will continue to qualify for the program."

Our bill had been paid in full by Mercy's Financial Assistance Program!

The letter went on to explain that we would no longer qualify for their Financial Assistance Program and we needed to seek further insurance coverage.

We never signed up for any financial assistance and we still have no idea how this all came about, but we know WHO engineered this awesome gift: Our Heavenly Father!

ONLY GOD COULD DO SUCH AN INCREDIBLE MIRACLE!

"Thank you, our faithful Heavenly Father. Lavish your love and blessings on these precious children of yours who gave unselfishly to bless us."

How absolutely refreshing to personally see a Christian Couple be so dedicated to the Lord, listen to His voice and then obey without questioning. That is how our Father in Heaven wants us to be. How I thank Him for this awesome example to us. It was a very humbling experience.

Thank you, precious Father, for impressing on whoever it was at Mercy to submit our file to the Financial Assistance Program. We have been told that periodically Mercy will flag a file that has had excessive expenses in one particular year, and choose to write off the expenses. We suspect that is what happened. Again, God intervened and gave us loving favor that only He can arrange. Oh, how we love you, Jesus. You are so faithful!

~ THIRTY -FOUR ~

February 2017 Potentially Dangerous Dentistry

For several years Arne had noticed a small bump on the upper gum of his teeth. It didn't hurt so he basically just ignored it. However, at the last dental cleaning his dentist had mentioned it again and told Arne he really needed to have it looked at closer. They did further x-rays that day and discovered a rather significant infection between #12 and #13 teeth. The dentist was not able to discern which tooth was the one with the infection, so referred Arne to an oral surgeon for a 3D photo to isolate the tooth with the infection. We followed up with the 3D photo and set up an appointment to have the tooth extracted. He was placed on antibiotics for two weeks prior to the extraction as well as two weeks following the extraction.

On February 2, 2017 Arne had the infected tooth pulled. It was full of infection down to the root. The surgeon scraped and irrigated the cavity and told him it was a good thing we got that tooth out when we did. He explained that infected teeth can cause all kinds of trouble including heart problems and even death if the infection reaches the brain. He said it was entirely probable that Arne's compromised immune system could very well have been contributed to by this infection, which had been there for years.

Arne's urologist as well as our own personal physician concurred that this could have been why Arne never seemed to feel well the last couple of years and why it had taken so long for him to regain his strength. Who would have guessed this as a possibility! We were thankful for a dentist who insisted on pursuing what appeared to be a "small" thing, that could have ended disastrously. Once again, we thank our God for His watchfulness over us.

The morning before Arne's tooth surgery, we received the following from a lady in our church who had been having health issues of her own. We choose to claim this for our future:

"Good Morning! We are still praying for Arne. I don't know if this has any meaning or not, but thought I'd share it and let you decide. God Bless."

"I think I had a dream last night. I'm not sure if I was awake or asleep or both. But I was doing a Jericho march around your home. On the last round a wall a little over half way up the house appeared. It was brick/rock and as I marched the wall toppled down as I went. When I was almost done with the last round your home illuminated as bright as anything I've ever seen. The whole house was like a crystal with bright light permeating through it." Sherri

I do not claim to be able to interpret dreams, but I do know that God is able to do so, and He has often communicated to His children through dreams and visions throughout history and The Bible. Including today!

I see this as God using all we have been through in our lives as being living testimonies to the amazing and powerful light of God's love and truth as to WHO He really is.

He is a loving father who wants to use our lives to shine forth His unwavering love to everyone we meet. We want our lives and home to reflect that illuminating light of Jesus as we share all that God has done for us in our lives.

We are just ordinary people with an extraordinary God. We are not more special than anyone else. God loves us all the same. What He does for one, He can do for anyone else. It takes a total commitment in selling out completely to Him. Giving Him every part of your heart, talents, desires, money, ambition and allowing Him to call <u>all</u> the shots. The rewards far outweigh anything this world has to offer. Eternity is the goal and destination. This life is just a dress rehearsal for all to come. Yet what a rehearsal it has been. It is never dull when you are riding with Christ as the pilot of your ship!

Steve Jobs, CEO and maker of iPad, iPhone etc., died a billionaire and here are some of his thoughts and words before he passed away:

"I reached the pinnacle of success in the business world. In other's eyes, my life is an epitome of success. However, aside from work, I have little joy. In the end, wealth is only a fact of life that I am accustomed to...at this moment, lying on the sick bed and recalling my whole life, I realize that all the recognition and wealth that I took so much pride in have paled and become meaningless in the face of impending death.

-You can employ someone to drive the car for you, make money for you but you cannot have someone to bear the sickness for you.

-Material things lost can be found. But there is one thing that can never be found when it is lost – health and life itself.

-When a person goes into the operating room, he will realize that there is one book that he has yet to finish reading – "Book of Healthy Life".

-Treasure Love for your family, love for your spouse, love for your friends.

-Cherish others.

-As we grow older and hence wiser, we slowly realize that wearing a $300...or $30.00 watch...they both tell the same time. Whether we carry a $300... or $30.00 wallet or handbag, the amount of money inside is the same.

-Whether the house we live in is 300 sq. ft...or 3,000 sq. ft...loneliness is the same.
You will realize, your true inner happiness does not come from the material things of this world.

-Whether you fly first or economy class, if the plane goes down, you go down with it.

-Therefore, I hope you realize, when you have mates, buddies and old friends, brothers and sisters, who you chat with, laugh with, talk with, have sing songs with, talk about north-south-east-west or heaven and earth...that is true happiness.

-Don't educate your children to be rich. Educate them to be happy so when they grow up, they will know the value of things...not the price." End of quotes by Steve Jobs

I would like to add, the only way to walk through this life is by knowing Jesus Christ as your personal savior. Money won't save you. Fame won't save you.

As Steve Jobs so eloquently stated: *"recognition and wealth have paled and become meaningless in the face of impending death."*

When you get to the end of your life and you are facing eternity, you can either be holding on to the Hand of Jesus as you exit this life, or you will go into eternal outer darkness, called hell. The decision is made in this life.

Where will YOU be spending eternity?

That is the only question that really matters.

I urge you to turn your life over to Jesus Christ, who died to give you eternal life with Him, and then have guidance, peace and faithful love here on earth until that day you step into eternity with Him forever. Bow your head and ask Him to forgive your sins, come into your heart today and ask Him to help you live to please Him all the rest of the days of your life here on earth. It will make all the difference for eternity's sake!

~ THIRTY -FIVE ~

February 2017 A Word from Above

On Feb 9, 2017 during our regular devotions together we prayed a specific prayer. We had been following a 40-day devotional book called 'Communion with Jesus' by Steve and JoAnne Rupp. We were on day 28 of the reading and the scriptures were:

"All authority has been given to Me in heaven and on earth." Matthew 28:18

"Then he called his twelve disciples together, and gave them power and authority over all devils, and to cure diseases. And he sent them to preach the kingdom of God, and to heal the sick." Luke 9:1-2

"Behold, I give you the authority to trample on serpents and scorpions, and over all the power of the enemy, and nothing shall by any means hurt you." Luke 10:19

The authors went on to explain that we have full authority and power in the name of Jesus and nothing formed against us can prosper without God's permission.

Arne and I took the bread and cup to take communion together. We felt we needed to pray the Name of Jesus, with all its power, and command Arne's prostate, bladder and entire urinary track system to return to the healthy way God had initially created it to be. We prayed and commanded his body to obey the spirit of God which was dwelling within Arne's body. The Bible says we are made whole by the body and blood of Jesus Christ in communion. We didn't shout. God's not hard of hearing. We didn't wail. God understands our feelings and doesn't need a performance. We just prayed like any other time, but we could feel His power with us and we knew this was the time.

The next day Arne began noticing a difference. He had been unable to hold his urine for any length of time and the elimination stream had not been full like before his problems and surgeries began over nine months prior. Depends had become a regular part of his daily attire. However, he noticed time between bathroom runs and his elimination process was getting better. Within 3 days it seemed like everything was returning to normal. This blessed relief continued for 5 weeks.

May 2017 Change of Plans

In May 2017, as our RV was packed, sitting in our driveway and ready to depart for some long, anticipated RV Maps work at Trinity Bible College, Arne's bladder did an abrupt change. Again, he was visiting the bathroom every 15 minutes with little advance notice and close calls. Understandably, he didn't want to travel 800 miles having to stop every 15 minutes for a bathroom break! We decided to just go to his urologist's office and see if we could get an appointment that day. Nope, nothing available until the next day. Since we were halfway to the VA, we decided to just do the same there since it was early in the day.

As a walk-in to the VA, we knew we would probably be there all day, but this was an important issue that could make the next couple of months miserable or tolerable!

After checking in, they ordered all lab work to be done before we would be seeing his doctor.

We were the last patient of the day for his new doctor a female nurse practitioner who was very, very thorough.

She took one look at Arne and said, *"First of all, you have a urinary tract infection, but the culture won't be back for 2 days for a conclusive diagnosis. You look puny and you are quite dehydrated (as she pinched his arm)."*

We both sat up and listened. We proceeded to tell her of the previous year's journey for Arne's health, since none of it was in the VA records, having seen 'outside doctors.'

The doctor took many notes, added additional tests to Arne's already drawn blood and urine samples and asked a myriad of questions.

She spent two hours with us and said, *"Something is definitely not right here. You should be gaining strength and getting significantly better."*

When Arne excused himself to go to the restroom, she looked me straight in the eye and said, *"I am very worried about your husband. He does not look well at all."*

I said, *"You are suspecting cancer?"*

She replied, *"Yes, bladder, prostate or something in that area."*

When Arne returned, the doctor told him she was scheduling a full battery of tests to get to the bottom of all of this. She gave him a prescription for Cipro for the UTI and sent us to the scheduling person. Tests were set up for the end of the month.

Two days later we received the urine culture and there was no UTI.

During those two days Arne passed two kidney stones and a third one a day later: the cause of the bladder control going haywire and the reason for the initial skewed urine test.

However, Arne was not feeling well at all. We cancelled our trip to Trinity Bible College, unpacked the RV and put it back into storage.

Disappointed is not an adequate word to describe our feelings, but we were also thankful because we surely didn't want to go through another year like 2016 with Arne's health. And perhaps we would be getting to the bottom of this after all.

Later, when discussing this with our family doctor and friend, Dr. Margaret, and looking at Arne's medications, she found he had been prescribed (by another doctor) a medication to assist the bladder that was double the dose needed. Arne's blood glucose was also going crazy high and he would awaken in the morning feeling unbalanced and extremely tired. After taking his AM medicines, he would gradually fade until he had no energy and could hardly keep his eyes open. He would be forced to lie down and often would sleep for two additional hours. Even after awakening near noon, he would not feel well and was still tired. He had no energy whatsoever. He would begin to feel better by suppertime and by bedtime he would feel pretty decent. This went on for the next three weeks. We gradually weaned Arne off the offending medication.

Then we analyzed everything. We cut out all sugar, which is poison to all of us, but particularly poisonous to diabetics. I even quit giving him wonderful antioxidants like Black Elderberry syrup, as it was sugar – natural, but still sugar. I eliminated everything that had sugar in it and continued to do so for a long time. There is sugar in everything! Dr. Margaret suggested giving Arne more protein and we purchased low sugar/low carb protein drinks and protein bars for him, being sure he had at least one every day. I added eggs to his breakfast every day. Protein, LOTS of vegetables and managed amounts of fruits became the routine of the day. Carbs were strictly controlled also. It was essentially a Keto diet way of eating.

It took nearly five days before his blood glucose began to come down into safe numbers. His blood pressure improved and although he was still tired in the morning, he slowly began to feel more normal. Everything was still frustratingly tentative.

It is not easy being a care giver when you don't know what you are dealing with. Many were praying for us for wisdom and for anything hidden to be revealed in the coming tests. I determined to thank and praise God for what we were going through. We simply took it a day at a time, waiting.

Nearly three weeks later, Arne began to return to normal. He was finally free of the medication that had caused all of this.

All the VA tests came back as perfectly normal with good numbers on everything. The only thing I noticed was Arne had a distended bladder with calcifications. More stones would be passing through his urinary track system, and this explained why the bladder was such a problem. Arne finally began to improve, but he was having terrible trouble with his bladder, once again. He was having to visit the restroom multiple times a day and night, not always making it in time. He had searched the internet for various types of external catheters, since he was unable to have an internal catheter due to his propensity toward urinary tract infections.

He ordered multiple types of external catheters, some good, some not so good and none that completely did the job to great satisfaction. He was becoming depressed and really down with the entire situation. He was reluctant for us to entertain friends, didn't want to go anyplace public. We had gone to an outdoor concert and the catheter had leaked. Only I noticed and we got home without incidence. I felt his pain and embarrassment deep in my heart. I begged God for an answer. Arne became withdrawn and just didn't want to leave the house.

July 2017 A Needed Break

In July I talked Arne into a two-week visit to our son and family at Trinity Bible College in North Dakota where they were both on staff. We weren't going to work at the college, but simply visit our family. Family understands the situation.

Bryan had his father helping him put in electrical outlets, put up new light fixtures, install crown molding and it was a great thing for Arne to do something productive which helped to keep his mind off the bladder dilemma. His mind was still sharp, although the memory still left him frustrated at times.

Meanwhile I searched the web for possible solutions to men's incontinence. I found several great articles with several options. One morning I called a urologist that our family doctor had recommended. Dr. Margaret had sent a referral, but we had never made an appointment. I asked the nurse if the urologist did any of these procedures I had researched. She said he regularly did. Since she already had a referral, I asked what she needed from us to make this happen. I gave permission for Arne's medical records to be sent to the doctor, after which an appointment would be made if the doctor thought he could help Arne.

We left our kids in N.D. after a restful two weeks change of scenery, at least for me. Arne was excited about the possibility of getting help from this new urologist.

July 2017 "Patience Please"

Again, we waited.

My patience level was rapidly descending to zero. I found myself becoming critical (in my heart) of all the frustration and *"talking about"* bladders and catheters and doctors. I wasn't sleeping very well, and I was just plain tired of everything. I wanted to just stay in bed with the covers over my head. My heart ached for Arne. I loved him so much and it was so hard to see him suffer in so many ways. I felt helpless and desperate.

It was hot outside and I felt tied to my house. I knew I was not relying on the Lord like I should. I became resentful of all the work that needed to be done in the yard. I had to do most of it because Arne simply could not. This wasn't his fault and I knew it wasn't his fault, but I just resented the entire situation. I knew I should be thankful he wasn't missing arms and legs. I knew I should be thankful I simply had him still alive. I knew I should be thankful in ALL things because this is the will of God concerning Me. I knew what was right. I knew the Bible and the verses.

For about one week I wallowed in self- pity, once again, until I received an on-line devotional about cherishing. Among other things I came face to face with my bad attitude, ungratefulness and tired spirit. Our humanness so easily can crowd out the really, important things in life. I needed strength only Jesus can give. He is always the answer. I needed a change in attitude to one of thankfulness for ALL things!

My respite has often been our above-the-ground swimming pool. I could live in it. I would read my Bible early in the morning, then go into the pool and talk to the Lord. I poured out my heart, frustrations, limitations and lacking to Him. He already knew them, but I needed forgiveness and strength from my impatience and whining.

Whatever is thrown our way in this life can only be handled when we have the strong arms of Our Heavenly Father around us. I sometimes feel like the older I've gotten the more difficult it is to be patient. My faith is definitely stronger, but I simply do not have the energy and strength I once had. I know I cannot cram as much into a day as I once did, and I am not superwoman! When I get tired, I become impatient and unreasonable. I suspect you have been there also. It doesn't take a rocket scientist to know we just can't navigate this life at 75 years of age that we did at 45 years of age! Duh! Let's use the common-sense God gave us along with His divine wisdom and help.

The solution was pretty simple: let go of things that just are not priority. It can wait until tomorrow, next week, next month, next year. The most spiritual thing I can do when I am over tired is to take a nap. I must cherish my loved ones while I have them with me.

We only have today. Make the best choices, give it your best shot, and with a breath of kindness to yourself – blow the rest away!

Once again, *"Thank you, Jesus, for getting me back on point."*

August 2017 A New Urologist

In August of 2017 Arne saw his new urologist. He had read all of Arne's medical history and was a young, articulate doctor who answered our questions. He said he wanted Arne to try a new medication that was supposed to help with bladder control. He said there were other options, but he didn't want to consider those until we had exhausted all other non-invasive therapies. We put our trust into God's hands through this urologist and decided to go the route he preferred.

One month after taking the required medication, there was no change in Arne's bladder control. Basically, the urologist told us Arne had an "over active bladder" and there is no cure for that. There is one possible surgical procedure available, but he wouldn't even consider it viable until Arne's body became stronger. We had exhausted our options and it was now completely in God's hands. We let go of expectations and decided we would accept what we could not change and praise the Lord for whatever was ahead. Amazing how a change in attitude on our part would give us such a peace and the joy and laughter back into our lives, in-spite-of no change in the diagnosis ahead! That is exactly what God wanted of us: let go and let God. We took our hands off the situation and placed everything completely into God's hands.

Physical Therapy and Occupational Therapy began coming to our home, along with a nurse weekly, to develop a plan to strengthen Arne's body physically. We were so grateful that he did not have to travel the 90 miles round trip twice weekly for therapy at the VA. The VA arranged this homebound care and it was a direct answer to untold number of prayers and many phone calls. God always comes through. We will continue to investigate new ideas, new procedures and evaluate all that we have the ability to control, but this is now completely in Our Heavenly Father's hands. Humanly speaking it appears we have come to the end of our rope. Our pastor, when we were newly married, used to say,

"When you get to the end of your rope, tie a knot and hang on with the tenacity of a bulldog. And then, just wait for God."

Thank you, Brother Carter, we are hanging on and waiting for God.

~ THIRTY -SIX ~

My 75th Birthday, September 24, 2017, a Sunday.

Arne had been having pain in his left back side for several weeks and had been going to the Chiropractor for just as long. The iliopsoas muscle had been damaged and the pain was excruciating. The iliopsoas is classified as the "dorsal hip muscle," and is the strongest flexor of the hip joint and an important walking muscle which rotates the thigh laterally.

It is entirely possible that, having taken Cipro for an extended period for his continuing urinary tract infections, this muscle could have been become affected. This is one of the possible side-affects listed on the warning label of Cipro. It is not a common happening, but it can occur. This is what we believed happened to Arne since he had just begun physical therapy for rehabilitation of his weakened body. We did not know, for sure, and wanted to be certain it was not a kidney problem or hernia or whatever.

Arne was awake most of the night with severe pain and by morning was in excruciating pain. He was able to tolerate much more pain than the average person, having passed so many kidney stones in his lifetime. This, however, was beyond excruciating with every move he made. He knew it was not a kidney stone and said it was the worst pain he had ever experienced. Not knowing the cause, we went to the Emergency Room at Mercy Hospital in Rogers, Arkansas.

After several hours of tests and examinations, it was determined Arne had a yeast infection on top of his already diagnosed urinary tract infection and back spasms. He had recently passed another kidney stone, but the MRI showed no structural damage to the kidney or any other malady. The ER Nurse Practitioner asked if we had pain meds at home, which we did, and sent us on our way after seven hours. We came home and the pain meds had kicked in which allowed Arne to sleep for the next several hours.

As I was picking up the new meds, the Pharmacist said the following to me:

"I just want you to know that I called the ER doctor and asked him if he was SURE he REALLY wanted to give this patient these new medications. I asked the doctor if he was aware that this patient was diabetic and on, then named all the medications Arne was taking. The doctor told the pharmacist that he was aware of all of this and to go ahead and fill the prescription."

The pharmacist wanted to be sure I was aware of the fact that this combination can be <u>extremely dangerous</u> to a diabetic so, *"to watch Arne's blood sugars very carefully."*

It sounded much like one of the commercials on TV that made the side-affects sound worse than the disease. However, I did not forget his admonition.

The next two days seemed better and the Chiropractor confirmed that the iliopsoas muscle was the culprit for all the back-pain Arne was experiencing and that it would simply take time to heal. Arne's physical therapist recommended several additional exercises to help stretch that muscle several times a day and combined with the pain meds, it seemed like everything was going as hoped.

Wednesday, September 27th, Arne awoke and went to the bathroom. He was sitting on the commode, bending over running his fingers through the bath mat. I asked him what he was doing. At first, he didn't answer me, then replied when I asked him again, that he was looking for his glasses.

He was wearing his glasses and I told him that! He just looked at me blankly and continued to run his fingers around on the bath mat. Once again, I asked him what he was doing. Again, he replied that he was looking for his glasses. I then took his hand, tapped his own glasses, and said, *"they are here, on your head. You need to eat."*

We ate breakfast and Arne seemed to recover completely. This was due to low blood sugar.

However, Dr. Margaret always told me if anything like this happened, we should have him checked immediately to be sure it was nothing more than a sugar low. I called her at home, since it was her day off, and asked her opinion. (I was so thankful she was my friend as well as our doctor).

She said to go to the clinic and she would call in orders for some tests to be done. We did, and everything came back normal. It was a sugar low. I didn't think to tell her of the new prescriptions Arne was on at the time.

The next morning, September 28th, I got up early as usual and had my devotional time with the Lord and at 6:45 AM went to check to see if Arne was awake.

He was still in bed and I said, *"Hey sleepyhead, it's time for our morning coffee."*

He replied in a barely discernable slurred speech, *"Was appenin u me? I an't mov my arm. Head urts."*

I lifted-up his right arm and let go. It dropped like a dead weight. I had no idea what was happening, but he was sweating profusely, had a severe headache and I knew something was drastically wrong.

I immediately called a friend from church and asked him to come right over, thinking perhaps we could take him to the ER together. I tried taking his blood glucose, with the meter, but I had never done this, and although I had seen Arne do it many times, I just couldn't get it to operate. I felt an urgency to call the ambulance because Arne couldn't move any limbs and I realized time was very important here. I also called Dr. Margaret as I knew she was on her way to work. After several attempts my call just wouldn't go through.

The paramedics were on the way and they kept me on the line. I was using Arne's cell phone. I ran to open the garage door so the paramedics would be able to come in as soon as they arrived.

In that short span of time while opening the garage door and getting back into the bedroom, Arne had lost his urine and was completely unresponsive, staring up into the ceiling and not blinking. I shook him three times, calling his name loudly. The third time he blinked and looked at me but could not respond verbally at all to me. Just then Dr. Margaret returned my phone call on my cell phone.

I told her what was occurring, and she told me to immediately put 2 tablespoons of sugar under Arne's tongue. I ran back to the kitchen, grabbed the sugar container and ran back into the bedroom, having two phones going and sugar container in hand. I put the 2 tablespoons of sugar under Arne's tongue and almost immediately he began to focus.

He asked in a very slurred voice, "*Wass oing on?*"

The 911 dispatcher told me the paramedics were almost there and Dr. Margaret stayed on the other phone, monitoring what was happening also. Our church friend, Gery, also arrived and came into the house and quietly stood by praying. I thought Arne was dying in front of my eyes. I was terrified, yet God gave me a pretty decent calm. My hands were shaking slightly, and I just kept praying audibly. Gery joined me in constant agreement for God's touch.

Arne's body was quivering now but he was becoming easier to understand. He kept asking what was happening to him. About seven minutes went by and the paramedics were by Arne's side, taking blood pressure and vital signs and taking a glucose measurement. They then squirted something pasty into his mouth (more glucose) and five minutes later Arne was able to raise his right arm halfway up.

They said his glucose was 47 when they arrived – which was seven minutes AFTER I had given him the sugar under his tongue. In another five minutes the glucose was 67 and another five minutes it was 85 and 30 minutes after this all began, Arne's glucose was 125 and they told me to make him a sandwich. I instead brought him a protein drink which was perfect.

Arne was completely coherent with all limbs functioning and sitting up in bed with his feet on the floor. It was 8:01 AM. Dr Margaret stayed on the phone with me the entire time. She then said she would see us at 11:15 that morning. There was no need to go to the ER. The emergency was over. Once again, God had spared Arne's life. He had come dangerously close to going into a diabetic coma and possible death. Thank you, Jesus, for your keeping hand on my honey once again...and for Dr. Margaret and the medical staff in our community! I believe with all my heart that God placed Dr. Margaret in our lives some 20 years ago for such a time as this! Father, thank you for your watchfulness over us with Your infinite care!

We saw Dr. Margaret a few hours later and Arne was his normal self completely. She then went over all his medications, taking him off the meds that had been prescribed at the ER that previous Sunday and double checking his entire intake of all medications and supplements, adjusting as necessary. She knew Arne's history and we decided he would NEVER take another medication without her knowledge and approval.

Arne's yeast infection was gone, his UTI was almost gone and the iliopsoas muscle would heal in time. This was just a set-back that God had completely covered, as always! We just praised God for His continual watchfulness over us and attention to detail. People, even doctors, make mistakes. God never does.

I learned how to operate the glucose meter that day and for the next two nights I woke Arne several times during the night, checking on his sugar level, per Dr. Margaret's instructions. It was normal each time. Thank you, Jesus.

I asked Dr. Margaret if we could try oregano oil supplements instead of the glipizide to lower Arne's blood sugar, since there is no drug reaction with the oregano oil and it is a great natural antibiotic and lowers glucose also. She gave the OK and I began giving Arne first one per day, checked the glucose and it was a little high so added a second oregano oil supplement in the evening. His blood sugar was perfect. Yeh – our eliminating sugar from our diet and the natural herb was keeping Arne's sugar in tow! He still took the metformin, but not the glipizide.

We were making progress. I was becoming more knowledgeable about natural healing remedies as well as how to manage this nasty disease of diabetes.

We had prayed for wisdom. God gave it. What a faithful Savior we serve! He cares about every facet of our lives. He is alive and gives us what we need, just when we need it, if we just turn to Him in faith and trust. We may feel forgotten, sometimes, but God never slumbers nor sleeps. He is there on sunny days and He never leaves nor forsakes us on tempestuous, dark days.

"Who remembered us in our low estate: for his mercy endureth forever."
Psalms 136:23

"O give thanks unto the God of heaven: for his mercy endureth forever."
Psalms 136:26

"and lo, I am with you always, even unto the end of the world." Matthew 28:20b

"I will lift up mine eyes unto the hills, from whence cometh my help. My help comes from the Lord, which made heaven and earth. He will not suffer thy foot to be moved: he that keeps thee will not slumber. Behold, he that keeps Israel shall neither slumber nor sleep. The Lord is thy keeper: The Lord is thy shade upon thy right hand. The sun shall not smite thee by day, nor the moon by night. The Lord shall preserve thee from all evil: he shall preserve thy soul. The Lord shall preserve thy going out and thy coming in from this time forth, and even for evermore." Psalms 121 All

Arne continued to give a weekly urine sample to the clinic as Dr. Margaret monitored his bacteria and yeast count. He continued with his physical therapy, making weekly progress as he worked very hard to regain muscle, strength, stamina and endurance.

When a person spends great chunks of time in a bed or chair, not using the body regularly, the muscle tone will go flabby and the body simply will not have the strength it once had. If you don't use it, you WILL lose it. That's just a fact! Arne had now been in ill health for nearly 18 months, off and on. Just as he would begin to recover, he would be shot down with something else, usually another UTI. This was an up and down seesaw of hope, then the dashing of hope, and finally hope again. We hung on to Jesus with the tenacity of that bulldog that locks his jaws and doesn't let go!

Arne began to get strong! His bladder began to operate correctly. He was regaining control with many days in a row without any problems. God was completing the healing He began on February 9, 2017. Remember? The morning of our devotional when we took authority over the bladder and urinary tract system.

So why, on February 9, 2017, didn't God heal Arne's bladder completely? I believe God, indeed, touched his body and he did have a 5-week reprieve from any bladder problems whatsoever.

Did our faith waver? Did we fail to do something for continued healing? No. God touched Arne's body and I believe he gave me the assurance his bladder problems were going to be solved. The timing was still in God's hands.

There are no definitive answers to many of life's issues, my precious friends. That is why this life is called a walk of faith.

Faith in the ONE who holds our hands through every circumstance we will face, and gently takes those hands to follow Him into eternity. He is the light of my path. It isn't mine to question. I just need to hold on to that nail scarred hand of Jesus. We continue to trust, hope and pray. The future is entirely The Lord's. God was continuing to heal Arne's body. One day soon, I believed, Arne would be completely whole, healthy and functioning 100% as God created him to be. That day was getting closer and closer.

In January 2018, Arne's new insurance became effective. He was approved by United Health Care through AARP. We decided it was time for more vigorous physical therapy. Although Arne's tests were all coming back positive, his strength was still lacking. Progress had been made with the Home Health Physical Therapy, but his balance, and overall walking ability, shuffling of feet still were present.

We scheduled an appointment with a neurologist but could not get in to see him until May 16th. Until then Arne would do all in his power to go to rehabilitation faithfully and we prayed for wisdom. Was there more on the horizon or was this all a result of the nearly dying three times and having 8 UTIs in less than 18 months? Only God knew. Ours was to trust and carry on a day at a time.

Arne had a great report from his oncologist in February. All of his tests were right in range with everything being normal. At his next 6-month checkup it would be five years since having the cancer inside his appendix. Dr. S. said Arne would only have to come back for CT scans and follow up tests on an annual basis instead of every six months from now on. Thank you, Jesus. Another victory.

~ THIRTY -SEVEN ~

Saliva Stones

It was December and our son, Buz, had been having pain in his mouth for some time.

He called me one morning saying, *"Mom, I look like a chipmunk and my cheeks are swollen and really painful."*

He had been having pain for some time and decided it was time to see his dentist who referred him to an Orthodontist. He had Saliva Stones in his saliva glands. We had never heard of such a thing! It can be an extremely painful experience, as Buz could attest to personally.

WebMD states, *"A salivary gland stone – also called salivary duct stone – is a calcified structure that may form inside a salivary gland or duct. It can block the flow of saliva into the mouth. The majority of stones affect the submandibular glands located at the inside of the cheeks, or the sublingual glands, which are under the tongue. Many people with the condition have multiple stones. The exact cause is not known, but they mostly contain calcium. The main symptom of salivary duct stones is pain in your face, mouth, or neck that becomes worse just before or during meals. This is because your salivary glands produce saliva to facilitate eating. When saliva cannot flow through a duct it backs up in the gland, causing swelling and pain."*

Because the stones were small, the Orthodontist was able to massage and push the stone our of the duct. Several weeks later it was a different story.

Again, Buz developed pain in his mouth. This time he knew what it was and immediately went to his Orthodontist. However, this stone was quite large and imbedded rather deeply into his mouth. They scheduled surgery for three days later.

When Buz went for hospital pre-admittance, he was told his portion of the expense would be $2100 plus anesthesiologist cost.

He prayed, *"God, you've healed me before...I can't afford that, please take care of this."*

Thirty minutes later the blockage gave way. Surgery was cancelled. Buz was choked up as he told us this and just thanked God for such a gracious and early Christmas gift from his Heavenly Father. God cares about every aspect of our lives! Even our saliva glands. Praise the matchless name of Jesus.

And, as Paul Harvey would say, "NOW FOR THE REST OF THE STORY."

Four months later, Buz had his normal thyroid check-up. He had an enlarged thyroid gland and had been told if that thyroid gland became one milliammeter larger, the thyroid would need to be removed.

Dr. J. asked, *"Buz, why are you here today? What's been going on?"*

Buz explained this was his regular thyroid check-up, but told the doctor about his saliva gland story and how God had taken care of the problem.

Dr. J. remarked, *"The Lord touched more than your saliva glands, Buz. He touched your thyroid gland as well because it is completely normal. It is no longer enlarged at all."*

"Thou art the God that doest wonders: thou hast declared thy strength among the people." Psalm 77:14

~ THIRTY -EIGHT~

Neurological Exam 2018

Arne had his first appointment with Dr. D, a Neurologist associated with Washington Regional Hospital in Fayetteville, Arkansas. A most likable young doctor who seemed knowledgeable and caring. After many questions and evaluations, Dr. D presented us with the findings of Arne's recent MRI brain scan. There were no masses, no evidence of any strokes nor any acute intracranial abnormality identified. There was mild generalized atrophy and moderate severity appearing leukoaraiosis.

Leukoaraiosis: A hidden cause of brain aging. March 2014 <u>Life Extension Magazine</u>

"According to a study conducted at the Mayo Clinic, a surprising number of aging people suffer a condition in which tiny areas of their brain become oxygen deprived. This cerebral vascular deficit sharply increases risk of stroke, dementia and cognitive impairment. Healthy lifestyle choices can prevent and may help reverse it."

"....Imaging techniques have revealed ominous changes found in the brains of more than 60% of people in late middle age and beyond – changes that were once thought to be simply "age spots" on the brain, but have now taken center stage in the battle against age related cognitive decline....known as leukoaraiosis, or "white matter hyperintensities."

Leukoaraiosis is a small vessel disease and is a common finding in stroke patients. A lack of oxygen/blood flow which enhances proper nutrition to these small vessels can cause this disease. The more "unidentified bright white" regions scattered through white matter of the brain (which shows up as bright white spots on a brain MRI), the more damage occurs, resulting in poor function on tests of memory, cognition, gait, and balance. Over time, leukoaraiosis may produce slowed thinking, forgetfulness, disorientation, perseveration (inability to get off of one subject), depression and many other problems.

Leukoaraiosis has many causes and differs from risk factors for larger vessel diseases that cause stroke and heart attacks. The main risk factors for small vessel disease are: Hypertension, Diabetes, Coronary Artery Disease, Obesity, Elevated Homocysteine, Inactive lifestyle, and age over 45 in men and over 55 in women. It can be a result of a stroke.

Arne has had diabetes for over 20 years but had been good in controlling it with diet and being active. He played tennis regularly and cut wood for exercise. He hadn't smoked in over 55 years, didn't use alcohol at all and had low blood pressure. However, the past 2 years with the multiple surgeries, anesthesia from those surgeries, many urinary tract infections and many, many antibiotics brought this nasty diagnosis to our door.

The good news? It can possibly be controlled (and *possibly* reversed) through exercise (50%) proper nutrition, and good supplementation. To that we added, PRAYER. To us, that was the most affective of all. We were on a journey that had changed the course of our lives irreversibly. God was walking with us. It was not an easy diagnosis AT ALL!

In June 2018 Arne had a Psychological Evaluation to determine where on the scale his cognition landed. He was diagnosed with mild cognitive dysfunction in a few areas. His balance and gait had been the most noticeable area affected. On the MRI the "white spots" showed up in the Cerebral part of the skull in what is called the Puns area, which directly affected his balance and gait. His short-term memory was spotty, particularly with names of newer acquaintances and places. At times he was extremely sharp and other times he was not. Physical rest was absolutely essential and relative to his ability to remember and function well.

The brain is a marvelous, living, growing part of our body. It produces millions (and more) new cells daily and is able to make new connections as we "train" it and push it to learn new things. Neighboring cells can take over the function of diseased cells. That brings tremendous hope, and lots of work!

I made it my "job" to become as knowledgeable as possible on this disease as well as anything that was currently available in learning about any and all neurological diseases connected with memory and motor loss. That included Alzheimer's Disease, Dementia, Parkinson's etc.

It is astounding to me that so little has been accepted in the medical community regarding natural supplements. And there ARE many supplements that do not work. The research exists and several well known doctors in every specialty have been stepping forward with phenomenal research data that supports the use of all the above: exercise, nutrition and supplements.

I asked my Heavenly Father to miraculously heal my precious hubby in the powerful name of Jesus. I asked the Holy Spirit to enlighten MY mind to everything I needed in order to be the Care Giver I needed to be. I found that I was sadly lacking in several areas only my loving Heavenly Father could give me. HE can do exactly that!

Some of my mistakes are all too human and heart wrenching. I am thankful Jesus forgives. We pick ourselves up, dust ourselves off, and go on. The following entries are from my broken heart. This was a brand-new arena for us. We had not been here before and the waters were uncharted. I felt as though the bow had broken, the sails were ripping and the boards splitting. At times I felt like I had lost my own heart to the sea's black rage. I would not let my spirit die over this because the Captain who steers our ship had not changed.

~ THIRTY-NINE~

Weddings and Family Reunions

I had prayed and asked God to please keep Arne "OK" for both grandson's weddings. One was April 2018 in Alabama and the other was June 2018 in North Dakota. I wanted special wedding pictures since Arne was their only living grandfather and both boys were very close to him. I wanted Arne looking normal and "being there" in every sense of the word.

This was before we had an actual diagnosis and, quite frankly, I didn't know if Arne would live that long, because I didn't know what we were facing at this time. I just knew he was losing weight at an alarming rate, had no energy, was shuffling his feet as he walked, and his memory was going downhill crazily. It was frightening. God gave the assurance in my heart that Arne would, indeed, be present for those special occasions.

Our wonderful pictures and times together with family was a special gift from God to us. Our only two grandchildren, Paul and Timothy, both were united in marriage by their own father (our son, Bryan) officiating and our other son and wife, Buz and Vicki, present and helping in any way. That is a very special memory to cherish for any parent/grandparent! Both weddings were wonderful, and Arne looked and felt good for both weddings. Thank you, Jesus, for precious memories and answered prayer. You are so faithful to us.

The Jacobson Family Reunion was scheduled shortly after Timothy's wedding in North Dakota. Bryan and DeeDee suggested we stay in ND and ride to Colorado with them to the reunion. Again, another gift from God. We had ridden to Paul's wedding in Alabama with our son, Buz and Vicki, so God provided for us perfectly without due stress on Arne. It was the perfect solution to all situations. Thank you, Jesus. And thank you, Father, for giving us such beautiful sons to bless us all these years! You are an Awesome God!

Bryan and DeeDee planned the trip to Colorado to be no more than 6-hour days so Arne would not become over-tired and stressed. We had separate accommodations at the facility in Estes Park, but the elevation, time change, different beds, different food/meals, different temperature changes, over tiredness and simple stress on Arne affected him immeasurably. His walking and balance became instantly worsened, his memory took a nose dive and he became agitated and restless. I didn't find out until later that we had touched all trigger points for escalating the effects of leukoaraiosis (manifesting the same reactions often as vascular dementia). More about that later.

I did all the driving on the way home. We stopped at dear friend's in Rochester, MN, Ger and Mary Henry, for two nights. Arne seemed to recover somewhat. Our air conditioning had gone out in our car and it was 94 degrees most of the way home. It was beyond miserable! Arne became confused on several occasions, thinking we were on the wrong road and I had to pull over 3 different times to show him, on the map, that we were on the correct path. We finally arrived home at 5:00 pm on a Friday night, having been gone from our home for 5 weeks.

Arne said he would help unload the car later and headed for the shower. I found him in the guest bathroom, drying off with a small hand towel. I asked him why he was showering in the guest bathroom? He said, *"We are at my mother's house, right?"*

I gently and softly explained this was OUR house and we had lived here 21 years. I asked him if he knew who he was.

He said, *"Yes, Bryan."*

I told him to put on his pajamas and I would show him the house. I did. He asked who slept in the guest bedroom. I explained guests who came to visit us stayed in that bedroom. I led him into the living room and sat him down in the lazy boy, telling him to watch some TV. I knew he would fall asleep immediately. I told him to put up the foot rest. He fumbled with it but finally got it up. He fell asleep immediately. I unpacked the car as he slept for about one hour.

I heard the TV go off. Sometimes he can't operate the TV remote. I sat down beside him and asked him if he knew who I was. He said, *"Betty Lou Jacobson."*

I asked him if he knew my relationship to him.

He replied, *"Yesterday I would have said my loving wife, but today I'd say you betrayed me and convinced the boys I shouldn't drive. I can drive as good as the next guy and certainly better than you."*

He got up and went to the correct bedroom, got into the correct side of the bed and slept for 14 straight hours. No bladder problems. His prescription for Toviaz, and prayer have definitely taken care of the bladder problem for him!

The next day Arne was absolutely his old self. Weary and needing more rest, but otherwise completely normal.

Sunday, after being home only one day, we had a Sibling get-together at my sister's house in Branson, MO. Again, Arne demanded to be in command of the route. He had always done the driving and I really had not paid all that much attention, so I wasn't completely sure of the directions. At one point I really thought we should be turning right, but he insisted we turn left. It was the wrong way. We ended up on our way to Springfield, MO where our youngest son and wife live.

We looked at the map and took back roads to Branson, in our hot, non-air-conditioned car, arriving in 3 ½ hours for a normal 2-hour trip. We were both hot and tired and I was cranky inside.

We enjoyed my siblings and our time together and started for home. I had written down the exact route home, with the help of my brother-in-law. However, Arne refused to go "that way." He insisted instead that I take another route the entire way, hounding me to slow down when sometimes I was only driving 45-50 mph on a straight road. It is mostly up and down and very curvy in the Ozarks and we were going through the Mark Twain National Park for this ride home. It was our favorite route, but Arne complained the entire way that I frightened him, was driving too fast and he was as tense as a cat on a hot tinned roof. He becomes agitated and fearful through any construction zone and would never close his eyes and rest because he didn't trust I would know the way.

I wish I could tell you I lovingly and patiently flew victoriously through each of these episodes. I didn't. I simmered inside and more than once raised my voice and told him to please just let me do the driving. This simmering anger was building to a volcano. I just didn't realize it then. I loved this man. I realized he was not himself. I knew it was the leukoaraiosis/dementia controlling his behavior, but it still just compounded as the frustration mounted.

We finally arrived home and he went immediately to bed. I was exhausted and climbed into our pool and cried and prayed and cooled off. There were no loving hugs and good nights when I climbed into bed later. Neither of us spoke a word. It was a first in our marriage and it hurt so deeply.

The next morning Arne seemed normal again. He made his regular oatmeal for us for breakfast, putting everything in it correctly. He couldn't seem to operate the TV remote and I showed him again how to use it. Later in the day we both went into the pool, laughed and joked and he apologized for being a jerk on Sunday at my sister's house and travelling home. He remembered every detail. I found that most interesting.

He had accidentally messed up his phone multiple times, deleting icons, mail, contacts etc., and was having difficulty remembering the code to open his phone. I removed the entry code and placed a sticker on the back of his phone stating to contact me, along with my phone number, in case it became necessary. He was having trouble remembering his credit card password also. This became heart breaking to me. My adorable husband was just not the same man I married. I was slowly losing this precious man.

We had signed up for a Dementia and Care Giver Support Group through the Washington Regional Hospital at the Senior Care Center in Fayetteville, AR. I drove the truck because our car's air conditioning was being evaluated. I drove 70 mph because we were running late. Arne told me I was driving great, but going a bit too fast. I said I was sorry but to please overlook it this time because we were late. He understood and seemed relaxed.

We arrived on time, but no one was there! The Director, herself, had told me over the phone that this group was moving to this date today! None of the secretarial staff knew anything about it. Great – I didn't need this extra stress! Two Social Workers happened to walk by and one of the secretaries snagged them, explained the situation and these two beautiful ladies spent 1 ½ hours having a one-on-one with us personally. They asked many questions, had Arne's medical evaluations, and listened as we recounted the previous 2 months of frustration during our travels as well as stress between us. Arne and I held hands as we shared with them.

They explained the biggest triggers that stress out leukoaraiosis (vascular dementia) patients. We had violated every single one: Unfamiliar places, climate change, different bed, different food, change in times of taking medicines, driving and riding in a car and lack of necessary rest. No wonder Arne had flipped out. He had been subjected to all of the above in the previous two months!

These wonderful gals gave us valuable advice and gave us warm kudos for being able to discuss each situation and face it head on, still loving and supporting each other, in spite of raised hackles. They commented on our faith in God and how important that was for each day ahead. We left encouraged and blessed. The meeting 'mistake' became a God moment for us. The Care Giver Meeting mix-up wasn't ours. But we were thankful it happened!

About a week later when Arne and I were just sitting and visiting together, Arne asked me to tell him exactly what happened on the way home from our vacation/trips and when he thought he was Bryan. I did. He got tears in his eyes. He didn't remember any of the shower incident at all and only vaguely the incidents in the car. He was so sad and asked me to forgive him because of how he treated me and not to allow him to get away with such nonsense. I told him once again it was the disease – not my normal babes! I assured him I loved him deeply and was here for the long haul. It was a tender, sweet and precious moment with my "old" hubby. I treasured those moments. I had no idea how many "normal" moments were ahead, but I was believing the best was yet to come.

I didn't understand how this insidious mind robbing disease worked. Arne seemed to be fine one day and not so good on another day. Sometimes I could see it was related to how well he slept the night before. Other times there seemed to be no relationship to anything we had or had not done. I prayed for wisdom and took it a day at a time. God was teaching me so many things through this.

I have lost my temper in impatience, feeling Arne wasn't trying hard enough or because he was taking forever to do the most simple task. I had so much to do, taking up many of the duties he once did, like yard work and bill paying and still doing all the normal household tasks plus organizing all medical visits and medications while researching ways to make him better.

I was trying to be superwoman, without realizing what I was doing. Anger and resentment were building inside of me and my Heavenly Father took me to the woodshed. He made me realize I just could not do this in my own strength. I needed Him for everything! Every thought had to be given to Him. I needed to take care of my own body, mind, spirit, and emotions as I consecrated it all to Jesus. I WOULD make more mistakes, but I was learning to lean on my Savior in an entirely different realm. Thank you, Jesus.

"Come to me and I will give you rest – all of you who work so hard beneath a heavy yoke. For it fits perfectly. And let me teach you; for I am gentle and humble, and you shall find rest for your souls; for I give you only light burdens." Matthew 11:28-30

The yoke for two oxen consists of placing a heftier yoke on the stronger Ox. The weaker Ox bears the lesser burden. In fact, all the weaker Ox has to do is walk along beside and not pull against the load. The result is no chafing, irritation, abrading, fretting or excoriating. Jesus carries the heavier load when we submit to walking along beside Him and not pulling against His plan. He knows what is best for us and never makes mistakes.

"I want you to be merciful MORE than I want your offerings." Matthew 12:6
(ouch..that means at ALL times, no matter what is happening!)

"For we are responsible for our own conduct." Galatians 6:15

The choice is always OURS. The buck stops at me. I can choose to be bitter or better. I want to be like Jesus – so my choice then obligates me to rely on Him at all times.

"My grace is sufficient for you for My power is made perfect in weakness. I delight in weaknesses, in insults, in hardships, in persecutions, in difficulties. For when you are weak, then I am strong." 2 Corinthians 12:9-10

"For God is at work within you, helping you do what He wants. In everything you do, stay away from complaining and arguing." Philippians 2:14-15

My protesting sabotages my maturity process. Sometimes my prayers are more like complaints.

What about yours?

We must allow Him to clean all the secret places of our heart, every single corner!

"The thief comes to steal, kill and destroy. I am come that you might have life, and that you might have it more abundantly." John 10:10

I cannot do anything on my own. But God has PROMISED to help us when we ask. He desires us to become like Jesus in every way. He will equip us as we seek Him and read His Word and surrender every part of our being to Him.

"I can do ALL things through Christ who strengthens me." Philippians 4:13

"But the fruit of the Spirit is love, joy, peace, longsuffering, gentleness, goodness, faith, meekness, temperance: against such there is no law. If we live in the Spirit, let us also walk in the Spirit." Galatians 5:22, 23, 25

God is outside of time and sees everything from an eternal perspective. It's not over, precious one. Rise up right where you are, stand still and see the Hand of the Lord. Read the end of the Book – Jesus Christ wins! He has ALREADY won the victory and these skirmishes we encounter in our daily lives are only temporary. Look ahead with eyes of faith. We win right alongside Jesus, our Savior.

God often uses hardships to mold us into the person He wants us to be in His Son. God is glorified as we are transformed through suffering. God works in the midst of suffering. His light shines through the crevices of our weaknesses for others to see and be encouraged by His power in our weakness.

We have all had stones in our shoes. Even little stones can irritate and cause discomfort. Let us remove all unwanted stones, remove critical, hateful judgment, bitterness, hurt and self-pity. Stop and take off your shoes. Don't ignore addressing these issues. Guard your heart carefully and then out of the heart the mouth can be a fountain of life, enriching others and pleasing our Heavenly Father.

"Keep your heart with all diligence; for out of it are the issues of life." Proverbs 3:23

"Death and life are in the power of the tongue: and they that love it shall eat the fruit thereof." Proverbs 18:21

Whatever seeds are sown will yield a bumper crop! What kinds of seeds are you sowing?

Winston Churchill said, *"Fear is a reaction. Courage is a decision."*

I urge you to put your trust in Jesus with all your fears and negatives. He will give you the courage, strength and fortitude you need to face each problem and situation daily, hourly. Don't allow fear to steal your constant communion with Jesus. Bring all things to Him and lay every hurt, hardship, discouragement, finances, marriage, health, children – everything – at His feet.

When you operate and walk in His emotions, they will eventually become yours as you become more like Jesus. It cannot be done by yourself. You must give it all to Jesus. Give up and let God do it His way! He will complete what He starts in you. As you do, His joy will explode and expand in you, so you will be able to face any obstacle, any situation in His strength within you.

Believe me, this is the only way! His word confirms it again and again. Feast on His Word and grow in His grace.

The situation may not change, but you will!

God has created us with a capacity for love, hope and beauty because we are created in the image of God. That knowledge assures us that He is able to do exceedingly above and beyond our highest expectations when we put our trust in Him alone.

He has the plan.

He never makes mistakes-EVER!

He has your best interest in His heart and hands. Give Him the reins today. I did, again!

~ FORTY~

Another Neurology Appointment

I had been learning about natural supplements that could help my hubby. Many websites touted the benefits of their products, so I turned to experts in their fields of medicine. After researching nearly 20 different medical experts and each nutritional supplement that was suggested, I began adding selected choices. I had never heard of some of them. Many were difficult to even pronounce and all were expensive.

We settled on a proprietary brand of vitamins, both pills and liquid. Then added the strange sounding supplements like Ashwaghanda, Resveratol, NAC, Protandin and a few others. We found that a supplement called D-Monnia completely cleared up all the bladder urinary tract infections. It was like going on a treasure hunt. Sometimes treasures, sometimes not! We were building up my husband's immune system with Pre-biotics and Pro-biotics, protein and good fats, like Coconut Oil and MCT Oil. Arne began to improve!

We had been on this Ketogenic Way of eating for some time: no sugar, selected good carbs, good fat and lots of fruits and vegetables of all kinds, whether they were liked or not! We were making progress. We began to exercise earnestly, concentrating on core strength. Arne's cognition improved exponentially but his balance and gait remained pretty much unchanged. Some days were better than others.

Arne had his next Neurological exam. After a few minutes the Doctor asked exactly what we had been doing.

We told her, *"Prayer and lots of good vascular supplements and exercise."*

She replied, "Well, keep it up. It's working. He's 100% better than last time." We went home encouraged.

Arne was still tired much of the time, which we really didn't understand. Dr. Margaret suggested another blood work up. After getting the results, she suggested taking him off blood pressure medication, because his BP was excellent. We eliminated Metformin, substituting the natural supplement, Berberine, instead, and because his T3 (part of TSH measurement) was low, added Cytomel. He immediately felt much livelier. Dr. Margaret suggested an Oximetry test, which the VA performed. Arne was found to have extreme Sleep Apnea.

Another reason for his dragging tiredness. A full-scale sleep study followed. Thank you, Lord, for all the wisdom and knowledge you have given us.

Don and Connie, good Minnesota friends as well as RV Maps friends, came to visit for a few days. Don had undergone cancer this past year and was recovering himself. It was wonderful being with great friends. As we played games, I noticed Arne was struggling to remember the rules of a game he had played dozens of times. He was unusually quiet and tired. These ups and downs seemed to be the norm for him and I made it a matter of prayer. There is nothing too hard for our God.

I have been reading "Power in Praise" by Merlin Carrouthers over and over for many years. Does God REALLY expect us to thank Him for cancers, vascular dementia, and everything that happens in our lives?

And why?

Because He wants us to trust Him completely, unreservedly, one hundred percent, without hesitation or restraint.

"But without faith it is impossible to please Him: for he that comes to God must believe that He is, and that He is a rewarder of them that diligently seek Him."
Hebrews 11:6

Believing God is just the beginning. Even the demons believe that much. God will not settle for mere acknowledgment of his existence. He wants our faith in a personal, dynamic relationship with him. This type of a relationship requires complete trust and belief that He really does know what is best for my life at all times, and that He has my best interest at heart. Remember in the book of Jeremiah God says he wants to give us peace, a future and hope? Just digest the following scriptures from Isaiah:

"Lift up your eyes on high, and behold who hath created these things, that bringeth out their host by number: he calleth them all by names by the greatness of his might, for that he is strong in power; not one fails." Isaiah 40:26

V.28-29 "Hast thou not known? Have you not heard, that the everlasting God, the Lord, the Creator of the ends of the earth, faints not, neither is weary? There is no searching of his understanding. He gives power to the faint, and to them that have no might he increases strength." V31 "But they that wait upon the Lord shall renew their strength; they shall mount up with wings as eagles; they shall run, and not be weary; and they shall walk, and not faint."

"Fear not; for I am with you: be not dismayed; for I am thy God; I will strengthen thee; yes, I will help you; yes, I will uphold you with the right hand of my righteousness. V13 "For I the Lord thy God will hold thy right hand, saying unto thee, Fear not: I will help thee." Isaiah 41:10
"Fear not for I have redeemed you, I have called you by your name. You are mine. When you pass through the waters, I will be with you; and through the rivers, they shall not overflow you: when you walk through the fire, you shall not be burned; neither shall the flame kindle upon you." V5 "Fear not: for I am with you.' V11 "I, even I, am the Lord; and beside me there is no savior." V25 "I, even I am he that blotted out your transgressions for my own sake, and will not remember your sins."
   Isaiah 43:1-2

"I will go before you, and make the crooked places straight: I will break in pieces the gates of brass, and cut in sunder the bars of iron: And I will give you the treasures of darkness, and hidden riches of secret places, that you may know that I, the Lord, which call you by your name, am the God of Israel." Isaiah 45:2-3

God wants us to walk by faith and complete trust. Not by fear or feelings. He will ALWAYS be there to open the way, when we allow Him to be in charge – completely!

He has the plan, which may seem even weird to us, but His way is the best way and the only way for complete happiness, peace and joy.

Is everything back to normal? No. There are still strains of music in my heart that yearn for what once was, and times when I feel like some of what we once did has gone out with the tide.

Nothing is lost, even when we think it is. The shipwreck has threatened to destroy our health, our finances, our lives, our hearts, and our home.

However, it will not drown us, but it will transpose and transform us. It opens up another vast potentiality of possibilities that only God knows is ahead. He has The Plan. We are yoked to Him.

~ FORTY-ONE ~

The Cadillac

It was a hot, muggy day when I attended a baby shower at our church for a new mommy. I drove our Buick and was grateful not to have to be in that hot car for very long while traveling to our church just 8 miles away. It was a delightful afternoon. There was a pool party after the baby shower, at a friend's home for all seniors. Yes, we were attending. It was a Luau and we were excited to attend.

We decided to take the truck to the Luau because it had air conditioning that worked. We stopped at a gas station to fill up the tank. Suddenly, I had ants crawling all over my left arm, down my back, inside my top and biting me all over. Thousands of them just swarming like madmen. I couldn't kill them fast enough. I called to Arne and said we had to go home, immediately, so I could get out of my clothes and into the shower. By the time we got back home, he was being attacked by tiny, crazed ants that were eating him alive also!

We quickly disrobed, shook out the ants and climbed into the shower for blessed relief. Forget the pool party! Our evening was ruined. I was discouraged and frustrated.

I prayed, *"God, we need a good used car. I don't care what model, make, color or anything. Just please let the air conditioning work, get decent gas mileage and let it be dependable. I don't have the time or energy to go looking for a* *car, so would you please bring the car right to us? And make it be under $3,000.00."*

Our Buick had serviced us well, getting good gas mileage, didn't burn oil and was nice riding. But it had 217,000 miles on it and we had fixed the air conditioner 3 times already. It was time to give it up.

The next morning in Sunday School, my friend sitting next to me asked why we didn't show up at the pool party. I explained what happened and even told her my prayer.

She said, *"Rick and Sheri sold their home and are going to travel in their new RV. They are selling their Honda Odyssey for $6,000.00."*

That was more than we wanted to spend for a used car, but we decided to talk to Rick about it. Someone else was interested in the car, but we would have next option to purchase it.

I was also taking Sign Language instruction and we always prayed for needs before we began our class. The instructor asked for requests and I said we needed to find a good used car. That was all that was said.

On Wednesday, Rick called and said we could come look at the car on Friday when Sheri would be returning from visiting relatives. We agreed to do so.

It was 7:00 AM on Friday morning when the phone interrupted my devotions. It was a friend from my Sign Language class. She told me that a friend of hers, someone she worked with, was selling a beautiful Cadillac that had been her parents. Her parents had to go into an Assisted Living Facility and could no longer drive. They had a home, furnishings and two vehicles to dispose of – 3 ½ hours from Bella Vista in Oklahoma.

This lady was a teacher and school would begin in another week. She wanted to dispose of as much as possible of her parent's assets before she began teaching and wouldn't have time to commute the 3 ½ hours to finish all sales. The Cadillac was a 2008 DTS, top of the line vehicle and fully loaded with many extras. It was fire engine red. And she was asking $2,500.00.

My first question was, *"What's wrong with the vehicle?"*

Absolutely nothing. She simply didn't have time to transport the vehicle to our area for sale and hadn't been able to sell it up to now, so the first person who showed up to their garage could have the car for cash. It sounded too good to be true. My friend said she and her hubby would take us there to see the car that afternoon. We agreed.

We could tell this couple, who was trying to sell the Cadillac, was under stress with all that had happened with her parents and the time deadline for them ahead. We asked if we could pray with them. They said that would be fine.

As I began praying, they both were quietly murmuring, out loud, *"Yes, Lord. Thank you, Jesus. Yes, Lord."*

When I finished praying, I said, *"You obviously know Jesus as your personal Savior?"*

They both smiled and said, *"Oh yes!"*

They said their father regularly had the oil changed on the car, never had any problems and except for a few scratches her father had put on the car, nothing was amiss at all. The V8 engine looked clean as a whistle and brand new. The service records were impeccable with regular check-ups and oil changes. The cream, leather interior was perfect, and they were getting 20 miles per gallon. Everything worked perfectly. And we were an answer to this precious couple's needs as well. Yes, God is good!

Long story short: we drove this beautiful red Cadillac home that day. It was gorgeous! And it drove like a dream!

Upon arriving home, we immediately called Rick to tell him what had happened. He said, *"Praise the Lord!"*

Then he explained that some other good friends wanted his Honda but he had promised it to us first. The other couple bought his car and we all were blessed. God gave us a beautiful vehicle for an unheard-of great price. The next week we sold our Buick to a Salvage yard for twice the price they quoted over the phone. God is so very faithful and gives his children way beyond what we can begin to imagine.

These past three years have been challenging financially with all the medical expenses, necessary supplements, doctor visits and unexpected extras that have exceeded our budget considerably. Yet God has supplied every need, every time. He is so faithful and good. We have tithed regularly and given beyond normal when God touched our hearts toward others. Now He was pouring His blessing back to us and I knew He was smiling as He saw our joy too. What a loving Heavenly Father we have. We are so blessed!

It was beginning to get colder outside and I noticed it was warm on the passenger side of our Caddy, but cold on the driver's side. We took it to the dealer to have it checked out. It was a module that required removing the dash completely to replace a $2.40 module. With labor, this would cost us nearly $1,200.00 Ouch!

We were just beginning to get out of the hole and save a little toward new needed kitchen appliances. OK, I grumbled a little and wondered why God would allow this. But we had the money from a fishing boat we had just sold to a friend. God had provided the entire amount and the heat felt marvelous. We still had a really good deal in our vehicle.

Soon after we discovered the shocks were not in the best shape. Not serious, but we knew we couldn't go indefinitely without changing them or damage to the car could occur. Saving the needed $1300-1500 dollars began again. I questioned God as to whether this car was really such a great deal. I continued to practice trusting that He really had the plan for our good from this. After all, Arne and I never gave **our** kids junk gifts or lemons! And God is OUR father. Yet the niggling doubts persisted. *I'm sorry, Lord. I believe, help thou my unbelief.* We decided to just wait until after Christmas to do anything about the shocks – maybe longer!

CHRISTMAS 2018

Bryan and DeeDee from Ellendale, North Dakota came the week before Christmas, as did Paul and Haley from Washington, DC. Oh, what a joy and privilege we had to have them stay a week with us over the holidays. Bryan and Paul helped Arne chop wood, fix several things that needed fixing, including a small leak in the attic that would have become a big problem! What a blessing they were to us, besides the fun we shared playing games and just being together. Arne had improved considerably in his memory over the last time Bryan and DeeDee saw him and it was a confirmation to us that they too saw an improvement. Arne's balance, however, was going from bad to worse and totally unpredictable. One day he could be great and the next falling all over the place and bent over like an old man.

We began praying for those "bright spots" that showed up in the brain MRI would be healed and replaced by healthy brain cells. We continued to ask our Healer for that gift of healing. Arne used his walking stick to give himself balance and was once again in physical therapy to help him gain muscle strength in his legs and arms. God was in control and I was able to thank the Lord for Arne's diagnosis because I knew God knows the future. God knows what He is doing and going to do. I was content with whatever the outcome, but I expected the Best was Yet to Come!

Buz was able to join us on Christmas Eve also. Vicki had a family emergency so was unable to come, but Buz slipped away for a couple hours so he could be with us a bit over the holidays too. It was a precious Christmas to remember for a very long time.

More Cadillac Repair?

"Did you know that your right rear taillight and turn signal light do not work?"

This was the Sunday after Christmas and our family had just left the day before. No, we didn't realize this and thanked our fellow parishioner.

Monday morning, I called the Cadillac dealer to ask how much it would cost to replace a couple of lights in the rear taillight area. I was told this is an LED module that was $400.00 per side plus $455.00 labor plus tax!

He said, *"And of course you would want to replace both sides, right?"*

I replied, *"No, not at that price! I'll have to get back to you for an appointment."*

I started to bemoan and begrudge the Caddy, wondering if we needed to unload it because if this was going to happen often, well, it was something we just could not afford. I tried to praise and thank God because I truly believed He gave us this car. My emotions were *so* conflicted.

Guess what? God understands. He made us. He also came and lived as a human person on this earth. He experienced all the emotions that we have, except He never gave in to them – EVER! He was totally without sin. He understands our feelings, hurts, doubts and discouragements.

Arne checked with an auto body shop across from our church and was told that they replaced those type modules and didn't charge nearly as much for labor. He could probably even get us a used light module for a lot less. We prayed for wisdom....and waited.

Two weeks went by. Arne came home from Physical Therapy, parked the car in the garage and came inside. Later he went into the garage to get something and thought it looked like one of the lights in the rear area was on, so got into the car to be sure nothing was accidentally left on. He tried starting the car. The dash lit up with every conceivable light on the entire front of the car dash. WOW, we didn't know there were so many idiot lights. He shut it off and tried again. After the third try, the car went completely dead, dark with no lights of any kind. Extremely dead, in the garage. Very, very dead!

I leaned my head back and prayed, *"God, we don't know what to do. We just can't afford any more surprises here. Please give us wisdom."*

I heard the Holy Spirit whisper into my heart, *"Are you still going to praise me?"*

I hesitated, then answered, *"God, you got me! I consciously decided and had told you I was going to praise you for everything – no matter what it was. Yes, I thank you that this car is as dead as a doornail. I don't have a clue what we should do. I haven't any idea how this could possibly work out, but you've got it. This is your problem and I choose to thank you for it because you have The Plan ALWAYS."*

We got out the book. Seems like the battery is under the back seat - really? We decided we better call Triple A for towing to the Cadillac dealer. Arne was quite certain the mother board of the electrical system probably was out! Triple A said we would have to have the dealer tow the car in. I called the Cadillac dealer. She said it sounded like a battery to her and gave us a tow number. It was another Triple A dealer just 15 minutes from our house.

A young man came, connected the cables, jumped the car and it started immediately. All the lights on the dash showed normal!

He said, *"If I were you, I would drive it a little to charge the battery, then take it to an auto body repair shop (yep, the one across from our church that Arne had already visited) because they are fair and will advise you what to do."*

We did exactly that!

Larry met us at the door, ushered us into his office and remembered Arne's having been there and about the problem with the car's signal/taillights. He made a call and said they could put in a used part, labor complete for $211.30 the next day. *Yes, yes, yes*, I told him!

He said, *"Let's take a look at it first before I order the part."*

Outside we went, opened the trunk and he reached in, tore away the lining by the light, dug around a little and pulled out something. He looked at it, put his hand back into the cavity, did something for a moment and pulled his hand out. He put the lining back in place, gave the taillight a couple of little taps with his hand and said,

"Start the car now."

It started up and all the lights were working properly. It had been a loose connection! No charge!

I hugged Larry and thanked him profusely. He said to keep an eye on it, but it would probably run for a long time to come. He suggested we have the battery checked just to be sure, but the car started right up every time so there was probably no problem.

I went home and baked oatmeal chocolate chip cookies, chocolate candy and homemade muffins. I hiked my bod to the auto body shop that afternoon and Larry was standing by the door as I arrived. I asked if I could see him in his office a moment.

I gave Larry the goodies and then said, *"Larry, I don't know what you believe, but I want to let you know that you were part of a miracle today for us."*

I then told him how Arne had nearly died three times in the past couple of years, how our finances had been drained, how we had gotten this car and what had occurred so far. I told him, I had also prayed for guidance regarding keeping or selling the car. Two other mechanics had told us we had a really great car and got a deal when we purchased it, and even if we put a couple grand into it, we would still get our money back if we sold it. They all suggested we fix the few things and keep it.

I had prayed and asked God to use this auto estimator to give us our final answer – that the Holy Spirit would speak the truth through him to us. When I had asked Larry earlier what he thought of the car, he had answered that a Cadillac in that good condition, with that low mileage was one great deal and he had seen many Cadillacs go over 250,00 miles without a single problem. He said if it was his, he would keep it. That had settled it for Arne and I.

I told Larry all of this. He put his big arms around me and said, *"BJ, I'm a Baptist minister who believes every word you spoke. I know how the Holy Spirit works in our lives, and I'm just thankful to be a part of this miracle."*

He then prayed for Arne's complete healing, for peace and grace and favor on us both with blessings from heaven upon us. What a day this has been! God knew all along what He was going to do. He just needed to see if I was ready to praise Him anyway. What a Big God we serve!

We are SO blessed!!!

To be blessed means to be fully satisfied. To thrive on the inside even if life is falling apart on the outside. It is knowing the sweet communion of the Holy Spirit and God's love even when things around us are bitter, hurting and we don't understand. It is not blind trust. It is trust that has been forged out of the experiences that God has brought us through, and the knowledge that He will see us through <u>all</u> the way to our heavenly home. It is trust based on factual experience. We have a Bible full of testimonies of why we can trust Our Father completely. There is nothing blind about that kind of trust. It truly is a blessing.

The road has not always been easy, but we have never had to navigate it alone. We shared a devotional time together daily and we prayed for our loved ones and others often during any given day. Jesus Christ is the center of our home. He is the light that guides our steps now and until the day He takes us home. I know someday one of us will say our final farewell to the other here on earth. I have mixed emotions when I think of that.

I am not afraid of death. The Bible says, *"to be absent from the body is to be present with the Lord."* That is a wonderful thought – for the one who gets to leave first. It is very lonesome for that one still here on earth. I prefer the package plan. I hope we are alive when Jesus Christ comes back to earth for His children, so we can go up in the sky together *"and forever be with the Lord."*

Until that time, we live each day and occupy until He returns for us. We plan for the future, but hold lightly to the things we have here on earth because this is not our permanent home. It has been a beautiful temporary home, filled with excitement, love, fun and adventure. I love this extravagantly designed world with all its varied terrain, intriguing animals and fascinating experiences just waiting for our exploration. It is anything but drab, boring and dull. It has been exciting for us.

If we think this life and world is full of wonder, please notice what we can expect ahead:

"But as it is written, Eye hath not seen, nor ear heard, neither have entered into the heart of man, the things which God hath prepared for them that love him."
I Corinthians 2:9

So, *"to live is Christ and to die is gain." Philippians 1:2*
That means we win either way!

I am content to trust My Lord to choose that final day for me. Until then I will simply trust and thank Him for each day He gives. All my tomorrows are in His hands.

How about you?

God doesn't care about the mistakes you've made – He simply wants all of your heart.

~ FORTY-TWO ~

The Beginning of Another Nightmare

Be careful what you say. Words are either life or death. Speak only words of encouragement and positive lifting. Watch your tongue. Choose your words carefully. You will give account for every word spoken.

"Keep your eyes open for spiritual danger. Stand true to the Lord. Act like men – be strong. And whatever you do, do it with kindness and love." I Corinthians 16:13

He sees our tears. May our pain, deep grief and sorrow in the midnight hours help us to see God's thoughts toward us are good. He loves us with a deep everlasting love and draws us to Himself in our most broken places. He wants to hold us in our darkest hours and give us comfort and solace. God can transform our grief with His love and hope.

"He keeps all my tears in a bottle." Psalms 56:8

April – June 2019

Some of Arne's siblings came for a visit over Mother's Day and it was a precious time for all. All 7 of them stayed in our home for 3 wonderful days of love, prayer and encouragement. Arne was feeling quite well most of the time.

Arne had already had the sleep study and badly needed to be using a continuous positive airway pressure (CPAP) machine regularly every night. He had just started to use the CPAP at night and was having a difficult time adjusting and was tired all the time. I noticed him being "spacey" at times with his thinking and expressing himself. He had more difficulty with his balance and memory. He was forever messing up his cell phone, losing icons or not remembering how to use the phone. He misplaced his keys, wallet, checkbook, hat, shoes – just about everything. This was so frustrating to me, but I realized that he truly could not help it. His mind just was not functioning normally at times. He tried so very hard. This was crushing my heart into jagged shards of pain.

I had gotten so upset with him that he sometimes thought I didn't love him anymore.

"God, help me to be more patient, loving and kind. Curb my impatience. Help me to learn everything does not have to be done perfectly. Help me to remember that my wonderful husband is more important than anything else, except You, Father. I feel so guilty. I feel so tired. I feel so alone, and like a failure. God help me please."

Arne had another brain MRI the end of June. The results were the same. Nothing had changed, for good or bad. That was actually good and said we were doing something correctly. However, his balance and memory keep deteriorating.

The lawn needed mowing and Arne lost the key to the rider mower. I ordered 2 new keys from the manufacturer. It had been raining. The weeds were proliferating again and I had injured my shoulders and right arm from over-doing. I had been going to the chiropractor twice weekly and she said my back, neck and shoulders were so tight they were trying to pull my arms out of the sockets, which was why they were so painful.

I realized I had been trying to keep the CPAP on Arne at night. He couldn't put it back on once he took it off. He needed that machine to regulate his breathing. He would quit breathing 47 times out of every hour. No wonder he had been so tired and wanted to sleep all the time. But I could not get up and fix it for him 2-3 times a night and not go back to sleep. I was exhausted and could see the signs of burn-out in myself. I needed wisdom, Lord.

Recently I had been (lovingly) told that I had to humble myself and ask for help when I needed it! Pride is a sin. This attitude of *"I can do it myself (even with God's help)"* is not pleasing to God. People WANT to help, but don't know how.

My beautiful new neighbor said, *"I'm going to mow tomorrow so how about I mow your yard at the same time?"* He added, *"all you have to do is ask! I will help you anytime you need me."*

I reached out to another couple about spraying my weeds and they were Happy to do it for me and said, *"Anytime. Just ask."*

It is SO hard to ask for help when I felt like I should be doing these things myself. I could handle taking care of Arne, the house, finances, groceries and cooking, but the yard did me in.

I realized that all the years we helped others when they needed help was a <u>joy</u> for us. Now I could not rob others of the blessings God gave us when we served others. It is truly easier to give than receive. Yes, it is also humbling. God was shaving off all the little corners of my life to make me what He wanted me to be. It was a tearing, ripping, painful process and I didn't like it one bit.

One day Arne was trying to teach me how to put air in the car tires. He couldn't find all his little hoses and adapters for the compressor so we went out and purchased another set of pneumatic gauges and necessary items. (we found the old ones two days later).

As Arne was trying to show me, I realized he didn't know how to attach them correctly. Our neighbor saw what we were doing and came over to help. He put the parts together and showed me how to inflate and deflate the tires.

The car was partially out of the garage and Arne said he would pull it back into the garage. That was fine. He couldn't get both legs lifted to get into the car so left his left leg hanging out. No problem, he only had about two feet to go. I noticed he hesitated as if he wasn't sure which gear to use, then put it into drive and moved it about 3 inches. I was standing beside the open door and told him he needed to go further because the car was not in the garage. He argued that it was fine. I told him it was not fine and the garage door would crush the trunk. He turned off the car, got out, looked at the back of the car, got back in, turned the car on and moved the car ahead 3 more inches.

I told him that the hanging tennis ball was supposed to be against the windshield when he was properly inside the garage all the way, so he needed to move forward more. He said, *"NO, this is fine."*

He repeated the process of checking the back of the car, getting back in and starting the car again. I could tell how agitated he was becoming, how hot and humid it was and how tired I knew we both were. I asked him to let me finish putting the car in the garage. He just shook his head and said *NO*. He then tried to pull the car door closed with me in the way and put the car in reverse.

I said, *"NO, that's the wrong gear. You need to go forward."*

He then shut the car off and told me to go into the house. I pleaded with him to please give me the key, but he refused. I quickly leaned over and grabbed the key out of the ignition. He grabbed my hand, but I was now stronger than him and used my other hand to pry his hand off mine. I told him he was not thinking clearly and should not be driving now.

He got out of the car faster than I thought he could move, raised his fist and said, *"I could pop you in the mouth for that."*

I **quietly** replied, *"No honey. I'm stronger than you and I would have to deck you if you tried that."*

He smiled, slightly, anger diffused. I told him to please go into the house where it was cool, drink some water and sit down please. He did. I finished the job of parking and putting everything away. That was as close to any anger I had observed from my mild mannered, polite and gentle husband to this point.

I checked on him in the living room, then went into the bedroom and cried. This just was not my loving, gentle hubby. *God, I hate this!* I rested a bit and his younger sister called. We talked some, then I brought the phone out to Arne and they chatted awhile. When he was free, I simply sat down by him, put my arms around him and held him. He responded back and held me tenderly.

I asked him to kiss me.

He said, *"I didn't think you would ever want me to kiss you again."*

I assured him I would never stop loving him and his mind was just not cooperating and he wasn't himself. It broke my heart. He knows something is really wrong, but he isn't able to reason it all out appropriately. This slow death of the person I once knew, is a hideous disease that slowly robs its victims of dignity, reason and living. It is horrible for the ones they love.

July - September 2019

Arne had been having delusions lately. We had watched a program on TV about sextuplets and their birthday party. Shortly after he asked me where all the children were that we brought home with us. I asked him where had we gotten these children and he said he thought maybe church, but where were they now?

I asked, *"Did you actually see these children?"* *"Oh yes,"* he replied.

He said he saw them playing and having a ball on our side yard. I finally got the connection and explained it was a TV program, but I could see the doubt in his eyes.

Another night we watched a zoo TV program about the care of their animals. They were trying to catch a particular animal for a check-up but the animal didn't want to be caught.

Arne said, *"Don't you think we should go now?"* And he started to get up. I asked him where should we go? He said, *"Don't you think we should help them find the animal?"*

The program was so real to him that he thought we were there and his gentle, giving heart was willing and ready to help, if he could. So very like him. Always giving.

Other times he thought we had guests in our house. These episodes became almost a nightly thing yet in-between he was lucid as can be. He would often ask what happened to the lady or man that was sitting in the living room chair. It freaked me out the first time this happened, but I got to answering that I didn't know but he/she must have left.

Another day in October when it was very cold out and there was ice on our pool, I came into the bedroom to find him in swimming trunks. I asked him what he was doing. He said a young lady came and told him that all the people were in the pool and we should come too.

I told him he would freeze his bippies if he went outside like that, then took him back into the family room where he could see the pool and I pointed out the frozen water on the top of the pool cover. He looked so puzzled and I gently told him his mind was playing tricks on him again and it was alright. Nothing to be concerned about. Hugging him, I simply helped him change into warm clothes. This defied logic, but I was learning this was quite normal for vascular dementia. Oh, how I hated it! What a demeaning disease.

We watched a 60 Minutes program one evening about Nuclear Submarines that were protecting and on alert in the middle eastern waters. This captured his attention because he had served on The USS Odax SS484, a conventional submarine, while in the Navy. During a commercial he stood up. I asked where he was going and he said to *"pee."* He then went to our atrium door, facing our neighbor's house, and started to open the door. I asked why he was going outside.

He answered, matter of fact, *"Sweetheart, when you are on a Sub, you can just pee over the side."* I replied that we were not on a submarine. He insisted that we were.

I got up, opened the door and inquired, *"Do you see any water out there, sweetheart?"* He looked and said he didn't.

I gently said, *"That's because we are in our house tonight and that means you cannot pee outside where neighbors could see you."*

He just said, *"OK"* and went to the restroom.

Frequently he had forgotten where the bathroom in our house was located and would ask where it was. I would lead him to it and he would take care of business. We had lived here 25 years. I was seeing more and more lapses and less lucidness. I was losing him an inch at a time. My heart was breaking.

We had discussed the driving issue. I had allowed him to drive to and from church, but his judgment and reaction time was not what it should be for the safety of all concerned.

This is a very difficult issue with almost all older people who have to give up their independence. I fully understood and sympathized but I could not risk Arne's life or the life of some other innocent person by continuing to allow him to drive. Our sons discussed this with him, from the standpoint of how devastating it would be if he took the life of some young mother or father, leaving children orphaned, or took a child's life. This always got his attention.

I had attended a Care Giver's Meeting at a local Methodist Church and the issue of driving had been discussed that time.

I tried one suggestion: *"Honey, you have driven 56 of our married years! I think it's my turn to have a shot at it! Can we at least try that?"*

I also told him he was too precious to me to take any chance of losing him. It worked. Although, he would remind me that he was a good driver and really didn't see why he shouldn't be driving.

October 2019

I had another melt down. I guess I figured I would never have another one because God is big enough to keep me strong! Well, He can, but I don't seem to learn the lessons easily that I need to learn.

I cried more tears and asked God WHY? Why was He allowing this in our lives? Arne had been a wonderful husband, a good father, a man of integrity, a strong, Christian man of God.

"Why haven't YOU done something about this yet? It's been almost 4 years now. How long, Lord? All you have to do is say the word! I fairly shouted at God to PLEASE speak to me."

Silence stretched for several minutes and then I did hear God speak in my heart.

He said, *"I want you to obey me. I want you to let go and give this to me. All I have asked you to do is take your hands off and trust me. Just let go and trust me."*

How many times do I need to be told????? I keep trying to do it myself with vitamins, supplements, CPAP machine, exercise and any new idea that I hear. Most of these are good, but God doesn't need a single one of these. He may use them, but He needs none of them. He is a creative God. He doesn't need my help. I think he tires of my pushing and fretting to get it all done right! I wept in His presence and once again repented.

I felt like all I had been doing those past six months was apologizing to Jesus and Arne for my temper, impatience and trying to do it my way! I needed to give up. I needed to let it go. I needed to just let God be God. I needed to trust Him. I think I do, but I keep interfering with what I am supposed to do. I needed to accept help. I needed to ask for help when I needed it. I needed to quit being the perfectionist I have been all my life. I needed to quit thinking *"I can do it myself."* This is such a difficult journey. I could not do it by myself. I needed Jesus and I needed others. They are Jesus with skin on! Help me Jesus to let go, trust you and rest in your arms.

Do not ask me to remember

Do not ask me to remember
Do not try to make me understand.
Let me rest and know you're with me.
Kiss my cheek and hold my hand
I'm confused beyond your concept.
I am sad and sick and lost.
All I know is that I need you to be with
Me at all cost.

Do not lose your patience with me.
Do not scold or curse my cry.
I can't help the way I'm acting
Can't be different though I try.
Just remember that I need you.
That the best of me is gone.

Please don't fail to stand beside me.
Love me 'til my life is done.

Author unknown

I began having Vertigo attacks. The first one was on a hot-day, the ambulance was called and I was taken to the hospital. I was cold sweating profusely, could not stand up without falling over, was nauseous and vomiting and had a bad headache. I knew I wasn't having a stroke because I could talk correctly and lift both arms up above my head but I did think I might be having a heart attack.

I called my Dr. Margaret at work. I had NEVER done that before and thankfully she was able to answer. She called the ambulance as I called our pastor and asked if he could send someone over to be with Arne. He came himself and sent one of his secretaries to be with me in the ER. Four hours later I was stable and sent home. I had every test imaginable and was 100% healthy. Dehydration and stress was the verdict. Dr. Margaret had been telling me for some time that she could see me becoming more and more stressed and she was going to order Home Health Care to assist me with Arne. That turned out to be a huge blessing.

Laughter doeth good like a medicine, the Bible says!
I will take all the humor I can get!

One morning we had a strange taste to our oatmeal. Arne has always made great Microwave oatmeal for us with cinnamon, real maple syrup, unsweetened coconut and raisins. I saw these black flecks floating in the milk, but didn't see any cinnamon. I asked him what he put into the oatmeal that was different. He didn't know. I tasted it and realized it was seasoned with Italian Seasoning. The cinnamon stands right next to the Italian Seasoning in the cupboard. Arne has no taste (because of diabetes) so he didn't have a clue as to what he had done. We had a good laugh along with unusual tasting oatmeal that day.

Arne had always put together our morning vitamins. I had them marked with a black marker so he would know who took what and how many of each. However, I noticed there were daily mistakes. He couldn't keep it straight and it was becoming stressful to him. I gladly took over that job as well as the oatmeal making. I was getting in the wood for our wood burning stove and he wanted to help me, but he was just too weak and unsteady. I could not risk him falling more than he already had done. I suggested he watch me and open and close the door for me. He often said how he felt useless, which broke my heart. I assured him that he had taught me everything I knew and was still giving me wonderful advice on the running of our household. I knew he felt badly and he knew he was fading. He had admitted to me that he knew he was losing his memory.

When we had gotten the diagnosis that Arne had some form of dementia and possibly other yet undiagnosed maladies, Arne asked approximately how long he had to live. He was told 3-5 years. When we got home, he looked at me and said,

"Hon, it's a win, win situation all around. If I die, I'll go to be with Jesus. If I live, I will get to stay with you. I worry about leaving you alone, Sweetheart."

I found out much later our Neurologist had suspected a form of dementia, called Lewy Body Dementia, but it is very difficult to diagnose, and often cannot be diagnosed until after death.

Arne's physical therapists, occupational therapists and speech/memory therapists were all marvelous and so very patient. Arne tried so very hard to please them and comply with their wishes and instructions.

We had a bath aide that came twice weekly to shave, shower and dress Arne. At first, he objected but I reminded him that I had male doctors who saw all my private parts and this was no different. They all happened to be born-again, God-loving, Christians who gave more than just physical therapy. They gave hugs, prayers and encouragement. Arne seemed to be doing really well and was using his walker better and now always using his cane when we went to church too. Progress.

When the lights went out

I awoke with a start. The house was as black as the ace of spades! I ran my hand over Arne's side of the bed – no Arne. I sat up and called Arne's name.

He answered, *"I'm in here."*

He sounded far away. I fumbled out of bed, became disoriented so went back to bed and felt for the flashlight on my nightstand. Finally, a tiny bit of light! I gingerly ventured into the kitchen, found a larger flashlight and proceeded to look for Arne. No Arne anywhere.

Back into the bedroom again and I called out, *"Arne, where are you?"*

Again, he simply said, *"In here."*

That was always his reply, which told me nothing! But I went into our master bathroom, and there he was, sitting on the bottom of the shower stall, elbows on his knees, just waiting.

I asked him what in the world he was doing in the shower. He said he had gotten up to use the bathroom and all the lights were off so he couldn't see and ended up in the shower. He thought it better to just sit down and wait until he could see so he didn't kill himself tripping into something. HOW he managed to actually get into the shower, step over the higher lip, and make it safely to a sitting position without falling and hitting his head on the tile floor, I will never know.

I got us back into bed and thanked the Lord for protecting Arne from potentially lethal falls and harm.

The Lord simply dropped into my mind, *"See, I can take care of Arne just fine."*
Unspoken thought…..*you can trust me*!

~ Forty -Three ~

The Long Goodbye

The episodes of hallucinations escalated exponentially. As did my Vertigo attacks. I was having an attack 3-5 times per week and sometimes daily. I was taking Dramamine which helped if I could take it immediately before it became a full-blown Vertigo attack. These would last anywhere between 1 – 4 hours each time. I was having to call on friends and neighbors to come be with me because I couldn't keep an eye on what Arne was doing since I couldn't get up without falling myself. Eventually, I would ask Arne to just sit with my feet in his lap because it made me feel safe – I so needed his presence and touch. Besides if he was near, I knew what he was doing. It was like watching a precious

3-year-old whose curiosity would get him into all kinds of trouble.

He took off doorknobs that he thought needed fixing, only to forget how to put them back on. Anyone who came to visit became my next repairman. I was grateful for every kind of assistance.

He was always trying to operate the television and the Direct TV repairman became a constant visitor on a first name basis. I was becoming dependent on others to pick up groceries and drive us where we needed to go. I was exhausted all the time. I was awakening at 4:30 and 5:30 AM, but I also was going to bed with Arne by about 8:30 or 9:30 nightly. Surely, I was getting plenty of sleep? Unfortunately, it doesn't work that way.

Arne was becoming agitated, not just in the evening (Sundowner's Syndrome), but all day long. We would go through the same scenario daily.

Arne: *"What is the plan for today Babes? When are we going home? (He was back in Minnesota in his mind). Shouldn't we pack the car to go home? Where are we going to sleep tonight? Whose house is this? Wow, we have two houses? This is a gigantic house (only 2000 sq ft). How can we afford all this? Where did we get all this furniture?"*

I discovered that the best thing to do was to never disagree, argue or try to reason with a dementia patient. They are simply unable to reason. They mean well, they truly see what they see, even if it is not there to you. They feel threatened if you raise your voice, and at least my hubby would feel sad and down if I corrected him or seemed irritated by his actions. I realized Arne could not help how he was, or how he thought, or what he did. It was this maddening, menacing, diabolical, disturbing disease that was slowly eating away my beautiful husband's ability to be HIM. I loved him so! I no longer corrected him and I made a deliberate effort to just make him feel loved and safe.

Dementia is often called, "The Long Goodbye." A very true, pernicious and baleful definition that devastates the soul.

At first, I explained to him that he had built this house. I took him on a tour of the house, pointing out special features he had created and how we had added the family room addition, the decks and pool. He would be amazed, but did not remember a thing of it. The next day we would go through the same set of questions. I quit doing tours.

I would just answer things like, *"We will be here tonight, Honey. This is where we are staying now, Sweetheart."*

He never stopped asking the same questions and never remembered any of the answers. I lovingly answered his same questions daily, almost always punctuated by a hug or kiss. My heart just continued to splinter.

I knew what was ahead and began to up my work on compiling information for our boys, in case of both of our deaths. We visited a lawyer and signed Power of Attorney papers to add to our already Power of Medical Attorney papers we had done over 10 years prior.

I began checking with the Veterans Administration to see what assistance may be available, if needed. And I got out our Long-Term Care documents and began to underline and highlight key information. I had been compiling a 3-ring binder of pertinent information along with copies of our donating our bodies to the University of Arkansas Science for medical purposes. I had copies of every credit card, driver's license and all insurance information. Our sons only needed to pick up and follow instructions in this 3-ring binder, at our passing. I finally completed this important binder of information in October 2019. I sent a copy of our Power of Attorney to our Long-Term Care Insurance Company.

Arne continued to decline mentally and physically, in spite of the Home Health physical, occupational and voice/memory caregivers who were coming regularly each week. I also had an aide that came to bathe and shave Arne twice weekly. He could still toilet himself, but could not wash his own hair or properly wash his body by himself. I had been helping him dress for about 3 months already. He could not navigate the Depends accurately, often getting 2 legs into an opening and becoming frustrated, or just pulling them up, thinking they were ok – his private area exposed – a sight to behold. We laughed at many of these things together. It is better to laugh than cry, and I was crying inside. I was losing my precious husband, best friend, lover and my spiritual covering an inch at a time. It was devastating and I cried more tears than I knew I had in my body.

Arne often struggled with his CPAP apparatus regularly. No, nightly! I would awaken to find him attempting to scrunch up the hose and place it under his pillow. He fought with it like it was some huge serpent attacking him. It, being filled with air, only bounced back to its original size to attack him again. It was actually very humorous to watch this, and knowing Arne as I did, I knew he would have laughed right with me. I was not laughing at the frustrated situation, or at Arne at all. It was something like a clip from a Laurel and Hardy movie.

I was finally able to wrap the hose around the bedpost and tuck it under his pillow with just enough hose to reach his face. This only worked temporarily and eventually a hole appeared in the hose, rendering it unusable. I ordered another hose. However, it never arrived in time for him to get to use it.

Without the CPAP, and waiting for the replacement hose to arrive, Arne was getting less actual sleep. Consequently, he was wanting to go to bed earlier and earlier each night.

~ FORTY-FOUR ~

Friday, Nov 8, 2019   A Cherished Memory

It was 5:30 PM and Arne said he had to go to bed and wanted me to go with him. I said I just could not go to bed that early, but tucked him in and he promptly fell asleep. I was working on my laptop when at 8:30 PM Arne came walking out – actually, walking normally and standing up straight, no balance problems at all.

He sat down on the love seat across from me and asked, *"Hon, would you come sit by me for little while?"*

Absolutely, and I closed my laptop. As I sat beside him, he tucked his arm around me and snuggled me very close, kissing my nose and forehead.

Arne: *"I have to ask you some questions that I need the answers to, but I hate to ask you."*

I told him he could ask me anything and I would answer him fully and honestly.

Arne: *"When were we married?"*

I replied: *"1963."* Pause.

Arne: *"Wow, that was a long time ago. We sure have had a lot of fun times together, haven't we? We've laughed a lot, loved a lot and made so many memories together. I sure do love you, Babes. (He kissed me ever so gently, almost reverently.) You've made me so happy, Sweetheart. You are all I ever wanted and more. I don't know how I was ever so lucky to get you for mine. (more gentle kisses and caresses.)"* Pause.

Arne: *"How many children do we have?"*

I replied: *"Two sons. Do you know their names?"*

Arne, *"Bryan and Buz. I just wanted to be sure I hadn't left someone out."*

Me: *"Do you know our daughter-in-law's names."*

Yes, he did. Did he know our grandson's names? Yes, he did. Their wives? Yes, he did.

Then Arne proceeded to ask me all kinds of logistical questions about how we came to Bella Vista. Yes, *he remembered where we were*. He wanted to know about our move from Rochester, Minnesota and about our house and his building it. Details.

We talked for almost an hour and I realized he was getting really exhausted and asked if he wanted to go to bed. He did. I tucked him in, kissed him gently and emotionally on the lips, then his forehead and he was sound asleep before I got to my side of the bed.

I said, *"Thank you, Lord."*

My heavenly Father said to my heart, *"Cherish this moment."*

I knew in my heart I had been given a priceless gift. I knew deep in my heart I was not going to have my hubby fully cognizant again. I fell asleep weeping in the arms of Jesus.

~ FORTY-FIVE ~

The beginning of the end

The following week was very, very difficult. Arne was "seeing" people in our home, "seeing" them outside, absolutely sure he saw something I did not see and would often say,

"You think I'm crazy but I'm not. I know what I heard and saw."

All I could think of to answer was that I didn't hear or see them but I was sure he did. I assured him I did NOT think he was crazy. I knew it was the disease he had.

By the following Friday, November 15, I was drained emotionally, having Vertigo attacks regularly plus I was extremely sleep deprived. Friday, Saturday and Sunday nights I was up 12-15 times during each night, following Arne around, asking what he needed, cajoling him back into bed and not knowing what to do. Monday night, November 18 I cut a Xanax tablet in half and gave one half to Arne and took the other half myself. We both needed rest!

I awoke startled but had no idea what awoke me. Arne was gone from bed. I went looking for him and found him asleep on the living room couch, in the dark, with only a pajama top on. I woke him and asked what was going on. He said he had to go to the bathroom.

I took him into our master bathroom, washed him up and put clean depends on him. All by nightlight only. I turned up the light and noticed his lips were all blue, bright blue. I asked him what he had eaten but he was incoherent and groggy. I thought the best thing to do was to get him contained in bed and search for what he had eaten.

I looked everywhere and found nothing amiss. Then I went back into the guest bathroom all the way and saw the garbage container there. Inside the garbage container's plastic bag was the depends he had removed. They were filled with purple, blue poop. A plastic wrapper in the garbage was labeled, *"Scrubbing Bubbles Tank Cleaners."* These are little blue cakes that one drops into the toilet tank to keep the toilet bowl clean. He had eaten one. This had to have occurred between 9:30 PM and 2:30 AM that night, while I was zonked out.

I immediately called the EMT for an ambulance. They were 6 minutes from our house and came instantly. They assured me that Arne would not die from ingesting this, but he would probably be pretty sick with diarrhea. They put him into the ambulance and I was going to follow in my car, but I instantly had a Vertigo attack. I told them to go and instructed them which hospital to take him to, and I would have someone bring me as soon as possible. It was 3:00 AM on November 19, 2019.

Hospitalization and God's mercy

I called my neighbor and she got me to the ER at 4:00 AM. I knew she had to work and told her I would call someone else to come bring me home. For the next 4 hours they simply ran tests, changed the pads under Arne as he had continuous blue diarrhea. The lady doctor came in and was telling me that he was out of danger and could go home.

Arne immediately had an explosive diarrhea attack. I had a bad Vertigo attack at the same time. Medical personnel were coming out of the woodwork.

The doctor looked at me and said, *"He is NOT going home. We are admitting him for more tests. And you, young lady, have had two Vertigo attacks in my presence and you cannot handle this any longer. I am putting that in my report."*

With that she told me to have someone come and take me home and they would attend to Arne and admit him. I called Kathleen and she came and brought me home. I had 4 Vertigo attacks in a row that day. I called my oldest son, Bryan, and told him what was going on. I couldn't do this anymore. I simply couldn't function anymore.

Bryan sent his wife, DeeDee and our granddaughter-in-law, Bobbie, by car as he was tied up at the college and could not come himself. It was a blessing only God could have orchestrated. Both gals are so smart, practical, loving and caring – just what I needed.

They arrived 11 hours later and simply took over. Bobbie is a medical student who was working at an Alzheimer's Home so knew the questions to ask and could speak the doctor's language, giving precise information to their questions.

The two gals began researching Nursing Facilities in our area, making appointments to visit, and caring for me all at the same time. I had to be wheeled by wheelchair because of my Vertigo. Arne took it all in but didn't seem to understand all the hoopla. However, God was in the details all along!

Because Arne was in the hospital, they were able to do all the necessary testing to determine if Arne should be placed in a care facility. He had all the Psychoanalysis, Psychiatric and Medical analysis done that otherwise would have had to be individually performed at various facilities. This was all able to be accomplished and documented so the transition to a Nursing Home was complete. God took care of details and otherwise stressful situations that would have made Arne think I was putting him away. The decision was, in actuality, taken out of my hands. Our children concurred I could not take care of him safely at home any longer. Doctors all agreed this was the only solution.

We eventually got from Arne that he had been looking for cough drops, in a bag inside our master bathroom's lower cabinet. He was confused and looked in our guest bathroom lower cabinet and apparently thought this was the cough drop bag. As a diabetic, he had no taste or smell ability so in his mind, apparently, he was finding what he needed without wakening me. I was filled with guilt over this for a long time. God had the plan.

We visited four different facilities and chose Magnolia Place, just 2 miles from Mercy Hospital and 20 minutes from our home. It was a whirlwind of activity. The Doctors visited with Arne, explaining he needed further care that I could not give him at home and Arne agreed to go to a facility for rehab and future evaluation.

Arrangements were made and at 4:00 PM on November 22, 2019, Arne arrived at his new home. DeeDee, Bobbie and I met him there. DeeDee and Bobbie pulled pictures off the walls at our home to place around Arne's room, making it homey and familiar. His favorite Razorback, soft-blanket was over the foot of his bed. My heart was breaking into tiny pieces. I couldn't imagine my precious hubby spending the rest of his life locked in a facility, no matter how beautiful and homey it was. Guilt was eating me up and I cried at the drop of a hat. Comfort eluded me.

Because this all happened so quickly, and I didn't have the finances to admit Arne into the nursing home facility, I called a dear friend and asked if I could borrow $2,000.00 for a short period of time and told him why. Without hesitation, he said, *"Absolutely!"*

Mike met me at the door of the hospital as we were preparing to bring Arne to Magnolia Place, with a personal check for $2,000.00. That is Christian love and friendship at its highest! How I love and admire these precious friends!

DeeDee and Bobbie were leaving the next day, Saturday, November 23. They had arranged with Buz to remain with me until he arrived at 10:00 AM, which they did. I was covered, once again, by family who was looking after me when I most needed it.

Buz stayed with me until Monday evening and insisted I attend Sunday School and Church on Sunday. He wanted me back in the groove of sanity and surrounded by others who would nurture and sustain my aching heart and depleted body. I shared with our Sunday School Class what had happened with Arne the previous week and asked them for prayer and support and thanked them for all they had already done. It was a tender time, with Buz standing beside me, encouraging me and keeping me from talking forever!!! I love our Sunday School Class. They were there for us during my cancer and double mastectomy, and for 25 years of prayers and close friendships. They have been a source of continual encouragement to each of us in our class and I love every person in it! Their outpouring of love and gentleness was that of close family!

Thanksgiving 2019

Buz went home Monday evening, then he and Vicki came back Wednesday to celebrate Thanksgiving with Arne and I at Magnolia House. It was a rainy, dreary day and Arne just wanted to come home. That's all he talked about. We tried to explain that he had to stay to have rehab and couldn't come home until the doctors gave the ok. Nothing we said made an impact. He suggested to Buz that Buz get the truck and drive it up next to the window and we could bring his things into the truck that way, so he could go home. Buz told Arne that it had rained so much that the tires would ruin the grass and we surely didn't want to mess up their lovely lawn that way.

Finally, Vicki said, *"Dad its pouring rain out and just not a good day for leaving. Let's just do it another day, ok?"*

Arne said, *"OK."* And that was that!

A dementia patient is unable to reason like a normal person. I learned many creative ways of diffusing situations other than trying to reason, which simply does not work! Changing subjects or creating diversions becomes an art when dealing with your loved one suffering from this debilitating, progressive disease.

Thanksgiving Day Lunch was lovely, festive and a special effort was made for all residents and guests attending. Arne was exhausted and we got him into bed before we left. We hugged and kissed him and Buz knelt down beside his bed, took his father's hands tenderly in his and said,

"Dad, I want you to really listen to me, OK? This is really important and I want you to hear what I am going to say. OK?"
"Mom, Bryan, DeeDee, Paul, Haley, Tim, Bobbie, Vicki and I have

all agreed on this. If Jesus should come for you tonight, you have our permission to go with Him. OK?"

There was a long pause. Buz then got his father's attention and gently repeated what he first said, once again. *"Dad, if Jesus comes for you tonight, you have our permission to go with Him, OK?"*

Arne looked up at Buz, hesitated, and said, *"Oh Son, He did come the other night, but I guess it wasn't my time. Thank you. Thank you for telling me that, Son. I needed to hear that."*

It was the most tender conversation I had ever heard and I had to leave the room because my heart burst and I lost it. Buz came out shortly and together we held each other as we sobbed in each other's arms as our hearts fell into shattered fragments of crushed dreams.

The next couple of days were so difficult. Arne refused to use his walker. He would use the wheelchair going to meals or leaving his room because he was too weak to walk any distance, but insisted he didn't need to use the walker while in his own room.

Broken Hip

Saturday, November 31, 2019, Arne got up to use the restroom. I begged him to please use the walker. He ignored me and began going into the tiled bathroom. He lost his balance, grabbed the towel bar, ripped it off the wall, hit the floor landing on his right hip and slid into the opposite wall, hitting his head with a thud.

I checked him over carefully and he seemed ok, just shaken up. He commanded me NOT to call anyone for help. I got him settled into bed for the night, kissed him and prayed with him and left. I stopped at the Nurse's Station and told them what had occurred. It was documented.

The next morning, Sunday, Dec 1, I received an early call from Magnolia Place. Arne had fallen once again, getting out of bed and was complaining of right hip pain. EMTs had taken him to Mercy Hospital for x-rays. He had a displaced impacted fracture of the right hip.

Dr. J. explained it thus: It is like an ice cream cone with the ice cream slightly off the cone. In teen and young adult patients, we usually don't even repair this as it will settle and heal itself. But because Arne is a dementia patient, he would probably fall multiple times in the future and the next fall would undoubtedly fracture the complete hip. Dr. Jones elected to place 4 pins into the hip, pulling everything tightly into place and securing the hip for the future. This is what he did. This would prevent future problems with that hip.

Arne had the surgery, all went well and he was back at Magnolia Place on Wednesday afternoon, not remembering that he had even had surgery. The very next morning, he again tried to get out of his wheelchair and fell again. In the next several weeks he fell a total of 18 times. He had x-rays and check-ups but nothing showed except abrasions, cuts and bumps! He simply wanted OUT! He didn't remember he had broken his hip or had surgery and said it wasn't so. He was very determined that he could get up and walk and do whatever he could before. It broke my heart to see him so unhappy, angry and frustrated. The palliative doctor from Mercy had warned me that the first month was "brutal" and his anger would be directed at me, because I was the closest to him. It was
building, like steam in a kettle

An Angel of Joy

Arne's niece, his older brother's daughter, Kirstin, had always had a special spot in Arne's heart. She was just a tiny, little thing when Arne was stationed in New London, Connecticut while he attended submarine school in the Navy. His brother lived nearby and Arne visited often on weekends. He loved his little niece and carried the cutest picture of her in pink curlers inside his wallet for many years. She grew up being very close to her Uncle Arne.

She called me one day saying she was coming to spend a week with me. She had cared for her own bedbound father (Arne's older brother) in her own home the last 5 months of his life. Roland had bone cancer and then dementia at the end of his life. She understood what I was experiencing and had been my *"go to"* person for invaluable advice these past few months. She understood!

Kirstin arrived December 8, 2019 for five full days with me. What a beautiful gift from God she became. Besides lifting Arne's spirits, helping him to remember fun times and memories long forgotten, she ministered healing into my very being. We laughed together, cried together and prayed together. Being an incredibly talented young lady, she made a lovely Christmas decoration for Arne's Magnolia Place bedroom door. It included a tiny framed picture of Arne and I together within the arrangement. I cried when this precious, beautiful, young lady had to leave to go home.

Arne told her, *"I am going to miss you."* He meant it with all his heart.

I knew anger had been building inside of Arne, just as the palliative doctor at Mercy Hospital had warned would happen. There was a coolness toward me all week Kirstin was here and I could feel the distance widening between us. He would rarely meet my eyes and he didn't want to hold my hands and would pull them away sometimes. This was very, very hard to experience in my vulnerable, hurting state. It broke loose when I returned from taking Kirstin to the airport on Friday, December 13th.

I sat down beside him and he began attempting to stand and get out of the wheelchair. It was good exercise for him to stand, sit, and stand to build his leg muscles, but that was not his intent. He was determined to WALK.

At one point he asked me to stand in front of him, which I did. He then grabbed both of my arms and told me to back up so he could walk. I knew he was not capable of this and said,

"No, Babes, I will not be responsible for you falling again!"

I pulled away and he sank back into the wheelchair, glared angrily at me and said,

"OK, if you won't help me, then I want a divorce!" Loud and clear!

Instead of seeing the absurd humor in this, as did our sons and anyone else I told, my inner self crumbled, I began to cry and left him in the care of nurses as I hurried to the car, buried my head in my arms, sobbing and crying out to Jesus to please help me.

Looking back, it seemed almost childish. Emotions involving grief don't follow protocol or right thinking sometimes! I was broken, over exhausted, lonely and very devastated hearing those words coming from this cherished husband of mine that I had done everything I could to help him. It seemed so unfair and ungrateful. I felt very sorry for myself and guess what? There is room for those emotions and God fully understands better than anyone else!

The next day Arne acted like he didn't remember any of what had been said the day before. This was because he had dementia and that's exactly how dementia works. It was as if it had not happened because in his mind, it hadn't. He had expressed his pent-up emotions of anger, taking it out on me as the doctor said he would. He never again showed any signs of anger toward me. Dementia handicapped people can experience built up emotions which they cannot cognitively explain nor understand. However, they still hurt, feel anger, love and other emotions. They just cannot reason and figure out the whys of their feelings. The beauty is that they quickly forgive and return love very quickly as the blessedness of forgetfulness kicks in. I've observed that blessing as I watched outbursts with various patients in Magnolia Place turned into something beautiful. That is how I viewed it.

Christmas was fast approaching. Arne continued to be up, down, up, down in his wheelchair all day long. He would constantly try to get out of bed alone, fall and be rescued by the nurses. They finally decided to place him in a leather recliner, that he was unable to escape from, and keep him out front by the Nurse's Station where they could watch him 100% of the time. I felt sorry for the nurses and helpers as it was disconcerting to see him constantly trying to be a Houdini all day and all night and whenever he was not sleeping.

The doctors were trying various medications to help control his agitated state of being. He didn't want to be there. He didn't remember that he had a fractured hip, even though it caused him pain. He just wanted to go home. It was a constant theme of every conversation. I asked everyone to pray for peace and contentment from the Holy Spirit to invade and replace Arne's anxious spirit with the peace that only God could provide. It made going to visit my hubby an anxious and stressful experience every day.

December 20th brought the EMTs to Magnolia Place to bring Arne to Mercy Hospital because he was severely constipated and absolutely miserable. Five burly EMTs took him 2 miles via ambulance to Mercy to resolve the problem. About a $2,000.00 ride! I had a rather firm conversation the following day with the staff, explaining I could not afford this type of resolution to this type problem that Mira Lax and other medications, given regularly, could easily solve!! That was the last time for that problem.

An Early Christmas

Bryan, DeeDee, Tim and Bobbie came for an early Christmas. Words cannot express the relief of being in my children's presence. I wasn't alone for a few days. I didn't have to do the worrying when they were here. (God took care of this in me...we will get to that later.) Buz and Vicki joined us as we exchanged gifts, shared love and good food, but without my honey. It was a very difficult time in my heart but I smiled and really tried very hard to be thankful for all we DID have. Buz and Vicki brought their three dogs, something that had never happened before, and they just seemed to know I needed extra love. They were a delight! Those precious pups loved on me like they knew I was hurting. We had fun times just laughing at their silly antics. It was good to laugh together.

The hardest part of Christmas was knowing neither Bryan nor Tim had seen Arne in the state of mind he was in now. DeeDee and Bobbie had walked me through the horribleness of Arne's hospitalization and subsequent placing him into a long-term care facility. They had seen Arne at his worst. It was a shock to both men, but especially to Tim. It shattered my heart to see their pain. I was a basket case the night they had to say good-bye to Arne. I couldn't contain my emotions and was physically sick to my stomach.

Later Bryan told Buz he was very worried that they were going to lose a mother too because I was not handling this well at all. I KNEW I had to do something about my state of being. I was not living my faith about trusting God completely. I was still trying to control things I could not control. God didn't need my input, but I kept on trying to "*help*." God doesn't need our help. Our help becomes a hindrance 9 times out of 10!

Buz and Vicki insisted I needed to go to Silver Dollar City, in Branson, Missouri, before the end of the year to see all the new lights and to get away for a couple of days. Arne and I had Seasons Tickets for the last three years which we just kept renewing for a fee because he never felt up to going. It was time to use these expensive tickets at least once! We had extra guest tickets so it made for a perfect excuse.

I was so afraid Arne would miss me and be upset. He never realized two days had gone by without me. Dementia patients have very little concept of time. My sister, Naomi, husband Bill, and their daughter, Heather, joined us and we had a wonderful time. I couldn't believe all the millions of additional lights since being at this theme park three years earlier. It was a bit of normalcy, even without Arne. I even slept peacefully all night long at Buz and Vicki's home. They prepared a breakfast for a queen, for me, and it was so good to be with them again.

~ FORTY-SIX ~

Magnolia Place and Hospice

Arne had been receiving physical and occupational therapy at Magnolia Place, but it really was not working. The therapists tried so hard, but Arne was either agitated or sleepy. Arne was pleasant enough but his limbs wouldn't cooperate and he just seemed to be getting weaker instead of stronger. He was talking less and less, usually only answering with a yes or no. His falls were regular despite the many creative ways the staff tried to watch him. He managed to crawl out of the recliner chair and fall before someone could get to him. It was extremely frustrating to all of us. He had scrapes, bruises and rug burns all over his arms and legs. And because he was terrified of falling, he would grab the grab bars next to the toilet with an iron grip, not allowing the certified nursing assistant (CNA) to lower him to the toilet so he could use the needed facility. We would have to pry his fingers loose, assuring him quietly that we would NOT let him fall. Oh, the patience of some of these beautiful gals! I was coming to love each of them dearly.

January 4, 2020 Arne turned 78 years old. He still had his full head of beautiful light brown hair, waving across his forehead. He was still one very handsome man who did not look 78 years old. However, he was deteriorating in front of my eyes. He could no longer feed himself adequately, and I was diligent about being there for lunch in order to feed him. The staff would see that he ate and were so kind and loving, but I wanted to be sure!

January 17, 2020 was a day I will cherish forever! The activity director brought us a pair of headphones and a laptop. She knew we both like Gaither and Swaggart gospel music and we sat for 2 hours listening to all our favorite songs of praise. Arne, who had not spoken in full sentences for several weeks, was singing along with the music, knowing all the words! It was the most beautiful afternoon we had experienced together in months. At one point I took off the headphones and asked him if he knew who I was.

His eyes shined in obvious awareness and he said, *"I SURE do! You're my babes, my bride. And I love you with all my heart."*

Then kissed me full on the lips! What a precious gift from God.

The next day, January 18, 2020, Hospice met with me about their becoming involved in Arne's care. I asked if they felt his death was imminent. They said he could be here for several months to come, but felt he needed the extra care and attention because he was deteriorating rather quickly. Their involvement meant specialized care for his type of disabilities including bathing, nurse supervision and another doctor overseeing his medications. They would be covering the cost of specialized wheelchairs, beds, medications and anything he required or needed. Magnolia Place had suggested the additional care, for which I thank them profusely!

Hospice care is the one thing our government has gotten really right! What a wonderful program of caring, dedicated, efficient care givers. They took over his care, and after multiple falls, he was placed into a specialized wheelchair that supported his head, feet, lumbar and coccyx. He was now in this wheelchair 24/7. He was no longer able to do anything for himself and rarely interacted with anyone yet was able to answer with a yes or no. He could not escape from this wheelchair no matter how determined he was. His Houdini days were over – and I never received any more calls telling me he had fallen. It was a great relief.

It was time! God and I had been talking – well, I talked and He lovingly listened but His Holy Spirit was nudging me gently. I was lying in bed Monday night, January 20, 2020 when I felt my Heavenly Father asking me if I really believed He was who He said He was! I said, yes.

It was then I realized I had **not** been acting as though I believed He was truly God Almighty. I was still trying to *"hang on to Arne"* and was not completely giving him to Jesus – 100%. Oh, I thought I had, but I had not! I worried, fussed and was still the mother hen watching everything to be sure it was done right! It's called micromanaging, otherwise known as a stage mother, obsessive pest...well maybe not quite that bad, but I needed to quit being the caregiver and just be Arne's loving, caring wife. I needed to allow God to be in charge of everything – to take my hands completely off every aspect and to trust God to coordinate and complete His plan for both of our lives.

I repented in many tears as God's loving arms surrounded me in compassion and comfort. How many times had I said, *"God never makes mistakes – ever!"* Now I would give Arne and his future to Jesus and I would trust and thank Him for all He HAS done, IS doing and what He is GOING to do. Such a peace flowed over me and a joy began to even bubble up a little inside of me. Yes, Jesus, this is your way. Why did it take so long? Because I am just human and He lovingly brought me to this place when I most needed it. Thank you, Father God! I began filling up my spare thoughts with praise and thanksgiving.

"He is my strength, my shield from every danger. I trusted Him and He helped me. Joy rises in my heart until I burst out in songs of praise to Him." **Psalms 28:7** *Living Bible*

"Don't be anxious about tomorrow. God has it!" **Matthew 6:34** *Living Bible*

"When I am afraid, I will trust in the Lord God Almighty." **Psalms 56:3-4** *Living Bible*

"I will be with you constantly until I have finished giving you all I am promising."
Genesis 28:15 *Living Bible*

Two weeks later Hospice informed me that they wanted to honor Arne for his four years of service in the United States Navy. They arranged a date, brought a photographer, a VA Chaplain and the Hospice Director for a presentation of a certificate of appreciation for service, a special commemorative coin and a full-sized United States flag in a fluffy blanket that was beautiful.

The photographer took about 30 photos and told me they would bring me two framed photos, copies of all photos and the CD with all the photos taken. What a special day it was, January 30, 2020. Arne was fully aware, awake and when everyone left, put his hands on each side of my cheeks, pulled me down and kissed me gently on the lips. His eyes and gentle kiss said it all. God, you are SO good!

Feb 10, 2020 Hospice brought a new bed for Arne. It was closer to the floor, had air pressure in the mattress that changed with each movement to prevent any bed sores. They had placed a raised pillow-like edge around the bed to help prevent Arne from getting out of the bed. It didn't work. Somehow Arne would manage to get his legs over the edge of the bed, stand up and crumble to the floor. They tried many different tactics and ideas, but he always ended up on the floor. Back to the wheelchair as that was the most - safe solution so far. When asked why he would get out of his bed, he would tell them he had to go to the bathroom, or needed a drink of water. He just couldn't grasp that this was beyond his abilities. Dementia will do this to the patient and it is frustrating for everyone.

The Cadillac we purchased was still giving me great service! It was eating my lunch in gas, running back and forth to see Arne daily, driving 40 miles round trip each time. The Caddy only got 18-20 miles per gallon and lately, sometimes less. I was paying about $100.00 a month for gas. I decided to look for something else. My neighbor had a Toyota Corolla that got 33 mpg and he was very pleased with its performance. One evening they took me to the Toyota lot and we cruised through the used lot. There was a snazzy looking 2017 with low mileage and reasonable cost. I liked it!

That evening my neighbor sent in the vin numbers of both the Cadillac and our 1999 Dodge Ram Truck. Arne and I had discussed selling both vehicles and purchasing something newer after the first of the year so I knew he would be in favor of this. Even though none of this would probably make sense to him, it was just comforting knowing he would approve of my move.

The email back from Toyota quoted a trade-in price on each vehicle and asked if a salesman could contact me by phone. I said, yes.

The next day Eric called, asked a few questions, then asked if I would be interested in getting a brand new 2020 Toyota Corolla for the same price as that used one. Kind of a no brainer! Our son, Bryan and DeeDee, were arriving the next day for a quick visit so I agreed to come visit with Eric the next day.

Eric presented a very good offer and I said I would sleep on it and check my figures and resources. After going over my budget, I just felt I did not dare bite off that much. I sent Eric an email the next morning explaining my situation with Arne, and said I didn't feel I could take the really great offer. Eric called one half hour later, offering me a fantastic offer I COULD afford. Bryan and DeeDee agreed it was a God opportunity of blessing.

After going over all the details of our transaction the next day, I asked Eric how they could do this for me.

He said, *"Of course we are here to make money, but there are times when doing the right thing is more important than money. When I told my Manager about your situation, we decided this was one of those moments."*

I said, *"Eric, you are a born-again Christian, aren't you?"*

He replied, *"Yes Mam, I surely am!"*

The two had decided they wanted to take the pressure off me and do something special besides. God used these two wonderful guys to help me purchase a car with a full warranty and no worries for a long time to come. They said it was a *God-given pleasure* to be able to do this for me. And if there was anything, and I mean <u>*anything*</u> they could do to help me, to please call either one of them and they would see that it got accomplished. *They told me I just got myself two more sons!*

I broke down and cried at the beauty of humanity that loves and serves Jesus and for the goodness of my God. I truly felt like my Heavenly Father brought me two of Jesus with skin on. They hugged me and I drove home with only 6 miles on my new car, fully warranted, extended warranty, GAP insurance, 2 years of oil changes, tire rotation and lifetime car washes. Plus two new friends the ages of my oldest son! They told me I could get a better deal selling my truck outright, which I did later – for cash! What a phenomenal, loving, caring, faithful and protective God I serve! Only God can do these kinds of things! I do not know what others do who do not believe in, or trust in Jesus. He is my best friend. I trust Him implicitly.

Magnolia Place and Stomach Flu Outbreak

The 2020 Corona Virus, labeled Convid-19 by the Center of Disease Control, was in full epidemic mode. Many were calling it a Pandemic. It began in China and had spread to almost every country in the world. In Arkansas, there were already two cases, two just miles from the nursing home. I went to visit Arne on Sunday, March 8th. When I first approached him, I could see confusion on his face. I could tell he wasn't sure who I was. I knew this day would come so I was prepared for it.

I said, *"Hi Sweetheart, I'm your wife, your sweetheart, your bride, your babes, Betts, BJ!"*

Recognition came into his eyes and he said, *"Hi Sweetheart!"*

It was the last words I would ever hear him speak to me.

On Monday, March 9th, I was told, along with the hospice worker at the door, that no one but personnel would be permitted inside until this outbreak of stomach flu was completely contained. It was a self-quarantine, completely for safety reasons for not allowing any more germs into the facility. It was NOT Corona Virus, but they were not about to take any chances. I was thankful for their cautionary approach. After all, there is NO distance in prayer and I would be blanketing all the patients, staff and everyone connected with this wonderful facility in prayer. God had this one too.

On March 18th, I was able to FaceTime with Arne, with the aid holding the cell phone. His eyes were closed, but when he heard my voice, he opened his eyes and started looking around for me. It was a short call, no response from my sweetheart, but at least I was able to see him for a couple of minutes. I knew I was losing my best friend and I ached inside for missing him so much. My heart was bleeding and I could do nothing to stop it. Yes, I knew God was in control, but that didn't stop the rush of tears and tearing of my insides of loneliness and pain that seemed so raw. I knew I had to hang on to my Heavenly Father to help me through whatever was ahead.

~ FORTY- SEVEN ~

Homecoming

On Tuesday, March 24th, the hospice nurse called to tell me Arne's body was shutting down and oxygen was being administered. Arne was unresponsive at times and was nearing the end. I could not go to be with him. No one was being admitted into the nursing home because of the Pandemic of Covid-19. My heart was wrenching.

I received a call early on Wednesday, March 25th, that Arne was being transported to the Springdale Hospice facility and I was to meet them there. I was told I would be able to stay with Arne there as long as I wanted, night and day. My heart rejoiced. I NEEDED to be with him when he breathed his last and went into the arms of our Jesus. It was something I had prayed and requested from my Heavenly Father.

I quickly threw together extra clothes, toiletries, Bible and notebook. I then had to drive to Magnolia Place to retrieve all of Arne's things so they could use his room for another patient. They boxed up everything and placed it in the trunk of my car and backseat.
It was packed full to overflowing and stayed that way the entire next 5 days. I hurried to be with Arne.

Arne never opened his eyes again and remained unresponsive until he went to be with Jesus five days later on Sunday, March 29th, at 7:00 PM. Those Five days contained a lifetime.

He could hear everything that was being said. I told him again and again how much I loved him and sat beside him just recalling all the many memories that flooded my heart and soul. At times he would move his lips as if trying to talk to me. Once in a while he would get a little smile in the corner of his mouth. I wiped tears away from his eyes many times, and wept with him. I told him again and again that our sons would take care of me and so would Jesus. I told him he didn't have to worry because God had proven over and over, all of our lives, how faithful He was to us, and that would <u>never</u> change. One time I was sure he winked his right eye once during one of the tender moments. He always winked at me throughout our marriage so I shall choose to believe he was just telling me one last time how much he loved me too. The first couple of days Arne would squeeze my hand occasionally, gently. I knew he was *"in there,"* and was understanding me.

I called each of our sons and wives and put the phone up to Arne's ear so they could have an opportunity to share their hearts with him. I did the same with our grandsons and wives. Each one told him that our circle in heaven will not be broken, something they had heard their father/grandfather pray many times. It was so emotional, yet so very tender and appropriate. Tears ran down Arne's cheeks as he listened to the love of his family. How could I say goodbye to this beautiful man, father of our sons and my best friend, lover and partner that I didn't think I could live without? Only God knew.

I also called each of his siblings, some nieces and nephews and family members – giving each an opportunity to share their love and gratefulness to Arne in these last days. Arne, again, would move his lips as though trying to talk to us. Tears fell from his eyes more than once and other times he smiled a tiny bit of a corner smile of his mouth. It was so very special to hear how

Arne had so influenced so many of the family with his steady, quiet manner, life and speech. Each family member did just that. It was a blessed week.

Friday, March 27th, was my younger sister's birthday. She loved Arne and Arne had been like a father to her three children over the years. They spent every Christmas with us while the children were growing up. Arne had shown them love, helped during difficult times (like their first car accident) and been there for them always. We had taken them sailing, fishing and just loved on them when their own father was not being what he should have been. I didn't want my honey to pass away on her birthday and joined with Buz, our youngest son, to pray that God would allow Arne another day or two to avoid this heartache remembrance for my sister. God really does care about things like that!

All day Friday and Saturday, I sang to Arne his favorite songs, read the Bible to him, played Gospel music on Pandora and laid beside him for a 2-hr nap, just feeling his warmth and hearing his gentle whisper as he exhaled each breath. It was a peaceful, gentle time of just being together, hand in hand. I didn't want anyone with me. God was there with Arne and me. It was beautifully exquisite, and he looked so completely at rest. I had held his hand almost constantly, except when I slept at night in the comfortable recliner beside him. The chair was oversized, thickly padded, had lumbar vibration and heat in it. How grateful I am for the Hospice folks who provided such a comfortable and private place for me to share my last cherished moments with my husband. There would be times that Arne held tightly to my hand. I noticed with each passing day his hand became more relaxed, yet there were times he gently squeezed my hand in the beginning of those last five days.

Dr. B. came in on Saturday afternoon. He patted Arne's shoulder and said,

"Mr. Arne, you will be going to your eternal home in the next day, or so. I know you love the Lord and He is getting ready to bring you home. Your beautiful bride is holding your hand and I have your other hand and we are going to pray that your journey will be peaceful and full of joy as you reach the other side."

He then took my free hand and we formed a three-fold chord, with Jesus surrounding us as Dr. B. prayed a beautiful prayer of commitment to the Lord Jesus Christ. I was weeping as Dr. B. came around the bed, took me in his arms and just let me cry in his arms. Corona Virus didn't frighten Dr. B. He knew my pain and simply let me weep and weep. I will never forget such simple empathy and kindness. He told me it would be within 24 hours.

Sunday, March 29, 2020. The nurses bathed Arne, swabbed his mouth, put on clean sheets and a new gown, like every other day had been. They always combed his full head of beautiful, wavy hair without any grey yet – just the sideburns had some grey in them. He looked so young and even the doctor had commented on that. Several nurses said he was still very handsome – yes, he was, indeed! He had his mother's smooth face and it looked almost porcelain to me, with just a splash of color on his cheeks that shone like a polished apple. Beautiful is not what we usually call men, but that is what Arne looked like. He had a sheen on his face that made him look almost angelic. I snapped a picture of him because it was so awesome and unusual. I love that picture now and enlarged it on my phone to see each beautiful peaceful expression. God truly gave me one of His best specimens for a hubby.

Dr. B. came in again about 3:30 pm on Sunday. He told me Arne would be going to heaven in just a few hours now.

Then he leaned down and told Arne, *"Son, hang in there now. Just a few more hours and you will be free of this earthly body and you will be home. Your sons and God will take care of your loving wife."*

He then prayed from his heart for God to hold me and bring me through all of this victoriously. He ended with The Lord's Prayer as I joined him, squeezed my shoulder and left. I just laid my head on Arne's lap, wept and thanked God for Arne once again. It almost didn't seem real. There was a peace that enveloped the room that was beyond words.

At 6:00 pm I felt Arne's pulse in his wrist, then his legs, but there was no pulse. I called the nurses and they checked and said he was leaving his body. They helped me climb into bed beside him, being careful not to lean heavily against him, put my head on the pillow with him so I could feel his breath on my forehead.

I held his one hand and placed my other hand on his heart, so I could easily reach up and feel his carotid artery in his neck. I prayed out loud as we had done every night of our married life. I prayed for our children, grandchildren and loved ones by name, and for generations to come, if Jesus didn't return soon. I thanked Jesus for dying for our sins, for rising from the dead and living now in heaven, waiting for us to join Him someday in heaven. I thanked Him that Arne was soon coming to be with Him too and thanked Him for all the wonderful, beautiful memories we created together.

I just laid next to Arne, knowing it was the last time. All of a sudden, I was afraid. He took a breath, held it awhile, then exhaled. It made me afraid - afraid it was his last breath.

I distinctly heard in my heart, *"Don't be afraid. I am here with you."*

I knew my Father's voice and all fear left.

I remained snuggled close to Arne, praying quietly within my heart. He took a breath, and I really do not know how I knew, but I quickly put my fingers to his Carotid and felt his beautiful, generous, adoring, loving, gentle, caring heart stop. Jesus came and took him.

I sat up and looked at his radiant face and said,

"Darling, you always said I was crazy when I told you how beautiful you were. You are even more beautiful in death, precious Arne. Go to Jesus now. I'll be coming soon."

I raised my arms, thanking Jesus that Arne was finally free from this pain. My heart was broken and my tears flowed, yet I knew Arne's journey was over. I knew the victory was won forever for him. Praise be to the Lord God Almighty. He received the ultimate healing.

I called the nurses who noted his death as 7:00 pm, March 29, 2020.

I didn't want to remember Arne lying there in the hospice bed. I chose to wait until they were ready to remove him from the Hospice Facility. They (funeral director) placed an American Flag blanket, like the one Arne had been given weeks before, over his body and wheeled him through the hallway toward the back door. All the hospice workers had removed their masks and were standing respectfully along the aisle. The gentleman stopped and pulled the blanket over Arne's face.

I touched Arne's thigh and said, *"Goodnight Sweetheart. God bless you. I'll see you in the morning."*

Something I had said every night of our married life to the treasured love of my life. I knew he was finally home.

I called my dear friend, Kathleen, and asked her to please meet me at our home so I wouldn't have to come in to an empty house. It was 9:30 PM and Kathleen had gone to our home, pulled all the shades, which I had left open for 5 days, turned on soft lights and had hot tea and cookies waiting. She was in her robe and slippers and after I showered and washed my hair (because of the virus being so virulent), Kathleen enfolded me into her loving arms as only a "sister" (we adopted each other long ago) can do. She stayed with me for about 45 minutes and I fell into a peaceful sleep and slept all night. Just one more gift from my caring, loving Heavenly Father.

~ FORTY-EIGHT ~

Funeral Arrangements

Because of the Covid-19 pandemic around the world, and everything was on lock down, a funeral was out of the question. Our sons suggested a Virtual Celebration of Arne's life using Zoom on the internet.

On April 6th we had a wonderful celebration with Arne's large family together. There was laughter, tears and love oozing through the airways. On April 19th we had the last celebration of Arne's life with my side of the family, adding former pastors and long-time friends and those especially close to us or had worked closely with Arne over the years.

It was better than any normal funeral could be, with so much healing balm for our hurting hearts. Arne was greatly loved, respected, admired and revered by every family member, and everyone that knew him. Nieces and nephews shared things I never knew Arne had done for them. Hearing young family members say how "cool" their Uncle Arne was, and how much he had influenced their lives was just so special. Most importantly, our circle will not be broken in heaven.

One close friend summed Arne up perfectly. Mary said,

"Arne was a man of total integrity, Steel covered Velvet."

He was all of that and more.

How blessed I was to be Arne's Bride for 56 years filled with every adventure and excitement a marriage could contain. It was a beautiful sharing that my grandsons recorded for my remembrance in the future. I held back most of my tears until alone in my bedroom, where aching tears flooded my pillow as my body longed to be held once more by this man who loved me thoroughly, gently and without reservation.

"Dear Father God, how am I to make it without this man I have cherished for so long?" My emotions were raw until I almost could-not breathe. *"I can-not do this without your help!"*

"Behold, God is my salvation; I will trust, and not be afraid: for the Lord JEHOVAH is my strength and my song; he is become my salvation."
Isaiah 12:2

~FORTY-NINE~

Where do I go from here?

To God!

You, God, are a Promise Maker and a Promise Keeper. From the beginning of time and throughout the Bible, your dependability and faithfulness HAS BEEN validated. You need no assistance from us or anyone! You don't ask our opinion, nor need it! Your Word is true. Your Word is sure. What you say, happens. The same power is in Jesus Christ. The power to keep His Word. It is irrevocable because God cannot lie! Faith is the deeply held belief (not hope) that God keeps His promises. We have the Holy Spirit living within us to be our comfort, courage, legal assistant and guide. He is all of God leading us to our Heavenly Home!

He never changes. James 1:17
He is faithful. Hebrews 10:23
He is strong. Romans 4:21
He cannot lie. Hebrews 6:18

God's promises are many, and true. You can have confidence in them and claim each one for every situation. God's promises can give you security amidst the most horrific storm of your life. God's promises are like the lighthouse that leads the mariner to the safe harbor from the raging seas.

If you have accepted Jesus as your Savior, you are HIS Child, I am HIS Child – 100%.

Satan wants nothing more than to discourage us and steal from us by making us feel abandoned, unloved and forgotten when things go haywire or wrong.

God has a purpose in everything that touches our lives. Absolutely nothing touches our lives that doesn't *first* go through His loving hands! His Holy Spirit wants to guide us and use us for His glory. He wants to bless everything in our lives, and use us for a blessing to others - to point others to the love and forgiveness of Jesus Christ.

Satan tries to convince us we aren't good enough or that God doesn't really care about us or our problems.

The Bible says: *"Resist the Devil and he will flee from you."*

But look at what it says *before* we resist: *"Submit yourselves on to God ..." James 4:7*

Our Lord has promised us that we are sealed by the Holy Spirit **Ephesians 1:13**. He doesn't leave us nor forsake us. He is always there, even though the enemy wants us to believe He is not. We submit to God by confessing any known sin, ask God to fill us with the power of the Holy Spirit, thank and praise Him for WHO He is and WHAT He wants to do in our lives. Then we can relax into His arms, surrender our will to Him, decide to trust Him, and walk by faith into the next chapter He has for us.

"Father, I give you everything and thank you for all you are doing in my life. I give you total control. In Jesus Name, I command you, Satan, to leave me alone and be gone from me. I am covered by the blood of Jesus, and nothing formed

against me can prosper. Holy Spirit, please give me your wisdom and direction. Fill me with your power to please my Heavenly Father every day for the remainder of my life, and follow only His purposes. If you were finished with my life here on earth, you would have taken me to heaven too. But you still have a plan and a future for my life. I submit it to you fully and ask you to show me what you have for me to do. I want to please you and be obedient to Your plan. Being totally in your will, will be the best and only way to total completeness and joy in my heart."

Nothing in our lives is a surprise to Jesus. He hasn't stopped loving us or caring for us. He is the all-powerful, always-omniscient God. He hasn't changed, doesn't change and will never change. He never makes mistakes – EVER! He knows what He is doing.

When you feel like you've asked Jesus, *"Do you care that I am hurting so much?"*

He answers, *"My precious child, I DO care. Trust me. I know exactly what I am doing. I have the Plan. Rest in me and thank me, for I have you in the palm of my hand."*

God wants to release all the power of heaven into your life, transforming you into all He created you to be. But we must allow the Holy Spirit to empower and equip us. On my own, I have failed so many times and I have not arrived. I will continue to fail, because I am human. It makes all the difference when I remember that the Holy Spirit lives within me and Jesus promised we would never be alone. His Holy Spirit will guide us and direct us if we ask for His counsel and strength. We don't have to feel alone and vulnerable because when we are weak, He is strong and He imbues us with His strength to overcome and carry on.

"For He will deliver the needy when he cries for help, the afflicted also, and him who has no helper. He will have compassion on the poor and needy, and the lives of the needy He will save." Psalms 72:12-13

"So do not fear, for I am with you; do not be dismayed, for I am your God. I will strengthen you and help you; I will uphold you with my righteous right hand."
    Isaiah 41:10

"<u>Never</u> will I leave you; <u>never</u> will I forsake you." Hebrews 13:5

"And surely I am with you <u>always</u>, to the very end of the age." Matthew 28:20
The Lord loves me.

He's good all the time and His mercies are new every morning.

Nothing befalls me without His permission.

He is the ultimate wisdom, power, and authority.

He has a purpose in allowing this trial.

He works all things together for my good because I love Him and am called according to His purposes.

Life is not about me. It's about God. His greater purpose is to use all things for His glory and the building of His kingdom. Therefore, I can be thankful for *all* things.

I knew all this with my head, but sometimes, when I am hurting so deeply and missing my beloved, it is difficult to convince my battered heart what my head knows. Have you ever been there?

I read recently about lamenting. Lamenting does not mean that we are without hope; rather, it's a way of being honest with God. The Psalms are full of lament. Lament is a legitimate response to the reality of suffering and it engages God in the context of our pain, trouble and sorrow. Lament with God gives us hope in seeking help, change and growth. We cannot possibly give thanks for all things if we don't have and know Jesus Christ personally. As we give ourselves wholly to Him and His sovereignty and goodness, then our heart can join our head in the sacrifice of praise because God is proven faithful time and time again. He will never fail us, ever!

Happiness skims the surface and depends on outward circumstances. Joy is rooted in eternity and is dependent on inward circumstances. Choosing joy when our hearts are breaking may seem an impossible and unreasonable request. However, Jesus will meet you in your sorrow and breathe life and joy slowly, but surely, back into your life – if you let Him. It is a choice. Allow His love to compel you to allow joy to enter your heart.

As I write this, I am overwhelmed by God's caring love and provision always! I am spilling tears of gratitude for His loving arms that hold me as I grieve normal love for my husband's life now gone from earth. It seems like a dream and sometimes the tides of
sorrow sweep over me like sea billows rolling in the thundering waves that seem to never quit. Jesus understands the language of tears. It has nothing to do with my faith. It has everything to do with that human part of my life that is now gone forever here on earth. Jesus knows and understands. He is here with me now, holding and comforting me and telling me to not fear because He has the Plan and I can trust Him to bring me through every day ahead. I am not alone. And neither are you. He has this too!

Implanted within every living creature is a purposed individual identity for which it was created, the total DNA blueprint put there by Almighty God himself when He created us.

Birds know what they are and what they are supposed to do. No one has to tell them. Fish know they are to swim. Puppies know how to bark. Everything that has life depends on God for life and its future. God has created you and me – we do not need to worry because God will take care of us.

There are many books on grief. I have read my fair share. I can only speak from my own life. I deal differently today than I did years ago with disappointment and pain. I have learned who holds tomorrow and I know God is undeniably faithful and has MY good in HIS powerful and capable hands. I know I am His child and He loves me, unconditionally!

Although God's love and grace held me close those first few weeks, and I knew where my beloved was – with Jesus in heaven, I would be caught off guard with overwhelming waves of sorrow and missing Arne terribly. It would wash over me and knock me off my feet emotionally. One cannot live with, and love someone deeply, for 56 years and not have human feelings of loss and loneliness.

I let my feelings go. I sobbed my heart out to Jesus, telling him how much I missed my precious hubby, how thankful I was for those beautiful 56 years. I thanked God for all the wisdom and blessings Arne had given me. I thanked God for the boys Arne and I were privileged to raise together. I thanked God for every blessing I could think of and ended up full of praise to an awesome God who had orchestrated all our days and given me all these things for which to GIVE praise. Yet, I still have days and moments when my heart bleeds raw pain. It is that human part of me that pushes me into the arms of Jesus for comfort continually.

I will have many times ahead when this same sorrow and missing will overpower me. I know I will miss my beautiful husband for the rest of my life. He will always remain in my heart and the memories will never leave. Some may fade and the excruciating pain will lessen with time, but never leave completely, because we had true love. Love also heals.

I can face all my tomorrows because of that love, and the love of Jesus, my Savior, friend, comforter, guide and companion. He will be with me until it is my turn to be brought to heaven. My desire is to serve Him faithfully with joy, and all that is within me. I believe Jesus is coming back to take all of us who believe in Him to heaven one day very soon. I want to be about my Father's business, doing His will for my life.

I pray the same for each of you reading this today. Give yourself wholly to Jesus and find that life is worth living: through joy or sorrow. It is the only way to live.

"The Lord is my light and my salvation: of whom shall I fear? The Lord is the strength of my life; of whom shall I be afraid? Though an army may encamp against me, my heart shall not fear." Pssalms27:1 & 3

~ I am greatly loved ~

~ FIFTY ~

Post Script

My wonderful neighbor has continued to mow my lawn, especially the steep ditch near the highway. I enjoyed using our Rider Mower so decided to mow the flat part of our yard and our neighbor's yard, which we had done for over five years.

I was well acquainted with the terrain of our neighbor's yard and never had any problems before. However, this was just the second time on the mower this year and the mower is operated with both feet. Arne would always make me practice on flat ground before I actually mowed, until I was very familiar with its operation. I had not done that this time!

I could almost hear him saying, *"Babes, what were you thinking?"* I wasn't.

As I came around the corner by my Knock-Out rose bushes, I realized I needed to back up or plow into my beautiful bushes. I disengaged the blade, put the mower into reverse and gently let up on the brake as I pushed down on the accelerator. I had just gotten a new battery and when I pushed on the accelerator, the mower jerked backward way too quickly.

This startled me and I must have put both feet on the pedals because I shot backward, hitting the top of my neighbor's retaining wall, about 3 feet high, and was propelled into the air, hanging on to the steering wheel and going completely upside down in a complete revolution.

I saw the front of the mower directly over me in the air, put my hands up against it and cried, **"Jesus!"**

I don't know exactly what happened, but the mower seemed to roll to the side in slow motion, crashing down beside me as parts went flying. I landed on my back on crushed rock, dazed and hardly realizing what had just occurred. Two neighbor men came running over and asked if I was alright. I just laid there and said I didn't know. Finally, I gingerly sat up slowly. My limbs all seemed to work. I had no pain anywhere, just couldn't take a deep breath, had an instant headache, and felt rattled to the core.

Each neighbor took an arm and helped me to sit up, then stand, then walked me to my outdoor furniture to let me sit down.

One neighbor said, *"God must have been watching over you. That was a miracle."*

The other neighbor said, *"That 2000 lb. machine was coming down right on top of you. You could have been killed. There's no way that didn't land on you. I would say you definitely had some help!"*

It took both of these strong young men two tries to right that heavy rider mower. I thought, for sure, that I had just destroyed a very expensive piece of equipment and my riding days were over (I still wasn't thinking straight).

They got their tools, put the seat back on to the mower, adjusted this and that, got the battery, which had flown a distance away, and reattached it. They worked on it for some time as I just sat and watched them. My neighbor then got on the machine, started it and drove it to the backyard where he backed it into place. I got up and walked to the backyard, being pretty grateful I could walk at all. I should have been crushed, paralyzed or injured in some way. What a powerful God who sent angels to protect my life.

When I got to where the two men stood, Harrison said, *"I parked the mower and THAT is where it is going to STAY! I will mow your yard from now on."*

My body started shaking all over and I began to cry. Both men put their arms around me and just held me. The enormity of what had just happened overcame me and I knew what my amazing God had just done for me! I went into the house to lay down on an ice pack, covered up because I was suddenly freezing and just wept. They wanted to take me to the ER, but with all the Covid Pandemic stuff in our hospitals, I didn't want to go unless I really needed to be checked out. I felt no pain but knew I must be very careful because who knew what could be wrong with bones, muscles and ligaments that exertion might trigger? My inability to take a deep breath told me I probably bruised a rib or two.

As I lay thinking about what had just happened, I also realized that I had not felt my life was ALL that important anymore and I had many times told the Lord He could take me home anytime. I realize now that many who have lost loved ones have had those same thoughts, and God understands our humanness. I knew I needed to apologize to my Heavenly Father and thank Him for the gift of life He still gave me. I did so and just wept uncontrollably in His presence as His amazing love washed over my battered body.

Then Jesus firmly spoke to my heart. *"I could have let you come home to me today. But I am not finished with you yet. Pull up your big-girl pants and get on to the business of doing My will. I have work for you to do. Now, finish the book."*

I had begun this book almost 10 years ago, not really wanting to write and not being able to imagine how anyone would want to read about my life. Jesus showed me this is not about me. It is about a normal young gal, with a Great, Big GOD. This book is for you, dear reader. To bring you closer to Jesus and to help you see how much God has for you too. It is a relationship of loving trust, caring, dependance and faith just waiting for you!

Take this awesome gift from Jesus today. Let Him be the absolute center of your life.

It is the ONLY way to true happiness, joy, peace and contentment.

~ Epilogue ~

Our eldest son and wife: Bryan and DeeDee have been married 33 years. Bryan retired as a Lt. Colonel from the Army National Guard after 33 years of service. He and DeeDee serve at Trinity Bible College and Graduate School in Ellendale, ND where they also make their home.

Our eldest grandson, Paul, and wife Haley, live in the Washington, D.C. area where Paul serves in the U.S. Army.

Tim, our youngest grandson, and his wife Bobbie, completed their studies at Trinity Bible College and Graduate School. Tim presently serves on staff at the college.

I had prayed the Lord would grant Arne good enough health to be present at both boy's weddings so he would be in all pictures, and both boys would have the joy of celebrating their special day with their beloved Grandpa. God granted that request, and how I thank Him.

Both boys have been excellent students and active in music, playing various instruments and involved in their church youth groups. They are very close to their parents and make this grandmother very proud and thankful for their lives! We have had some beautiful memories and magical moments together with more to come in the future. They often call for no reason at all – just to talk to their Grams. I am extremely blessed.

Our younger son and bride: Buz and Vicki reside in Springfield, Missouri where they are actively involved in their church. They both have successful careers in education. Buz always manages to bring a smile to this mother with his quick wit and sense of humor. I love when he calls for a recipe or just to say, *"I love you!"* He is such a blessing to me, especially now!

What can I say about these outstanding young people that I am privileged to call my children and grandchildren? They are OUR Tomorrow, if Jesus doesn't return. They are energetic, ambitious, intelligent, industrious and full of fun. Most of all, each of them loves the Lord Jesus Christ personally and puts Him first in their lives. Nothing could be more important to this mother/grandmother. They are precious to me and someday we will all spend eternity together in heaven. That is the most I could ever want.

Last, but far from least, my hubby, Arne: was 78 years old in January 2020. I turned 78 in September 2020. We were married 56 years in July 2019. What a ride it has been!

Arne was the love of my life and the joy of my being. I know God blessed me with this beautiful man and I will be forever grateful. He has been all I could ever have wanted in a husband and he told me every day that he was the blessed one. We loved taking the back dirt roads, just to see where they went! We were in love and enjoyed each other's company more than being with anyone else. I look forward to that day when I see him completely healed and whole once again in heaven. Until then, I thank the Lord daily for allowing me to have him by my side for 56 wonderful, love-filled, memorable years. He made me complete and I miss him with every ounce of my being!

I have remained cancer free. I am about 85% blind in my left eye, due to glaucoma, but I see amazingly well and continue to drive without any trouble and am gaining confidence as I navigate through busy metropolitan areas (although I really don't like that!). My right eye continues to be 20/20, for which I praise God with all my heart.

I love singing for my Lord and feel privileged to do so often. I feel I am in excellent health but am seeing a Neurologist to try to get to the bottom on my continued vertigo.

Arne may be missing physically from my life, but he will live forever in my heart. Others say it will get easier as time goes by. The ache in my heart never seems to leave for long but I am trusting God for all my tomorrows. He makes all the difference.

I refuse to be a victim of circumstances I cannot fully change. I will change what I can with our Father's help. I thank and praise my wonderful Heavenly Father every day for who He is and all He has done for me. What a mighty God and coming King we serve. He is number one in my heart and life. Thank you, precious Father.

Life is more than wealth. It is storing treasures in heaven.
Life is more than success. It is gaining the loving favor of Jesus.
Life is more than worldly fame. It is hearing the Father say, *"Well done, thou good and faithful servant, enter into the joys of the Lord."*

"That is why we never give up. Though our bodies are dying, our inner strength in the Lord is growing every day. These troubles and sufferings of ours are, after all, quite small and won't last very long. Yet this short time of distress will result in God's richest blessing upon us forever and ever! So, we don't look at what we can see right now, the troubles all around us, but we look forward to the joys in heaven which we have not seen. The trouble will soon be over, but the joys to come will last forever."
II Corinthians 4:16-18 *Living Bible*

Dance like no one is watching
Sing like no one is listening
Love like you've never been hurt before
Live like heaven begins tomorrow
"When life looks like one big jigsaw puzzle, Remember,
God has the cover."
Arne Jacobson

My life-time verse since childhood / BJ

"Christ shall be magnified in my body, whether by life or death. For to me to live IS Christ, and to die IS gain."
Philippians 1:20-21

BJ'S Prayer

Oh Father, as I look upon you bleeding hands and side,
It is with wonder, I conclude, your presence does abide.
For such unworthy principals you gave Your ALL , and more,
To bring us Your Salvation: wholeness and love restore.

My heart is filled with gratitude
My tears you've washed away
And in their place, you've given hope
And lasting peace to stay.

You see, I'm just a pilgrim in this land
In need of a gentle, loving Hand
Your guidance and plan I seek.

So, at times when I falter, slip...even fall...
My cries of despair fill the air,
When I struggle and plead, in my moment of need
Please be patient – look deep in my heart.
For I love you SO much, and I so want to please
My spirit wells up from within.
I remember Your Words, Your Promise, you see,
To finish what You have begun.

So, take what You've started, this clay to be molded
I am at Your disposal and call;
As I stand in Your presence, your servant, your child
I lovingly give you my ALL.

By BJ Jacobson 1988

How Can I become a Child of God and be saved from my sins?

A-B-C *(All scriptures from Living Bible)*

A. Admit you are a sinner and fall short of God's standard for eternal life.

> *"No one is good – no one in all the is world is innocent." Romans 3:10*
>
> *"Yes, all have sinned; all fall short of God's glorious ideal." Romans 3:23*
>
> *"For the wages of sin is death, but the free gift of God is eternal life through   Jesus Christ our Lord." Romans 6:23*

B. Believe in your heart that God has raised Jesus from the dead.

> *"For if you tell others with your own mouth that Jesus Christ is your Lord, and believe in your own heart that God has raised him from the dead, you will be saved. For it is by believing in his heart that a man becomes right with God; and with his mouth he tells others of his faith, confirming his salvation," Romans 10: 9 & 10*

C. Call upon the Name of the Lord and you will be saved.

> *"Anyone who calls upon the name of the Lord will be saved." Romans 10:13*
>
> *"Look! I have been standing at the door and I am knocking. If anyone hears me calling him and opens the*

door, I will come in and fellowship with him and he with me." Revelation 3:20

1. <u>Admit</u> you are a sinner
2. <u>Believe</u> that Jesus is the son of God who died for your sins
3. <u>Ask</u> Jesus to forgive your sins and come into your heart & confess Him as Lord and Savior of your life.
4. <u>Know </u>He came in because He said He would.

Prayer you can pray:

"Jesus, I know I am a sinner. I believe you are the Son of God who died for me on the cross for every sin I have ever committed. I ask you to forgive me for all my sins and come into my heart now and make me clean and pure from this moment on. Your Word says if I open my heart's door to you, you will come in and become my Savior, and Lord of my life. Help me to share my newfound faith with others who do not know you. Thank you for coming into my heart today. Help me to get to know you closely as I read your Word. In the powerful name of Jesus, my Savior, Amen."

Name: _____

Date: _____

Contact BJ:

Email: godnevermakesmistakesever@gmail.com

Website: godnevermakesmistakes.wordpress.com

Facebook:
https://www.facebook.com/bjbook.jacobson.3